Praise for

LAND POWER

'A fascinating book on the power of land inequality in history and the large land reshufflings of the past and present. It is a must-read to think about the coming struggles over land in the twenty-first century'

Thomas Piketty, *New York Times*–bestselling author of *Capital in the Twenty-First Century*

'Land has always been a source of economic wealth. This captivating book demonstrates that it has also been a fountainhead of political and social power, profoundly shaping the organization and political structures of many societies'

Daron Acemoglu, Nobel Prize–winning coauthor of *Power and Progress*

'An important book dealing with a timeless but under-appreciated issue: who owns the land. It illuminates how social hierarchies and injustice have been historically built around unfair land rights and provides a fascinating array of examples of how reshuffling land can help tackle these pressing issues'

Francis Fukuyama, author of *Liberalism and Its Discontents*

'With a sweeping scope across history and around the world, Albertus offers his readers a novel view on the rise of the modern world. Land—who controls it, who owns it, who works it, and efforts to alter all this—sits at the basis of social power and political power in the modern world'

Daniel Ziblatt, *New York Times*–bestselling coauthor of *How Democracies Die*

'A vigorously argued account of how patterns of landholding shape and are shaped by political power. Global in scope, *Land Power* is lively, well-informed, and highly illuminating'

Patrick Joyce, author of *Remembering Peasants*

'"Land"—four simple letters. Four enormous impacts: on racial divides, gender inequality, the struggle for development, and our precarious environment. In this powerful and compelling book, Albertus re-invents how to think about that most simple but profound force shaping our lives—the ground beneath us'

Ben Ansell, author of *Why Politics Fails*

'A powerfully evocative study that confronts us with the shock of the old: that land still matters enormously to how power is distributed today. Albertus is an expert guide on a dazzling tour of the world today and of different societies across history. He exposes the influence of past land grabs in shaping the present, but also emphatically shows how the global reallocation of land is an ongoing process—one that we can bend in a better direction'

Nicholas Mulder, author of
The Economic Weapon

'Albertus lays out a convincing argument at a global scale for the effect land ownership, control, and use has had on social structures, including the profound disruption of our tribes. He concludes, "Land reshuffling also continues because deep wounds from past land grabs haven't healed, and something can still be done about it." This is what has driven the Indian Land Tenure Foundation since its founding, and what makes me burn today'

Cris Stainbrook, president,
Indian Land Tenure Foundation

'A masterful telling of the making of the modern world, where all comes back to the land. Brilliant, bold, and provocative, *Land Power* explains how land reshuffling led to enslavement and to the dispossession of indigenous populations, women, and ethnic minorities, paving the way for some of the world's greatest social ills. Albertus documents how we arrived here and the policies some countries are adopting to repair past land reshuffles. A hugely engaging book and a major contribution to our understanding of today's world'

Beatriz Magaloni, Stanford University

'Magisterial, accessible, and compelling, *Land Power* vaults across time and geography to provide an extraordinarily learned account of the role of landed power in displacement, inequities, and exploitation. Spanning from 10,000 BC through a nineteenth-century cascade of land reallocations and into a dramatically transformed future, it reveals that the rise of the dispossessed is rarely a guarantee of justice for all, but the advent of a new set of winners and losers'

Margaret Levi, Stanford University

'Now more than ever it's essential to talk about land use with the widest lens possible. *Land Power* offers new insights into how public and private land initiatives worldwide can effectively safeguard ecosystems and societies for future generations of all life'

Kristine Tompkins, president and cofounder,
Tompkins Conservation

LAND
POWER

ALSO BY MICHAEL ALBERTUS

Property Without Rights: Origins and Consequences of the Property Rights Gap

Authoritarianism and the Elite Origins of Democracy (as coauthor)

Coercive Distribution (as coauthor)

Autocracy and Redistribution: The Politics of Land Reform

LAND POWER

WHO HAS IT, WHO DOESN'T, AND HOW THAT DETERMINES THE FATE OF SOCIETIES

MICHAEL ALBERTUS

BASIC BOOKS
LONDON

First published in Great Britain in 2025 by Basic Books UK
An imprint of John Murray Press

1

Text design by Jeff Stiefel

A CIP catalogue record for this title is available from the British Library

Hardback ISBN 9781399814324
Trade Paperback ISBN 9781399814331
ebook ISBN 9781399814355

Typeset in Adobe Jenson Pro

Printed and bound in Great Britain by Clays Ltd, Elcograf S.p.A.

John Murray Press policy is to use papers that are natural, renewable and recyclable products and made from wood grown in sustainable forests. The logging and manufacturing processes are expected to conform to the environmental regulations of the country of origin.

Carmelite House
50 Victoria Embankment
London EC4Y 0DZ

www.basicbooks.uk

John Murray Press, part of Hodder & Stoughton Limited
An Hachette UK company

The authorised representative in the EEA is Hachette Ireland, 8 Castlecourt Centre, Dublin 15, D15 XTP3, Ireland (email: info@hbgi.ie)

To the coming generations on the land

CONTENTS

Introduction: The Power of Land 1

PART I: LANDS WITHOUT MASTERS

Chapter 1: Land and Power in Human History 11

Chapter 2: The Great Reshuffle 29

PART II: HOW LAND MADE OUR GREATEST PROBLEMS

Chapter 3: Lands Divided by Race 55

Chapter 4: This Land Is Men's Land 85

Chapter 5: The Disappearing Wilderness 106

Chapter 6: The Underdevelopment Playbook 129

PART III: LAND AS A SOLUTION

Chapter 7: The Arc of History Is Long, but It Bends Toward Development 157

Chapter 8: One Small Step for Women 181

Chapter 9: Reclaiming Nature 206

Chapter 10: The Return of the Dispossessed 235

Conclusion 266

Acknowledgments 271

Notes 277

Index 309

INTRODUCTION

THE POWER OF LAND

LAND IS POWER. OUR IDENTITY, OUR FAMILY PASTS, OUR WEALTH and well-being, and our relationships are all rooted in the soil beneath our feet. For millennia, the earliest humans respected and lived on the land but did not have to think much about who owned it. The human population was small, territories were vast, and frontiers were plenty.

No more. As the population grew over the course of the past several thousand years of human history, land became a valuable resource. Sporadic battles over land ownership broke out in ancient Mesopotamia, Greece, and Rome. Land battles spread across the globe like wildfire with the advent of modern states. Who owns the land came to define who holds power.

Land power is economic power. Since the dawn of recorded human history land has had immense monetary value through the natural resources it supports, such as wild animals, plants, and precious metals. Prior to industrialization, land was also humanity's single most productive asset. The vast majority of humans over the past several thousand years have relied on it for agricultural production, raising domesticated animals, and harvesting timber. In more contemporary times, land actually multiplies prosperity. Not only does land's value reliably increase as populations rise—making less and less of it available—but it grants an immediate advantage to the landholder and accelerates the wealth of anyone lucky enough to own or control it. If life is a game of king of the mountain, and everyone is trying to hike uphill, gaining land is like stepping onto an escalator and cruising to the top. And it's a long way up: the total value of all the land on earth is somewhere around $200 trillion, greater than the value of all global economic output. No other form of wealth comes close to competing with land.[1]

Land power is also social power. Large landowners have long shaped social order and sat atop the pyramid of social hierarchy, commanding respect and taking advantage of special access to exclusive organizations and social circles. Across the centuries, large landowners have ruled over their territorial domains and extracted rent, labor, and deference from legions of souls who have worked their lands both freely and in various forms of bondage. Kings, chiefs, nobles, political leaders, and magnates around the globe from Versailles to Monticello to Baghdad have used their landed estates to signal status and to project authority. Families and individuals demarcate themselves and their influence by the land they hold. In Europe, members of the nobility hardwired land into their very names. Titles such as Duke of Windsor or Duke of York did not just signify family inheritance, but were also tied to respective castles and surrounding lands. The lands of the nobility placed these elites at the vanguard of creating government.

That's because land power is political, too. The resources and status that influential landowners hold has enabled them to shape the founding of nations and governments the world over. Political participation also became tied to land. As land ownership is the premier marker of citizenship and belonging, most societies have at some point used it to determine who can have a say in politics through voting or holding office. And politicians use land policy as a valuable tool to garner political support and undercut their opponents. Property taxes, zoning, eminent domain, and land grabs and grants can be wielded by a society's winners against their foes.

The tight link between land and power, once forged, is not easily broken. The advantages afforded by holding land accumulate over years and generations and cannot be easily overcome. Only when the land shifts under our feet is this bond broken.

Population growth, state-making, and social conflict over the past two centuries have sparked dramatic upheavals in who holds the land in societies around the globe. This new era of upheaval—call it the Great Reshuffle—brought revolutionary change, setting societies and their inhabitants on new trajectories. This book is about what happens when land power changes hands and how that determines a society's future for centuries to come. It is also about how that future can be rewritten today. The Great Reshuffle isn't over, and some societies are embarking on experiments to rewire land power that will radically impact future generations.

The American settlement of interior Southern California starting in the 1850s is a telling example of the monumental consequences of the Great Reshuffle. In the wake of the 1848 treaty that ended the Mexican-American War and ceded California to the United States, a tidal wave of settlers flooded west. Eager to secure the territory and develop it, the federal government encouraged the forced removal of Native Americans from the lands they had inhabited since time immemorial. It's a well-known story of American dispossession—but it did not end in the nineteenth century. It forged a path on which those who hold the land and those who lost it continue to this day.

Among the many victims of land policy in that era were the Cahuilla people of the Coachella Valley. Federal agents forced the Cahuilla into a lopsided treaty in 1852 that ceded large portions of their territories. The government then proceeded to ignore that treaty to steal even more of their land, encouraging railroads to lay tracks through the area by granting every other square mile of land to the Southern Pacific Railroad. This split the Cahuilla into ten different reservations, most of them in a dysfunctional and almost comically cruel checkerboard pattern.

Power in and around California's Coachella Valley shifted with the ownership and use of its land. Many of the impoverished Cahuilla were forced to work for settlers on lands that had once been their own, and the Bureau of Indian Affairs suppressed Cahuilla culture while seeking to control those who remained. The gap between the new landowners and the dispossessed grew larger and larger.

The effects of the reshuffling of Cahuilla land did not end in the 1800s. As the area became increasingly attractive to outsiders in the early 1900s for its desert climate and famed hot springs and palm canyons, one of the remaining Cahuilla refuges, the Agua Caliente Reservation, became more valuable than ever. The federal government in the 1920s, the City of Palm Springs in the 1950s, and corporate developers from the 1960s on all tried to snap up the land still under Cahuilla control. As Palm Springs transformed into a playground for Hollywood's rich and famous, the block-by-block disparity between those with land power and those without was apparent in everything from wealth to health, educational attainment, and political clout.

A series of subsequent development deals between the Agua Caliente and Palm Springs and the establishment of gaming on the reservation has marked a turn for the Agua Caliente in recent decades. They have proudly survived and deftly navigate today's world. But their example is emblematic of what can happen when land changes hands—and how far-reaching the consequences can be.

WHEN EUROPEANS BEGAN arriving on the lands that would eventually be rebranded as the United States of America, they found a land that did not belong to anyone in a way that they could understand or respect. Treating the New World as a *terra nullius*—a land without owners—they proceeded to assign it to themselves, expelling its prior occupants and importing a captive population to work the land in bondage. Since the time of the American founding, white Americans have ridden the growing value of that land, and the housing that was built on it, to economic domination while leaving Native Americans and Blacks behind.

The most fundamental economic engine afforded to white settlers was land itself. And from the earliest Indian removals to westward expansion and reservations, from the origins of plantation slavery to the failures of post–Civil War Reconstruction to urban redlining, Native Americans and Blacks never gained broad access to that land. The same is true for immigrants arriving in the twentieth and twenty-first centuries from racial out-groups.

Who owned the land in America determined America's fate: persistent economic inequality along racial lines, yawning racial gaps in social mobility and opportunity, and glaring racial disparities in political representation are all relics of past land choices.

Yet land reallocation does not have to generate the inequities and destruction that it wrought when the Great Reshuffle came to North America, South Africa, or Australia. There are numerous instances where granting land to the landless has improved life for just about everyone. Experiences in Ireland and East Asia, for example, show that society as a whole can benefit when landholdings are broken up and widely shared. Reshuffling the land does not have to be zero sum.

Land allocation offers a rare opportunity to craft a happy and healthy future—though most societies have bungled it, when their time has come. How they go wrong shapes the kinds of problems they will face long afterward. Over the past two centuries the way that land has been reallocated has served to entrench gender inequality, underdevelopment, and racial inequality in discernible, patterned, and persistent ways around the globe. Efforts at redistributing land have also exacerbated environmental degradation, resource depletion, and the loss of biodiversity, contributing to growing climate and environmental crises.

Land reallocation can go wrong for many reasons, but incompetence is least among them. The power that land confers makes it hotly contested. It is the battle to grab land and to wield its power for status, wealth, and control that starkly defines winners and losers and shapes the future of societies.

The fight over land is so often about power and wealth that it is easy to miss its broader social implications. But land power can be used to unwind inequality. Japan, South Korea, and Taiwan stand as exemplars of the positive transformative power of land for improving equality and development simultaneously. And social movements such as Black Lives Matter and Land Back are fueling a discussion over restitution and reparations that demands that we look more closely at how to reshuffle land the right way.

THIS BOOK TELLS a new story about the making of the modern world, in which the reshuffling of land paved the way for some of the world's greatest social ills. But there is another story in the pages ahead as well, one that is still in progress. The Great Reshuffle never ended—in many countries around the world, landholdings are still being broken up and redistributed. Other countries are experimenting with policies to right the mistakes of past reshuffles gone wrong.

That is in part because there is still rising pressure on the land. As urbanization ticks up, it gives the impression that fewer and fewer people live on the land. But the opposite is occurring. According to population figures from the United Nations, between 1960 and today the number of people living in rural areas has increased by about 75 percent, from 2 billion to nearly 3.5 billion.[2] Billions more in cities have close connections to the countryside through family and identity. Populations in cities are rising at a faster clip, putting urban land in the crosshairs for reshuffling, but they are still growing considerably in many rural areas too. That puts pressure on livelihoods as well as on identities and cultures that are rooted in the land.

Land reshuffling also continues because deep wounds from past land grabs haven't healed, and something can still be done about it. Land is power, but that does not mean it has to fuel disparity, indignity, and destruction. A better future can be made if land power is put in service of a whole society.

I have been trying to discern the best ways to realize that future for over fifteen years. Perhaps because most social critics and scholars call the world's bustling cities home, few have reckoned fully with how deeply humanity's connection to the land has shaped every nook and cranny of modern life. The gravity of that oversight became clear to me when a fateful research trip took me to the highlands of Peru and

Bolivia. The land was under everyone's fingernails and on the tips of their tongues. Peasants tilled the soil and tended flocks of animals everywhere I went in the Peruvian Andes. In La Paz, they crowded the land agency and banged loudly on the desk for their papers. But land wasn't just a source of subsistence, or a commodity to be bought and sold. It determined what was politically, economically, and socially possible for those who lived on it and for those who had left it but whose family heritage was rooted in the land. All roads in society led back to the land.

I began studying and learning about every aspect of the land in dusty archives, vast libraries, countless government land agencies, and, most importantly, through on-the-ground research in fields and furrows from Italy to South Africa, from Ireland to China, and from California to Patagonia. At every opportunity, I hopped on buses and into cars to go out to the countryside, strap on a backpack, and get out on the land. I have spoken with legions of peasants, government officials, land caretakers, and businesspeople who have dedicated their lives to the land and whose trajectories have been shaped by decisions above them to reshuffle, or not to reshuffle, the land. All of them spoke passionately about the promise of land and its centrality to their plans and dreams. Many bitterly recalled its misuse by governments and politicians. Their voices are in this book. Those experiences, put together with a more panoramic study of history and theory, made me recognize that how cultures and individuals buy, sell, seize, and exploit the ground under us can mean the difference between a nation's success or failure.

TO UNDERSTAND HOW land created the world as we know it, we must begin by examining how the link between land and power was forged over the course of human history. That link developed differently across the world and ultimately settled into five main forms of landholding before the Great Reshuffle began. The first chapters of this book, in Part I, detail those processes while sketching the monumental changes in land ownership that have remapped the world over the past several centuries, radically reshaping modern societies. Part II shows how choices that were made during the Great Reshuffle laid the groundwork for racial hierarchy, gender inequity, underdevelopment, and environmental degradation—the Four Horsemen of modern social maladies. Yet, as the final chapters of this book in Part III show, those maladies are not terminal. Some countries have taken important steps in the direction of resolving them and have progress to show for it. But many other countries are just coming to grips with them and debating policies and programs to address them. They could stand to learn from the lessons of the countries that have already made progress.

The Great Reshuffle in land over the past two centuries determined the future of societies but did not lock in a permanent destiny. In the right hands, land can be a tool for forging a more just and sustainable world. Plot by plot, some countries are treading the long and arduous path toward that better world and making real progress.

PART I

Lands Without Masters

CHAPTER 1

LAND AND POWER IN HUMAN HISTORY

THERE WAS A TIME WHEN NOBODY OWNED THE LAND. WHEN HUmans were sparse, land was abundant. Hunting and gathering defined life in the early days of human history. Small bands of humans foraged on the land to survive and moved as needed in response to the seasonal shifts of critical resources. Times of plenty were both exceptional and brief, and the tools to replicate and elongate these moments were rudimentary, ensuring that human populations remained small. Only a few million of our *Homo sapiens* ancestors roamed the earth as recently as 12,000 years ago.

In the absence of land ownership, there was no meaningful political power to be obtained in land. Yet humanity's relationship to the land still defined the nature of life and society, such as it was. With populations constrained and resources limited to what could be foraged seasonally or stored, human lifestyles were ecologically sustainable out of necessity, and the social, economic, and racial stratification we see today simply did not exist.

A shift began to occur around 10,000 BC. In a few isolated pockets of the world, sedentary communities and cultivated plants emerged. The act of a community settling into a particular place was most notable in wetland areas near the migration routes of fish, birds, and other larger animals.[1] After another 5,000 years, permanent agricultural towns were taking hold, relying mainly on planted crops and domesticated livestock.

Key to these transformations were abundance and surplus. Living in a single place year-round was only sustainable if humans harnessed natural local abundance or created it through agricultural production and animal husbandry. Prime lands easily suitable for generating this kind of abundance were limited, and the ways in which that land and its surplus would be used were consequential. So it was that in these early societies, small as they were, land began to shape power.

Those who controlled the land controlled the surplus, and therefore valuable resources that could be used in support of further accumulation and social status. This principle explains why the earliest administrative cuneiform tablets, from the city of Uruk in ancient Mesopotamia circa 3300 to 3100 BC, are lists of grain rations and taxes as well as labor and slaves. The Treaty of Mesilim, a stele inscribed in cuneiform from the region dating to 2550 BC, provides some of the earliest evidence of a conflict over land between two warring city-states. By around 2300 BC, scribes in the region were recording details about the land on clay tablets, most likely as properties were sold or boundaries disputed.[2]

The importance of land only grew with the passage of several thousand more years as some human societies, mainly in parts of the Middle East, Europe, Latin America, and Asia, began to grow larger. The gradual building of knowledge and trade as well as agricultural and other technologies sustained an increase of over thirtyfold in human populations by the year 0, when nearly 200 million humans walked the earth.[3] There is clear archaeological evidence from ancient Greece and Rome of systematic divisions and demarcation of land by this time. Rome even opened an archive in 78 BC for the deposit of property maps and associated documents. The first proto-states had formed, shunting surplus from agriculture into the creation of priestly classes, tax collectors, medical specialists, and standing armies. Those who controlled the land and its surplus used these new specialists to gain privileged access to the afterlife, extend their lifespans, and conquer neighboring groups to appropriate their resources and labor.

Land had acquired enough influence on power by this point that it began to spark some of the first documented attempts at revolutionary land redistribution. Land concentration advanced for several hundred years during the height of the Roman Republic. Roman aristocrats and provincial elites busily gobbled up conquered territories, slave labor from conquered lands, and the smallholdings of modest farmers, who were progressively forced into seasonal or wage labor. Some landholders sought ever greater wealth through lucrative tax farming contracts, while others chased power in the form of political office, such as senator or magistrate. Starting in 133 BC, this elite class faced an unprecedented challenge. First Tiberius Gracchus and then his brother were elected as tribunes by the Roman plebeians, the common folk who owned little or no land but were nevertheless afforded the vote. The brothers used their power to challenge the basis of aristocratic power through legislation aimed at land reallocation in favor of poor farmers. The reaction was swift and decisive. Each was put to death in turn.

Around the same time, half the world away in the Oaxaca Valley in southern Mexico, land had become coupled with power among the Zapotec at Monte Albán. This complex society formed one of Mesoamerica's largest settlements. A small but powerful group of Zapotec nobles resided at a complex of temples and ceremonial sites at the leveled top of a mountain that commanded a towering position over the agricultural fields of commoners in the extensive valley below. The nobles conducted ritual practices, wore elaborate clothing and adornments, honored their dead with lavish burials, and waged war to capture the territory of neighboring groups, while commoners had to sacrifice their labor and a portion of their harvests to them.[4]

Land power was producing societies, cultures, and wealth, but it was also entrenching inequality. Social and economic stratification deepened in unprecedented ways as these societies grew. Small sets of wealthy elites rose as rulers, while the ruled lost basic freedoms and autonomy that their ancestors had taken for granted. Those societies that grew large enough to contain racial and ethnic diversity, such as ancient Greece and Rome, produced nascent or proto-racial and ethnic hierarchies linked to social status—which, in turn, derived from land.[5]

With the advent of established agriculture and technologies such as the plow, gender roles transformed.[6] Men worked more in the fields, while women spent more time in the home processing harvests and doing housework. Higher fertility rates meant that women spent more time in child-rearing. In ancient Mesopotamia, for instance, the adoption of the plow between 6000 and 4000 BC converted men from hunters and herdsmen into farmers and pushed women out of the fields. The result was a shift toward male domination of society and beliefs, including a transition from female to male gods and priests.[7] As the plow slowly spread across the world over the course of several thousand years, male domination followed it.

The pursuit of abundance could also bring destruction. In the early years of human history, populations were so small that environmental damage was minimal and quickly reversible. But growing populations had the power to despoil the land at a rapid clip, particularly as rulers encouraged subjects to cut down forests and till an ever greater extent of the land in order to increase surplus. The extensive upland peat bogs of Ireland stand as a monument to a growing early farming and agricultural population that cleared the island's forests from about 3000 to 500 BC and acidified the land, pushing agriculture into every usable nook and cranny. Nearly half the world away and several hundred years later, a northern Chinese population boom during the Han dynasty drove deforestation of most of the North China Plain and serious degradation of the local environment. Still another millennium after that, the newly established people of Easter Island deforested their land between the start of a population increase in AD 1200 and the end of the seventeenth century, driving plant and animal life to extinction and triggering war and societal collapse.

The sixteenth century brought a new innovation that supercharged the link between land and power: the creation of the nation-state. Over the course of several hundred years, France, Britain, and Spain firmed up their borders, established a monopoly on the use of force, and raised standing armies and centralized bureaucracies. Germany, Italy, and most of Europe and Latin America followed suit by the nineteenth century. The power of land had swiftly transformed the world into something that would have been unrecognizable to early hunter-gatherers and sedentary communities.

All the while, human populations ballooned. Humanity numbered 1 billion by the early nineteenth century. In a world where agriculture remained the economic engine of the newly formed states, land was simultaneously more valuable, and under more demographic pressure, than ever before.

Land defined and conditioned virtually every aspect of social life. The ownership and productivity of land determined the houses people lived in, the work they did, the food they ate, the debts they owed, the social relationships they maintained, and the annual and daily routines they performed. Many people scraped by, tilling the soil for others and living impoverished lives of subservience. A far smaller share of the world's population owned the land either as autonomous farmers or as large landowners who profited from the labor of others.

For the world's new states, delineating the ownership of specific lands became critical to defining borders, administering populations, and collecting taxes. Professional bureaucracies began systematically mapping and tracking land ownership and sharing that information with tax collectors. The creation, stabilization, and standardization of currencies enabled the surplus from land to be easily exchanged in various ways and translated into different kinds of coercive, market, and political power. Britain established a national bank in 1694 and adopted the gold standard in 1816, and over this time the supply of currency and confidence in it increased. France reestablished the franc as a national currency in 1795 and created a national bank in 1800.

Bureaucrats and tax collectors could now translate harvests of wheat and barley into pounds and francs and deposit the revenue in banks that could be tapped to fund roadbuilding, wars, and empires. Power could be projected in new and profound ways as communications and transportation advanced. Leading states sought to control more land and could do so across the globe through colonization funded on the back of surplus.

Who held power in this world depended on the land they held. Kings, lords, and other rulers from the sixteenth to nineteenth centuries consolidated vast tracts of land and resources while others in society struggled as landless paupers. Landholding came to define citizenship and political power. It helped to define and prop up male-biased gender norms. It shaped racial and class hierarchies and structured opportunities and freedoms. And land became mismanaged and overexploited, with irreversible consequences for biodiversity and environmental health. The increasing pressure would eventually cause the entire system of land ownership to explode. A great reshuffle loomed, and it would usher in the world we live in today.

LANDHOLDING AND ITS connection with power did not evolve the same way across all societies. There were regions of the world where hunter-gathering and small, long-standing, sedentary communities remained largely untouched. And as landholding and power evolved in lockstep in early states, it settled into different patterns shaped by culture, climate, and the exercise of social and economic control.

Five major patterns of landholding predominated after 1500 and into the 1800s: indigenous landholding yet to be perturbed by nascent nation-building or expanding empires; lord-peasant landholding; landlord-tenant landholding; the hacienda system; and independent smallholder farming. With the exception of most indigenous and smallholding societies, all of these concentrated land in the hands of a few people in unprecedented ways. These modes of landholding encouraged, created, and allowed our most persistent modern problems—racism, sexism, climate change, poverty, and inequality—to take root.

Indigenous groups still occupied and stewarded the majority of the land around the globe at the dawn of the 1500s.[8] Western Europe at this point was dominated by large landowners and poised to build nation-states and empires. The dominant pattern within the Americas, Africa, Australia, Southeast Asia, and northern and central Eurasia was one of dispersed populations and plentiful land and resources. There were exceptions, however. Some, such as the Aztecs, Incans, and Hans, settled in specific locales and built villages, cities, and even empires, establishing agriculture. Land had become linked to power in these complex societies through the control of agricultural surplus, labor, and territory.

But most indigenous peoples continued to live nomadic or seminomadic lifestyles as hunter-gatherers or lived in small, relatively autonomous sedentary communities.[9] Their relationships with the land were intimate, complex, and variable, but in no case did they hold Western European notions of exclusive, individual, and alienable property ownership.[10] Land held value in its support of vital resources, such as plants and game, as well as for its spiritual and cultural significance. But it did not enable the personal use and exercise of power at a grand scale.

The Innu of Quebec, for instance, prior to French contact in the early 1600s, lived in small groups tied together by kinship, subsisting through hunting, fishing, and gathering. They seasonally followed the harvest of native plants, the eel run down the Saint Lawrence River, and shifting groups of animals.[11] The nearby eastern Cree of James Bay lived in a similar fashion. For this group, a special link to the land came through hunting grounds. Despite extended kin group "control" over certain areas, that control was permeable and limited, in practice resembling stewardship more than ownership as commonly understood today. It could accommodate other people who were mainly or seasonally affiliated with different hunting grounds.[12] Farther south, in coastal New England, the Wampanoag and others combined hunting and gathering with the seasonal cultivation of crops such as corn, beans, and squash. These practices shaped a semisedentary lifestyle punctuated by periodic relocations. Control and authority over land was layered and in constant flux. Some areas were used collectively and others individually, and land was also subject to the claims of and relations with a local chief.[13]

For these indigenous peoples, the years ahead would be riven by the disruptions of European colonialization, which amounted to a mass appropriation of the land they lived on and its reallocation to potentates, ambitious and rapacious explorers, and settlers. Some indigenous societies nonetheless managed to remain intact well into the 1800s as states formed in Europe and then the Americas. Most hunter-gatherers and independent sedentary communities in western North America, inland Africa, Europe's northernmost fringes, the steppe and mountainous regions of Asia, and parts of Southeast Asia and Australia survived the early formation of states and the onslaught of European colonization. Communities in the deep forests and mountain folds of the Americas and Eurasia, the uplands of Southeast Asia, and interior Africa prevailed into the twentieth century, and a few survive in the present day. Some of these indigenous communities began to adapt their livelihoods and links to the land following initial contact with settlers. But land relations typically retained traditional aspects, and few, if any, groups entirely adopted Western property rights unless forced to do so.[14]

In much of the world, however, by the dawn of the nineteenth century many indigenous communities had been stripped of their traditions and customs and incorporated and assimilated into the growing economies of modern states and empires. Centuries of feudalism, colonialism, and statecraft had made land ownership extremely unequal, drawing a tight link between land and power in most of the world.

LORD-PEASANT LANDHOLDING PREDOMINATED across most of eastern, central, and southern Europe and Russia between 1500 and the 1800s as well as in prerevolutionary France. In these places, a small number of elites owned large tracts of land while peasants eked out a living farming that land at the landowners' pleasure and direction. Landowners even owned the peasants themselves in some places through serfdom. The ownership of land, its products, and its people gave landowners enormous power and rendered peasants essentially powerless from cradle to grave.

East of the Elbe River, in what is now eastern Germany and western Poland, and was then Prussia, a classic story unfolded. Knights' estates dominated the landscape throughout most of the nineteenth and early twentieth centuries and in several centuries prior. Estate owners known as *Junkers* derived aristocratic legal and political privileges from their control over local and provincial government. They rang in the dawn of the nineteenth century as feudal lords who had almost complete control over their workers and received compulsory dues and labor from them. As one local count put it, "The dependents were chained indissolubly only to the authority of the *Rittergut* [estate], whose owner could sell the estate to a new lord without hindrance and, with it, the dependents."[15] Conditions were characterized by "harsh treatment and oppression" by landowners and "hate, recalcitrance, ignorance, [and] brutality" on the part of serfs.[16]

In 1807, after the *Junker*-dominated military led Prussia to an embarrassing defeat against Napoleon, Prussian leader Baron vom Stein abolished serfdom, calling it "the last vestige of slavery."[17] But landowner backlash and weak enforcement enabled forced labor to continue until mid-century. Even after that, landowners remained lords for another seventy-five years. Peasants continued to toil for them, first as resident estate laborers who performed work at low rates under poor conditions, and then as hired local or migrant wage laborers. Landowners continued to use the power that derived from their land to resist and dodge reform and persist in exploitation long after nominal reform.

Prussia's most famous *Junker*, Otto von Bismarck, was a product of this structure. Born into an upper-class landowning family, he rose through Prussia's political system, which heavily favored landowners. He eventually unified the disparate lands into a single Germany in 1871 and turned it into a European powerhouse. During the 1840s, as his political career began, Bismarck supervised two family estates.

One, spanning about 1,260 acres, employed numerous on-site contractual laborers and smallholders who performed traditional unpaid labor services for the family. The other, which produced grain, wool, and potato whiskey over 1,390 acres, housed 44 contractual workers in thatched-roof huts.[18] Bismarck's properties were far from the largest in the area; some estates were over 100 times that size, encompassing over 190 square miles. They operated nearly as kingdoms in their own right.

LANDLORD-TENANT LANDHOLDING DEFINED life in much of East Asia, Southeast Asia, Ireland, and India into the 1800s. While this pattern dated back to 1500 in many of these locations, it spread in the 1600s and 1700s with colonialism in places as far-flung as Ireland and India. Landlords owned the land in these arrangements and leased it out to tenant farmers. This practice gave landowners the power to set rent payments and evict disfavored tenants. Many tenants consequently lived in fear of landlords, owed them sizable debts, and had little recourse against abuses. The concentration of land in these societies further empowered landlords by granting them disproportionate economic and political power, which they used to set favorable rules and regulations.

Take the case of Ireland. For centuries, the Irish toiled as an exploited underclass of tenants in their homeland. By the 1870s, fewer than 10,000 British landlords controlled the vast majority of Irish land and profited from the labor of millions of Irish farmers. The Irish living under these arrangements suffered from poverty, famine, and the elimination of their language and customs.[19]

An economic downturn and a set of failed harvests then sparked the tenant-led Land War, with Irish tenants, particularly in the poorer western regions, bridling under the poverty and indignity of their subordinate positions. A grassroots movement of land activism swept the country. Activists and organizers gathered thousands of tenants in hundreds of meetings. At one meeting in Milltown, County Galway, on June 15, 1879, a land advocate named Thomas Hastings vividly recalled witnessing a local landlord, Lord Sligo, forcing his tenants to drop their rights to land improvements and agree to unfair land valuations: "I remember . . . my indignation to see those miserable slaves crouching down in the dust before the landlord, and signing away the last particle of right, which secured them a guarantee for their daily food." Underscoring the inequity of the landlord system at the same meeting, one of the leaders of the Land War, Michael Davitt, called it "a vampire system . . . which sucks the very life-blood of a people."[20]

Seventy-five years later and half the world away in Long Bow village in Shanxi, China, the Irish situation found a parallel. Although the population was relatively poor overall and there were no cultural differences among villagers, those who owned more land lived comfortably, while those who rented from landlords, or who worked for landlords because they did not hold enough of their own land, struggled even to survive. As one of the rare accounts from the time put it, "The poor who rented land or worked out as hired laborers got less than half the crops they tilled, while the rich got the surplus from many acres. That is why some were able to build enormous underground tombs marked for eternity, or so they thought . . . while others when they died were thrown into a hole in the ground with only a reed mat wrapped around them and a few shovelfuls of the earth to mark the place."[21]

The wealthiest landowner in town, Sheng Ching-ho, held about twenty-three acres of land, some pigs and sheep, and a distillery. He operated as a loan shark to poor villagers in desperate need, snapping up their land and tools when they could not repay on the terms. One poor farmer, named Shen, borrowed $4 from Ching-ho to buy medicine for his sick wife and indentured his son Fa-liang to him for seven years to guarantee the loan. At the end of seven years, because of interest, deductions for broken tools, and paying for replacement labor when Fa-liang was sick, Shen owed more than the original debt. He had to rip out and sell the timbers in his roof to recover his son. As Fa-liang told it, "All the years I worked for Ching-ho I never had a full stomach. I was hungry all the time. Every day he ate solid enough food but he gave me only a little soup with millet in it. You could count the grains that were floating around in the water."[22]

AN ENTIRELY DIFFERENT way of dealing with land, called the hacienda system, prevailed in Latin America under European domination. As Spain and Portugal colonized the Americas beginning in 1492, they doled out enormous tracts of land to European colonizers, along with the right to tax and demand labor from the indigenous inhabitants living on the land. By the 1500s this practice evolved into an estate system characterized by forced labor and a glaring disparity between powerful landowners of European descent and their impoverished indigenous workforces. Plantations in the southern United States, the Caribbean, and parts of Brazil that ran on slavery echoed the hacienda in important ways but were a sort of variant. One major difference was that plantations imported their forced labor from Africa rather than relying on local indigenous communities. The hacienda system endured well into the 1800s, and in many cases into the mid-1900s or even later. Traditional plantations ended in the United States after the Civil War but endured in a modified form under sharecropping and Jim Crow laws into the twentieth century. In a similar fashion in the Caribbean, the foundations of the plantation system shook with the abolition of slavery in the 1800s but did not crumble in many places until the 1900s.

One prototypical example of the hacienda is Huarán, nestled at 10,000 feet above sea level in Peru's Sacred Valley some forty-five miles from Cusco. The hacienda spanned nearly twenty-five square miles and incorporated hundreds of people who lived on and worked the land, serving the owner in semifeudal fashion over many generations up until 1971. When a military government came to power in 1968 and promised to dismantle haciendas, Huarán's workers seized the opening and rained down a hailstorm of petitions for relief to the Ministry of Agriculture.

In a letter on January 15, 1970, a group of poor peasants petitioned to the ministry: "We have worked the hacienda [Hacienda Huarán] from a young age and following our parents, without any payment and under conditions of servitude, suffering a series of abuses in the form of orders that we are forced to comply with in an exacting and inhuman manner. . . . We all work irregular and long hours, even during the night. We have served as shepherds, farmers, irrigators of extensive croplands, and more, which has given us sicknesses and prevented us from any time to educate ourselves. We are all illiterate, drowning in ignorance and servitude. . . . We want justice." They also explained how the link between the owner's land and political power kept them silent: "These abuses and the permanent submission we were subjected to by the powerful owner of the hacienda, who himself has been Department Prefect, prevented us from denouncing him and forced us to live under a permanent threat of reprisals if we were to go to any authorities to claim unpaid salaries or appeal against abuses."[23] They stamped the letter, written by a representative on their behalf, with their fingerprints because they could not write.

That same day, a group of small farmers neighboring the hacienda sent another petition to the ministry. It recounted, "As neighbors and just like the workers we have suffered a permanent form of abuses from the Hacienda Huarán of Oscar Fernández Oblitas, who keeps neighboring communities of small property holders practically asphyxiated for having the audacity to not sell him our lands for the continued growth of his hacienda."[24]

Other workers at Huarán reported being pushed to smaller and smaller pieces of land for personal use while paying exorbitant fees for land access, being entirely dispossessed of their land, having animals stolen or killed by Fernández, contracting illnesses from unknown agrochemicals, being denied educational opportunities, suffering arbitrary arrest and incarceration in a prison Fernández himself ran, being denied social benefits when they could no longer work, and having personal property stolen by Fernández.

For all of their differences, in societies defined by lord-peasant landholding, landlord-tenant landholding, or the hacienda system, a very small percentage of the population owned most of the land. In many of them, the largest 5 percent of landowners owned 80 to 90 percent of the land or more. This reality colored almost every aspect of daily life for the vast majority of the population in these societies, where cities were in their infancy and industrialization lay decades ahead.

Large landowners commanded large groups of workers, dominated business and the economy, and held the most important national and local political offices. Economic and political inequality intersected with social inequality: landowners were predominantly men, and they came from racially privileged backgrounds in societies that were diverse. Meanwhile, most rural inhabitants eked out a living working for large landowners, frequently through relationships of servitude, or rented their land from large landowners at often unfair rates.

IN STARK CONTRAST to societies defined by lord-peasant landholding, landlord-tenant landholding, or the hacienda system, there were also outposts of independent smallholder farming in places such as the northeastern United States, eastern Canada, northern Argentina, eastern Australia, and the southern tip of Africa. European powers, beginning in the 1500s and 1600s—and in the late 1700s in Australia—doled out small tracts of land to European settlers in these areas, where the land was not conducive to large-scale agriculture and where malaria and other endemic diseases were limited, rendering them habitable. As with the land, power within smallholding societies was far more widely distributed than in lord-peasant, landlord-tenant, or hacienda societies. Far more people within smallholder societies became literate, won the right to vote, and were the masters of their own destinies.

The New England region of the United States is among the best-known examples. After initial settlement in the early 1600s, small-scale farming became a mainstay of New England's economy in the colonial era. Settlements were initially laid out as fairly compact townships with modest plots of land to enable farmers to support themselves. The public land survey system systematized settlement at the end of the 1700s and stipulated a method for subdividing townships into sections and lots. Land speculators and companies built a business model on carving up large territories into family-sized plots to sell to the growing ranks of settlers and their many children. This model eventually expanded to the Midwest and it was replicated through the 1862 Homestead Act, which granted settlers 160 acres of land in exchange for a promise to farm it. Widespread small-scale landholding fostered local self-government and common investments in schools and infrastructure. Early political figures—such as Thomas Jefferson, himself a slaveholder and plantation owner—and observers (notably Alexis de Tocqueville) underscored how the dispersion of political and economic power associated with smallholder farming was a bedrock of democracy.

My own family history in part traces this pattern. My maternal ancestors left Freiburg in what was then Baden, a territory within the German Confederation, in 1820 and sailed to Philadelphia. From there, they trekked to northwestern Pennsylvania, where they bought 170 acres of unimproved land from the Holland Land Company and set to farming. Within a few generations they became store owners and engineers, and a few eventually moved to the Detroit area to work in the auto industry and for General Electric.

Ancestors on my father's side were less fortunate. They struggled under the thumb of lord-peasant landholding for generations in southern and eastern Poland. Southern Poland was long a poor and economically isolated outpost of the Habsburg Empire. The Habsburgs abolished serfdom following a wave of revolutions that swept Europe in 1848, and peasants came to own small plots of their land. An uprising in eastern Poland against Russia delivered farmers from serfdom shortly after, in 1864. But the shadow of generations of serfdom was dark. Grinding poverty persisted, and the brutality of World War I finally drove my grandfather and his father to migrate to the United States. They soon made their way to Detroit, the elder one taking a job driving a metro train.

*   *   *

OVER THE PAST two centuries, landholding has shifted in tectonic fashion. Driven by political and economic forces, and under increasing demographic pressure as populations grew, country after country has reallocated land within their societies. Some countries appropriated land from indigenous communities and gave it to settlers. Some seized land from large landowners and gave it to their workers. Some started 200 years ago, and some are still tinkering with the formula and awarding new tracts of land today. But few countries and landholding families have weathered the Great Reshuffle unscathed.

The appropriation of indigenous lands for settlement dates back to the early days of European colonization, but in the nineteenth and early twentieth centuries it reached a fever pitch as new nation-states sought to populate and dominate their territories and decimate or assimilate minority groups. The most familiar examples of this kind of land reallocation have defined the United States, Canada, South Africa, Australia, and much of Latin America. Elements of this type of settlement continue today in places such as the West Bank and Xinjang, China.

The reallocation of land from large landowners to workers began in the modern era with the French Revolution and spread across Europe with the 1848 revolutions, the world wars, and the introduction of communism in Eastern Europe. The end of World War II brought the Great Reshuffle to East Asia, and decolonization sparked land reallocation in the Middle East and North Africa in the following decades. Latin American countries reallocated land in the context of military coups and revolutions throughout the twentieth century. Some countries today, including Brazil, Colombia, and South Africa, continue to conduct this kind of land reallocation at a large scale.

How land has been reallocated has had profound consequences for life in every society touched by the Great Reshuffle. It determines a society's winners and losers for generations, and it can encourage prosperity or snuff it out, flatten hierarchy or entrench it, map out a green future or pave the way for extraction. In Mexico, for instance, in the decades after the country's early twentieth-century revolution, the government reallocated nearly half of privately owned land to collective groups of peasants. Male heads of household won nearly all the land. Weak property rights hampered productivity, and when the government tried to correct by pushing productivity-enhancing chemical fertilizers and pesticides on farmers, it wrecked ecosystems, soils, and watersheds. Even though over 80 percent of the population now lives in urban areas, Mexican land reallocation's legacy of gender inequality, underdevelopment, emigration, and environmental damage still hobbles the country a century later.

Some forms of landholding have survived the Great Reshuffle, while others have been made obsolete. Indigenous landholding was severely diminished, targeted in most parts of the world by settlers. Yet the smallholder farming that predated the Great Reshuffle flourished as many settlers adopted aspects of that model, and as more contemporary states experimented with alternatives to mass collectivization.[25]

Lord-peasant landholding, landlord-tenant landholding, and the hacienda and plantation systems collapsed in many places through land reallocation. Even in the places where they managed to escape reallocation, the forces of modernization and the fears of potential reallocation transformed them. In some cases, large landowners modified their relationships with workers while continuing to dominate them; in other cases landowners mechanized their production and expelled workers; and in still other cases landowners began to hedge their bets in agriculture by diversifying their investments into industry and finance. Because large landowners did not lose their land in this process, they did not lose their power. Sharp inequalities from the countryside reproduced themselves in cities, and land power continued to shape social life for generations.

The holdings of the British monarchy today are the transformed remnants of a bygone era of lord-peasant landholding. For centuries, British monarchs held a vast collection of landed estates that operated on feudal principles and provided royal revenues to them from a legion of peasant workers. Eventually the British Parliament forced the surrender of that revenue. But the Crown Estate persists today as a massive agglomeration of nearly 200,000 acres of tenanted farmland and urban real estate along with vast marine holdings, forests, and more. Its management funds a considerable portion of the House of Windsor's activities.

The United Kingdom has managed to achieve a peace of sorts between its old landed aristocracy and the parliamentary democracy that currently prevails, but the United States exemplifies a far rockier transformation. The United States today lives and breathes the consequences of failing to fully reckon with the southern plantation system. The debate over plantation slavery drove the country into civil war in the 1860s. After the North's victory, in what became known as the "Forty Acres and a Mule" scheme, the Union Army and US government sought to reallocate land from white plantation owners to formerly enslaved Black workers in a band spanning about thirty miles along the coast running from northern Florida to South Carolina. But President Andrew Johnson, who took office after the assassination of Abraham Lincoln and gathered support from white southerners, quickly peeled back this policy. Whites who had lost land recuperated nearly all of it. Many Blacks were forced into sharecropping and wage labor, often on the same land where they had been enslaved. Jim Crow laws blanketed the South with a racial apartheid that denied Blacks basic freedoms and opportunities, and segregationist real estate and banking practices ensured that land ownership would remain out of reach for many Black Americans long after mid-twentieth-century efforts at reforms had come and gone.

Our lives today are determined by the choices that were made when the land shifted hands during the Great Reshuffle. As every country's most valuable tangible asset, land, and its uses and management, seeps into every social, economic, and political layer of society. It lingers there even as the economy and society change. To have any hope of grappling with humanity's greatest problems, we must first decipher how the Great Reshuffle shaped the world we are living in.

CHAPTER 2

THE GREAT RESHUFFLE

ON THE EVENING OF AUGUST 4, 1789, FRANCE'S NATIONAL CONstituent Assembly gathered at the heart of French power at Versailles to grapple with a wave of unrest. The French Revolution had begun just weeks prior. King Louis XVI had been forced to recognize the authority of the assembly, which commoners had formed in order to reshape French society. But this act of recognition was not enough to keep revolution at bay. The country was now gripped by a panic known as the Great Fear as bands of peasants armed themselves and began attacking the landed nobility.

A raucous and dramatic session unfolded. Commoners had enlisted several sympathetic members of the nobility and clergy to give impassioned speeches denouncing their privileges and to renounce their titles. A cascade of denunciations unfolded as the session crept past midnight. By the early morning of August 5, the assembly had drawn up a series of orders to end centuries of feudal rights, noble privileges, and church tithes that had propped up a system of domination over peasants rooted in noble and church ownership and rights over land. It was the opening salvo of a campaign to shatter the centuries-old system and redistribute land from its old owners to new ones.

A new era in the reshuffling of land ownership and rights had begun. Three months later the assembly seized land owned by the Catholic Church, which had a state-sanctioned monopoly on religion and landholdings that amounted to about 7 percent of the land in the country.[1] Local governments began auctioning off church property the following year. The Revolution then took an even more radical turn starting in the summer of 1792. Revolutionaries sought to vanquish the monarchy and the counterrevolutionary pushback from the nobility and church in a second phase of the Revolution. Nobles, clergymen, and wealthy landowners fled in large numbers. King Louis XVI was arrested and guillotined. The new republic's government seized the large landholdings of wealthy emigrants, another roughly 4 percent of the country's land, and sold it off.

These reforms radically reorganized French society. By reshuffling the ownership and use of land in France, they reordered the exercise of power.[2] With the abolition of feudalism, the breakup of large properties, and the end of noble and clerical privileges rooted in land ownership, France ushered in a new age of emancipation and individual equality, one that not only transformed the country itself but also served as a model for revolution and emancipation elsewhere. Further reforms that reinforced this shift ranged from the abolition of primogeniture and the introduction of a proportional tax on income from land to, in subsequent decades, an initiative that mapped property ownership across France so as to undermine tax evasion and corruption by wealthy landowners.

The Revolution had many famous victims, but it also had many unsung beneficiaries, especially where the reshuffling of land was concerned. Small independent farms came to proliferate across rural France in the aftermath of the Revolution. Subjects became citizens. And eventually they became educated, creating the conditions the country needed in order to take advantage of the coming Industrial Revolution.

The French Revolution was not the first time in history that land power had been reshuffled. Land had been changing hands at an increasing pace for several centuries prior to the Revolution as colonialism spread. European colonizers had been appropriating indigenous lands community by community, first at the fringes of continents and increasingly in their interiors. But the French Revolution stands apart as a mass appropriation of lands from the European gentry. It marked a turning point in human history.

This moment also coincided with an inflection in human population growth. The global population has increased eightfold between 1800 and today, from 1 billion to 8 billion. Much like the moment in human history when the first permanent human settlements emerged, this period stands out as a new era. Accelerating population growth put unprecedented demand on access to land. Human beings spread out across continents, tilled over the prairies, and felled the forests at an unparalleled rate. Some long-settled areas, especially in Europe and parts of Asia, faced pressure as never before. In many places land became scarce for the first time in human history. Land's connection to power became ironclad.

That scarcity of land and the resulting conflict over it set off a Great Reshuffle that came to France at the turn of the 1800s and that has repeated itself time and again across the globe ever since. At a scale simultaneously grand and rapid, countries undergoing the Great Reshuffle were forced to make decisions about who should own land and therefore who has power. This transformation was fueled by the spread and consolidation of nation-states and conflict for power, and it was made possible by more powerful standing armies and more formidable bureaucracies than the world had ever seen before. The Great Reshuffle came to different countries at different times, and in some places it is still ongoing.

IN THE YEARS since the human population began increasing with stunning speed, what has made all the difference is not whether land power would be reshuffled, but how. Who gets the land, who loses it, how it can be used and shared, and how society will keep track of it has had profound consequences for prosperity, equality, and sustainability.

The winners and losers shifted as the reshuffling of land ownership made its way through time and space. Perhaps the most familiar pattern is the one that was most common at the outset of the Great Reshuffle: the taking of indigenous lands on a massive scale, which were then awarded to settlers. But this was just the beginning. Everywhere that land had become concentrated and scarce, people wanted more of it. That made land reallocation a popular, and at many times a populist, political move.

By the time of the French Revolution, governments were taking land not only from the indigenous population but also from some large landowners and reallocating it to others, often landless rural inhabitants. The reshuffle had turned within societies. No one was immune from it. In some cases, governments negotiated land purchases from landowners and sold or gave out the land in parcels to rural workers. But the classic examples of this approach to the Great Reshuffle, as in France, involved taking large estates by force.

Within the twentieth century alone, roughly half of countries around the globe at some point set about snatching the landholdings of large landowners and reallocating them to the landless or land poor.[3] This affected around 2 billion people and continues to leave a mark on billions more. Massive land reallocations in China after its civil war, in Russia and Mexico following revolutions, and in many Eastern European countries under the shadow of the Iron Curtain are among the many examples of governments opting for a dramatic break with the past.

But the story doesn't end with the reshuffling of the land. How the new landholders use their land and power has far-reaching effects on a nation's future. The decision to take land from large landowners and give it to the landless is often accompanied by impassioned ideological justifications that revolve around fairness, equality, and even reparation. Relatedly, the choice to take indigenous land and give it to settlers is justified by arguments about prosperity, individual liberty, and opportunity. But before the yeoman farmer plows his homestead for the first time, and before the first harvest on a newly fashioned communal farm takes place, a great number of social consequences have already been locked in by the choices that were made about how the land can be used. Good intentions, dearly held beliefs, and impressive rhetorical justifications themselves do not ensure that the reshuffled society will be more free and less unequal.

There are four distinct types of land reallocation policies that have shaped the future of societies in distinct ways. These are settler reforms, collective reforms, land-to-the-tiller reforms, and cooperative reforms. Countries sometimes adopt mixed reforms that blend these types, but most frequently they choose a single path. Although these approaches to land reallocation are often seen as completely separate, if we view them together we can begin to make sense of the world they created.

We live in a world shaped by choices made during the Great Reshuffle. To have any hope of addressing today's most pressing and persistent problems, we need to come to grips with the consequences of shaking up who owns the land.

SETTLER REFORMS

European powers started to explore and settle far-flung lands starting at the time of the Renaissance and the conclusion of centuries-long campaigns to expel Muslim populations from the Iberian Peninsula. Great Britain, France, and Spain in particular built sprawling empires that spanned continents. They fought dozens of wars contesting control over their new territories and bought and sold vast tracts of land knowing little about what these lands contained.

There was one thing that these lands all had in common, however: they all had indigenous peoples already living on them. Europeans viewed these people with both fascination and disdain, often relegating them to the category of inferior, uncivilized "savages." While early colonizers periodically struck deals with indigenous peoples to stand out of their way, more often they pitted indigenous peoples against one another, sought to destroy or enslave them, or aimed to Christianize and civilize them.

Indigenous populations resisted where the newcomers posed a threat to their existence. Though initially outnumbered on the ground, imperial powers eventually deployed their greatest weapon to control and expand their empires: settlers.

Settlers served to populate newfound areas with subjects that could facilitate imperial territorial control. They also helped to fill government coffers by sending back resources from abroad. At the vanguard, colonial powers would send war veterans and social misfits to new territories. Other groups with a wider range of motivations later followed. The outflow of undesirable or volatile populations from the home country to the colony helped to relieve potentially threatening militarism, social and religious conflict, crime, and demographic pressure at home, though such settlers were prone to ignoring orders from their home country. In return for putting themselves on the front lines of empire, they became the beneficiaries of the first major land reallocation policy: settler reforms.

As we've seen, most of the land in the world was stewarded by indigenous peoples as of 1500, but by 1800 it was becoming difficult to avoid the incursions of modern imperialism. Indigenous groups continued to resist, but the Great Reshuffle cranked up the pressure. Settler reforms started by nibbling at the fringes of continents. Examples include the settlement of New England and Quebec along the Saint Lawrence River in North America, the tip of South Africa, and a few pockets of Latin America. But soon enough they began to spread across the globe and move deeper inland. Throughout the course of the 1800s, settler reforms accelerated rapidly and swept across vast swaths of territory around the globe.

Settler reforms typically involve land taken from an indigenous group, often in a frontier area, which is then granted to new settlers. Many of the most rapid and complete settler reforms have targeted hunter-gatherer communities in sparsely populated areas. These communities are especially vulnerable to dispossession because they inhabit territorial areas rather than fixed plots of land, making it easier to begin encroaching on their lands. Encroaching on indigenous lands often weakens those communities and creates conflict with settlers that can be used as a pretext for further removals. The culmination of these settler reforms are massive checkerboard arrangements of private land ownership where no such pattern previously existed.

Settler reforms are accelerated by aggressive and permissive settlement policies. The 1862 Homestead Act in the United States and similar programs have generated land rushes among settlers eager to lay claim to cheap or free indigenous lands that a government classifies as in the public domain.

There is no more jarring example than the 1889 Oklahoma land rush. As the early United States expanded its frontier from its foothold on the Eastern Seaboard, it began forcibly removing Native American peoples. Many were relocated to "Indian Territory," a large expanse of land in the central United States that shrank over time into what eventually became Oklahoma. In 1866, the government moved the "Five Civilized Tribes," which had been removed from the Southeast in the 1830s, to the eastern part of Indian Territory to make room for Plains Indians who faced ongoing removal.[4] It left a 2-million-acre buffer of land "unassigned" in central Oklahoma. At noon on April 22, 1889, the government put this land up for homesteading by settlers. Some 50,000 settlers gathered at a starting line, and with the shot of a gun by a federal official, they rushed out in a dusty frenzy, each hoping to claim a 160-acre plot of land for a small registration fee. By the end of the day, nearly all 2 million acres had been claimed by settlers. Whites outnumbered Indians in what had been "Indian Territory" within a year. Settlers grabbed millions more acres of former Native American land in the territory by land run, land allotment, and auction over the next fifteen years.

GREAT BRITAIN BUILT one of the largest empires in history on the back of colonial land settlement. Three of the early crown jewels were its American, Canadian, and Australian colonies. At first hundreds, and then thousands, of British migrants crossed the oceans to start a new life in the colonies. Many arrived free. Others arrived as indentured servants, or, in Australia's case, as convicts.

These colonies differed fundamentally from some of Britain's other colonies, such as Egypt, India, and Jamaica. There the focus was on establishing a small administrative elite to extract resources from local populations rather than to conquer lands for new British settlement en masse.

As the American, Canadian, and Australian colonies expanded, settlers decimated indigenous populations through land appropriation, war, and the spread of new diseases. And they opened their doors to broader European immigration, especially after gaining independence from the British. Waves of Irish, German, Italian, Scandinavian, and Eastern European migrants arrived on their shores.

The initial divide between settlers and indigenous populations as "civilized" versus "savage," Christian versus heathen, and white versus Indian shifted with these migrations and with the changing landscape of racial ideology. Settler and immigrant identification as "white" versus "non-white" became more common even as other European identities remained nested within the white category. This dichotomy built rather neatly on prior dichotomies and eventually came to structure society into a racial hierarchy with whiteness at the privileged top of the pyramid.[5]

The Spanish and the French replicated these British patterns through colonial land settlement elsewhere. The Spanish appropriated indigenous land in Central and South America, the Caribbean, and the Philippines. Colonizers and the Catholic Church teamed up to seize territory, extract resources through forced indigenous and imported slave labor, and spread Catholicism and the Spanish language to indigenous peoples who were viewed as inferior. In small pockets of the Americas, such as northern Argentina and parts of Costa Rica, initial land settlement was considerably more egalitarian. Many settlers in those places received smaller plots of land that they farmed or ranched on their own rather than relying on indigenous labor. Those areas underwent spurts of development more like the northeastern United States, eastern Canada, or eastern Australia than like Mexico or the Peruvian or Bolivian highlands.

In North Africa, the French confiscated land from indigenous North Africans as part of an ambitious colonial project and granted it to French settlers who were viewed as more productive, deserving, and civilized than local Muslim populations. This racial lens came to infuse every aspect of colonial governance in North Africa. And it endured until France's colonies won independence in the decades after World War II. The French took a more extractive settlement approach in Indochina, focusing on drawing resources out of the territories through a small French administrative elite rather than settling large numbers of French citizens as farmers on the land.

While the British, Spanish, and French empires perfected the art of settlement through colonialism, many countries have since replicated this pattern through domestic settler reforms. Some of them are the very same countries that won independence from these three European colonial masters. The United States, Canada, Australia, and Mexico are but a few examples of countries that continued settler reforms long after gaining sovereignty. Still other countries have pursued domestic settler reforms that undermine indigenous communities and indigenous ethnic minorities, including China in Xinjiang, Israel in the Palestinian territories, and Indonesia in West Papua.[6]

Unsurprisingly, building a society on land taken by force is unlikely to lock in equitable outcomes in the long run. Settler reforms buttress racial hierarchies that place settlers in a superior position to indigenous peoples. Political narratives construe settlers as entrepreneurial, hardworking, and deserving, while indigenous peoples are construed as backward, premodern, and undeserving. And settler reforms have historically expanded gender inequity by privileging men over women in awarding land claims.

National prosperity is not as clear-cut. Settler societies have sharply diverged in their development outcomes over time. Some have grown into wealthy, democratic societies, while others have struggled with poverty and authoritarianism. Ironically, settlers have transformed some of the world's most resource-rich areas at the time of settlement into the most dysfunctional societies, and converted some of the most spartan territories at the time of settlement into economic dynamos. The difference stems from the specific decisions made at the time when the land was reshuffled.

Settler reforms that concentrate land and labor in the hands of a few settlers for the purpose of plentiful resource extraction may serve to enrich those specific settlers, but they also tend to pave the way for long-term underdevelopment, with the beneficiaries jealously guarding their privileges and monopolizing political power at everyone else's expense. Dictatorship, elite infighting, civil war, and even revolution are the results.

By contrast, in places where settlers have found fewer resources and where geographic conditions are more conducive to modest small-scale farming, reformers typically distribute land widely and in small parcels to settlers. These reforms attract floods of immigrants seeking opportunity through land and tend to advance economic development. They go hand in hand with the commodification of land and resources, creating markets. And by broadly distributing land to settlers, they spread out power, fostering secure property rights and inclusive political representation among the settlers.

But the effects of even these growth-enhancing reforms on development are uneven and unequal. Indigenous groups are excluded, relegated to the ranks of noncitizens or second-class citizens. National prosperity has a hollowness to it when it is only prosperity for the winners—the settlers.

Settler reforms also wreak havoc on the environment. Settlers typically arrive to new lands with little knowledge of the new environments they encounter. With few resources and no backstop, they have a pressing need to make ends meet quickly. As a result, settlers tend to tear up and deplete virgin soils. They pollute watersheds and exhaust resources. They hunt and trap animals and poison pests into oblivion. Native ecosystems strain and sometimes collapse under their weight.

Settler reforms have become less common over time, particularly where frontiers are diminished and indigenous groups are long since dispossessed. As lands filled in and became more densely settled, competition and pressure spiked among settlers themselves. That same competition dialed up in the lands that humans had settled long ago, and it soon came to infuse domestic political battles around the globe. New forms of land reallocation spread, facilitated by the unprecedented administrative control and military power of consolidating states. Governments could now impose their will on the powerful as well as the weak.

COLLECTIVE REFORMS

If the first century of the Great Reshuffle was defined by settler reforms, the second was driven by a markedly different set of winners and losers. The French Revolution was, in this sense, a harbinger of much more radical reforms to come. This more recent period came to be defined by reforms that take land from large private landowners and hand it over to rural workers.

Perhaps the most electrifying example of the new approach to the Great Reshuffle, and one that motivated many others, took place in the Soviet Union. On November 7, 1917, the communist Bolshevik Party staged a bold uprising in the harbor of St. Petersburg. Tens of thousands of soldiers disgruntled by their brutal service and poor treatment in World War I joined them. The Bolsheviks captured key government buildings throughout the day and forced their way into the seat of Russian government power, the Winter Palace, just before midnight. They overran it in the wee hours of November 8. Later that same turbulent day, a new legislative body enacted Vladimir Lenin's Decree on Land, abolishing private property and reallocating that land to communes composed of desperately poor peasants who had only been freed from outright serfdom less than sixty years prior.

A decade later, Lenin was dead and Joseph Stalin had risen to power over the new Soviet Union, a country plagued by shortages of food and resources crucial for industrial production in growing urban areas. Stalin adopted a radical five-year plan to change this. The plan outlined a drive to outright collectivize land and all aspects of farming. The Communists sent an army of operatives out into the vast Soviet countryside to tear peasants away from their farms and equipment and to reorganize them according to government central planner diktat. Many peasants called collectivization a "second serfdom," and while they overwhelmingly opposed it, they had little choice in the matter.[7]

Other countries followed the Soviet example. China nationalized all land after its post–World War II civil war and organized many millions of people in the countryside into collectives. Cuba collectivized the better part of its rural sector after confiscating large landholdings during the 1959 Cuban Revolution. As in the Soviet Union, China, and Cuba, other countries that collectivized land sought to control and micromanage farmers within collectives.

GOVERNMENTS THAT PURSUE reforms centering on large private landholdings and rural workers begin by targeting specific large landholdings for acquisition and reallocation. Although this could be done by negotiating with landowners and paying them market prices for their land, more often it is done by fiat. Many governments forcibly take land from large landowners with meager compensation or none at all and give them no legal avenue for resistance. This is what occurred in China and Russia after their revolutions and in Zimbabwe in the 2000s.

In collective reforms, the land that is seized is then allocated to groups of rural workers to be farmed as collectives. Landless wage workers, tenants, and other farmers are pooled together and are in many cases relocated to work land as a team and share the profits. Governments often keep large landholdings intact in collective reforms or even combine them.

Collective reforms tend to follow from private land concentration. That can take the form of lord-peasant landholding, landlord-tenant landholding, or hacienda landholding. All of these types of landholding put a big target on the back of large landholders. It is tempting for governments that for reasons of expediency or ideology seek to avoid the disruptions of rewiring land ownership associated with breaking estates up into many thousands of small plots and instead implement a collective reform.

Collective farming can make good sense in the right context with wise and careful management. Collectives have the potential to take advantage of economies of scale in agriculture. They can benefit from efficiencies linked to buying inputs, farming, and selling products at a large scale rather than breaking up the production processes of large estates into a proliferation of miniature farms. There can be advantages to collective ownership of common resources such as plentiful grazing lands that might otherwise be difficult to manage individually. Collectives can protect farmers in situations where individual farming risk is considerable and disruptions can easily force farmers into bankruptcy and land sales. And they can foster community cooperation and common cultural preservation.

But this is not how most collective farming ends up. Governments that embark on top-down collective reforms face the temptation to use collectives as a piggy bank for national projects and as a mechanism for political dominance and even wide-scale repression. They lurk as overlords, managing and monitoring collective decisions and isolating dissenters. They also typically retain ultimate ownership of the land. Worker rights are revocable in these radical reforms and coercion is common. At some point, most of these reforms come crashing down.

Collective reforms tend to drive countries that adopt them into a trap of underdevelopment. Collectivization saps workers of individual work incentives and distorts long-term production. It also generates endemic property insecurity. Everyone from farmers to bankers are wary of investing in them because they do not know what will come of their investment. The result is lackluster output and stagnation seeping into every corner of the economy. Collectives also give governments tantalizing opportunities for social engineering and political control. This can go terribly awry. Government planners tend to trap farmers in collectives in the countryside, stunting urbanization and economic modernization. And any misguided decisions have grave, system-wide repercussions.

The Soviet Union offers a cautionary tale. Collectivization aimed to increase grain production and fuel rapid industrialization. In its first decade, however, it was marked by violence, disruption, resistance, and even several years of devastating famine that cost millions of lives. Peasants quickly realized that the state wanted to increase its take of their production. They resisted by dragging their feet and reducing their work efforts in what Stalin called a "go-slow strike." Over the course of decades, the Soviets managed to modernize traditional agriculture and use growing surpluses to stoke industry and support its international ambitions. But it again came at considerable cost as the absence of property rights fostered corruption, a lack of trust, and underinvestment. These problems continue to bedevil Russia. Much the same happened in China in the 1950s. Land collectivization drove down agricultural production and contributed to the Great Famine, resulting in millions of deaths.

Some, though not all, collective reforms make an effort to elevate the social and economic position of women in society. The Soviet Union, China, and Cuba, for instance, gave women a greater role in agricultural production as wage workers in hopes of not only enhancing output but also improving their social status. But the progressive effort fell short in practice. Collectives gave women lesser roles than men and paid them less.[8] They also often routed actual payments through male heads of household. Meanwhile, men typically commandeer collectives and run them. Women who have sought positions of power within collectives have historically become the subjects of violence and persecution. Governments that adopt collective reforms also routinely fail to sufficiently support the household responsibilities of working women, particularly in childcare.

Collective reforms frequently lead to environmental catastrophe. They generate a tragedy of the commons as collective workers degrade soils and resources without fully internalizing the costs of doing so.

Governments shower them with cheap fertilizers and pesticides in an effort to compensate for underproduction, and these, in turn, damage local ecosystems and poison watersheds.

Still, collective reforms have at times demonstrated that they have potential to break down racial as well as class-based hierarchy. Prior to collective reform in Mexico, many people of indigenous descent labored as peons under large landowners. They were forced to work on large local estates with little payment and little recourse against abuse. Estates were commonly owned by whiter families that claimed European descent and could trace their lineages back to the colonial era. Land reallocation severed this racialized relationship of servitude by turning estates over to local communities of laborers. That the form of communal holding harked back to precolonial forms of indigenous community is part of the reason why most land recipient communities later chose to retain communal land ownership when given the choice, albeit in a layered fashion along with private property rights. The government that conducted initial land collectivization simultaneously encouraged a narrative of common racial *mestizo* mixing and rhetorically shifted to treating workers along class lines as peasants rather than along racial lines while they lifted them up through land grants.

Collective reforms that are not state mandated and state run but instead bubble up from coherent social groups are far less pernicious than collectivization imposed from above. Some governments, such as those of Colombia and Bolivia, allow landless petitioners to request collective rather than individual land grants as part of their ongoing land reallocation programs. These collective grants are not usually centers of strong economic development, but they do tend to be fairly egalitarian, sustainable over the long haul, and more attentive to environmental consequences, largely because the beneficiaries are committed to building tight-knit communities on the land over the long term.

The link between collective reforms and communism, while not ironclad, came to loom large as the Cold War settled in. Simmering communist movements and organizers in the late 1940s in places as disparate as China, Korea, and Italy seized on the grievances of landless peasants and put radical land reallocation at the core of their revolutionary platforms. The United States feared that land inequality and rural poverty would fuel a wave of conflict and spread communism. It settled on another approach, called "tiller reforms," as a more ideologically appealing alternative and worked to help craft and fund them in countries such as Japan, South Korea, Taiwan, Italy, Vietnam, and El Salvador.

LAND-TO-THE-TILLER REFORMS

As Europe and Japan lay in ashes at the end of World War II, American officials sought to cut out the taproot of fascism while providing an alternative model to communism. Japan became one of the early proving grounds. The head of the US occupation authority in Japan after the country's surrender in World War II, General Douglas MacArthur, in a letter to the Japanese government on December 9, 1945, called the country's landlord-tenant system "economic bondage which has enslaved the Japanese farmer to centuries of feudal oppression." A thin layer of powerful landlords had presided over a sea of poor renters before the war. The words of a landlord from Yamagata in northern Japan offer a sense of the lofty superiority that prevailed among landlords in those days. As head of the Otaki family, he controlled some 440 acres of prime agricultural land and managed 170 tenants. "As manager and representative of Otaki Saburoemon, owner of 4,000 bales' worth of land," he said, "I behave as such and with appropriate dignity. I have to be arrogant."[9]

Local landlord associations were amalgamated into one national, federated body that wielded unparalleled political influence. American occupiers viewed them as the pillars of Japanese imperial expansionism and enablers of the right-wing nationalism that had propelled the country to war. A land-to-the-tiller reform was the cure the Americans prescribed, and it dovetailed with nascent ideas among postwar Japanese officials about how to open a new chapter in its history.

The tiller reform marked a radical shift in the country. In October 1947, while still under US military occupation, the Japanese legislature passed a bill limiting the amount of private land that could be held to seven acres. Just over two acres of that could be leased to tenants. The government and local agricultural associations proceeded to buy out any landholdings above those draconian and sweeping limits.

Former tenants—such as those who rented land from Otaki—became landowners in their own right and saw their fortunes quickly turn, as they now kept their income. As one villager from Shinohata in central Japan put it, "Before the war, you could work and work and work and you never saved money, could never eat delicious food, couldn't eat enough food. Now even with working your guts out you have money left over—well, not that much left over, but enough so that we don't feel in need—and our everyday life is sheer luxury compared with what it used to be."[10] People began to remodel their houses, purchase better clothing, change what they ate, and acquire more material comforts.

LAND-TO-THE-TILLER REFORMS MORE or less follow this model. They reallocate land from large private landowners to the tillers on that land, and most frequently take place where there is a preexisting landlord-tenant landholding pattern.

Some of the most prominent tiller reforms occurred in East Asia alongside Japan after World War II. South Korea and Taiwan took this path, and even China briefly flirted with a tiller reform before taking a sharp turn toward collectivization. Land-to-the-tiller reforms occurred in parts of India after independence as well, and in South Vietnam under US occupation. One of the earliest tiller reforms occurred in Ireland in the late 1800s and early 1900s.

Tiller reforms do not always have to follow from landlord-tenant landholding. They can also occur in the context of lord-peasant or hacienda landholding. In those cases, workers on the land under peonage-style arrangements, or landless wage laborers such as farmhands on the property, receive the land. Italy transformed considerable portions of its land in this fashion in the 1950s, as did El Salvador in the 1980s. What sets tiller reforms apart is that the tillers who receive land get it as individual or family plots. In addition to receiving strong backing from liberal democratic powers during the Cold War, tiller-style reforms gained the approval of international development agencies such as the World Bank, which began to push tiller reforms during the Cold War and continued to do so for the two decades after its end, though they have begun to take a more context-specific approach to reform in recent years.

Unlike settler reforms, tiller reforms can help to level pernicious forms of race- and ethnicity-based servitude and disadvantage. Take, for instance, how the Irish Land Acts of 1870–1909 raised up poor Irish farmers against the British landlords who had long controlled Ireland's land and helped the British government stamp out Irish customs and language. The Land Acts eliminated abusive forms of land tenancy against the Irish underclass and subsidized tenant purchases of land from their landlords. The Land Acts gave landlords bonuses to sell their land in order to speed up the reform and reduce resistance. Later reforms forced the remainder of landlords to sell out. In their place arose an independent and autonomous class of Irish small farmers that could hold their heads high in the new Ireland.

Tiller reforms can supercharge development. After Japan's tiller reform, newly empowered small farmers could afford to send their children to school instead of to the fields for the first time in Japanese history. Within a generation, the country became urban and well educated, home to a booming economy. Members from the lower social classes entered the civil service, the military, and the industrial sector in large numbers. The government used surpluses to build export-oriented manufacturing and nurtured it through financial institutions it held on a tight leash. Similar transformations followed tiller reforms in South Korea and Taiwan.[11]

It would be hard to overstate the impact that these reforms had on the appetite for land reshuffling. Aside from moves by European settlers to appropriate indigenous lands, it wasn't until the United States began to view land reallocation as a necessary tool to break fascism and undermine communism, in the aftermath of World War II, that it came to be perceived as a powerful and effective policy for economic good. Although land reallocation was politically popular among the landless, it had led to strife and disruption time and again, as well as to stiff opposition by landowners.

But when land reshuffles in Japan, South Korea, and Taiwan rapidly transformed them from feudal, agrarian societies into "Asian Tigers," land reallocation became an object of fascination and even obsession for development economists. Study after study came to show that large landholdings are frequently underutilized and that small farmers, with strong incentives to wring as much as they could from the soil, could produce more per acre. Land reallocation came to be seen as the exceptional policy where greater equality and development could be achieved simultaneously rather than working in conflict with one another. By and large, that simple economic calculation has not changed. The United States began to promote tiller reforms everywhere it viewed landlessness as politically destabilizing and believed that Communists were poised to take advantage of deep rural grievances. The World Bank also started to prescribe it to countries around the globe as a cure for development traps.

The legacy of tiller reforms is decidedly more mixed when it comes to gender inequity and the environment. Many tiller reforms, including in East Asia and Ireland, contributed to gender inequity by granting property titles to male heads of household. Such policies set the stage for multigenerational gender imbalances in household duties, earning capacity, and intrahousehold bargaining power. Men rode the increasing value of their assets to ever greater social and economic power while leaving women behind.

Tiller reforms also tend to degrade the environment. Poor tillers who seek to stand on their own two feet as independent farmers and who now capture all of the earnings from what they produce quickly try to maximize their output. They adopt industrial fertilizers and pesticides where available and often overuse the land, since they cannot afford to fallow it. That strains resources and damages the land

and watersheds. Some tiller reforms that take place in contexts of land scarcity, as well as the presence of landless wage laborers alongside poor tenants, can lead to additional uncultivated public lands being doled out as individual plots to the landless. This transforms natural landscapes into more farmland, with negative consequences for biodiversity and environmental health.

Tiller reforms outlived collective reforms and the Cold War, and some of the more recent ones have paid closer attention to gender and environmental concerns. But during the Cold War, many countries that pursued land reallocation and did not want collective reform shied away from tiller reforms. They worried about economic disruptions and loss of political control associated with reshuffling land by creating a sea of new independent landowners overnight. These countries sought a different playbook.

COOPERATIVE REFORMS

The stark differences, and even competition, between collective and tiller reforms provided ample space for other ways to organize and use land. Many countries at the sidelines of Great Power competition during the Cold War chose a third way: cooperative reform.

In a dramatic speech to the nation on June 24, 1969, Peru's new military ruler, General Juan Velasco Alvarado, announced a land reckoning for the country that would turn it into one of the world's boldest experiments in cooperative reform. Spanish colonization had concentrated land in a small number of haciendas in Peru, especially in the Andean highlands. The country's rural population continued to toil on these haciendas for little or no pay and suffered indignities at the hands of wealthy landowners. Echoing the words of the indigenous hero Túpac Amaru, who had fought valiantly against Spanish colonists, Velasco promulgated a sweeping land reallocation, proclaiming, "Peasants, the master will no longer feed from your poverty." Over the next decade, the government seized most of the large private estates in the country and fashioned them into large cooperatives to be run by peasants.

One landowner from Junín recounted his expropriation in vivid terms: "It hit us like a bucket of cold water. I will never forget it because it was most unpleasant. . . . I ceased to be an owner of what had been mine for so many years, something that had belonged to my grandparents." The peasant beneficiaries, by contrast, were thrilled. One hacienda worker in Cañete recalled learning of its expropriation: "People were so happy they cried. They did not believe that they had become the owners of something they had never in their wildest dreams envisioned. To be owners of 500 hectares [about 1,200 acres], when before they did not even have one furrow! That was a real experience of a personal triumph."[12]

Peasant ownership, however, was a chimera. The government pushed peasants into cooperatives composed of workers under a single management structure and did not hand over ultimate ownership of the land.[13] Peasants who informally held family plots within or alongside haciendas at the time of the reform got to keep them and gained far more autonomy over them. They also contributed their labor to the new cooperatives and shared in their profits. But the cooperatives did not fare well over time. Most peasants did not want them to begin with. They wanted more of their own land and less intervention and management of their affairs. Within a few years most cooperatives fell prey to infighting over work contributions, profits, and management. People wanted out. Once the military government fell, so did cooperatives.

COOPERATIVE REFORMS ARE similar in many ways to collective reforms. They begin by reallocating large private landholdings to groups of rural workers. In some cases, the large properties remain intact, and other times they are combined or broken into pieces. Workers share in farming the land and buy inputs and sell products as a group. But there is a major difference relative to collective reforms: cooperatives do not work all of the land and share all of the inputs and profits collectively as a team. Cooperative members often farm their own plots and have side jobs. They "top up" that work by dedicating some share of their labor to collective tasks. Governments frequently, but not always, retain formal ownership of the land.

Cooperative reforms were especially popular in North Africa during decolonization and in Latin America during the Cold War. The reallocation of land through cooperative reforms during the decolonization of Africa severed a major thread of the colonial race-based order. In Algeria, Morocco, and Tunisia, for instance, French colonizers dominated large swaths of the highest-quality land and pushed native Arab and Berber Muslims onto inferior lands at the fringes of these agrarian economies. The large rural Muslim populations were consequently poor and marginalized. Many people worked as permanent or temporary laborers on French-run estates. They faced discrimination at every turn. Independence movements after World War II, and the French government's withdrawal from its colonial possessions, collided to remove white Europeans from the farming sector. Local populations took the land through farming cooperatives, removing the ugliest racialized components of rural labor.

Countries such as Bolivia, Chile, El Salvador, Nicaragua, and Peru in Latin America all conducted cooperative reforms around the same time, between the 1950s and 1980s. Portugal conducted a massive cooperative reform in the south of the country in the mid-1970s. Yugoslavia adopted a cooperative reform after World War II.

Cooperative reforms may light a spark under agricultural productivity in the short term, but more often than not, as in Peru, they soon flame out. As in collective reforms, distorted work incentives, government mismanagement and coercion, and stalled urban transformation are all culprits of this underperformance. Cooperative reforms rarely succumb to the deepest depths of collective reforms in terms of wide-scale famine and death. But that is a low bar to clear. They fall far short of land-to-the-tiller reforms in terms of contributing to economic development.

The governments that adopt cooperative reforms are rarely as ideologically motivated to support the empowerment of women as those that take on collective reforms. Cooperative reforms therefore tend to replicate and deepen existing gender disparities. Men end up dominating cooperatives in large number. That positions them to capture the lion's share of benefits from the government. And it puts them first in line when cooperatives break up to snatch up their most valuable pieces.

Cooperative reforms behave much like collective reforms from the perspective of breaking down racial hierarchies. These reforms, for instance, broke feudalistic forms of racialized servitude in the South American countries of Bolivia, Chile, and Peru. Peru's land reform of the late 1960s, as the anthropologist Enrique Mayer put it, "completed the abolition of all forms of servitude in rural estates, a momentous shift in the history of the Andes, akin to the abolition of slavery in the Americas."[14] Cooperative reforms similarly eroded racial hierarchies in North Africa.

Most cooperative reforms result in environmental carnage. Underproduction stimulates the use of fertilizers and pesticides, which wreak havoc on soils and watersheds. These chemicals also damage local biodiversity, killing off native plants, animals, insects, and microbes that are crucial for stable ecosystems. Weak property rights foster resource degradation through overuse.

* * *

THE WORLD WE live in today is shaped by the choices countries made when the Great Reshuffle arrived on their doorstep. If they chose to steal the land from its indigenous occupants, they bequeathed to their descendants a country consumed by racial hierarchy and gender inequality and diminished by the loss of ecosystems and a heavily damaged natural environment. If the pressure only reached the breaking point in the early or mid-twentieth century, they may have opted to expropriate the large agricultural landholders and collectivize. More likely than not those collectives are already long gone, but the societies that remain still struggle with underdevelopment, corruption, authoritarianism, and environmental wreckage. If a country instead fashioned cooperatives out of large landholdings, then it likely ended up with a milder version of underdevelopment, and authoritarianism and corruption had shallower roots. But the environment paid a similar price and gender relations could be worse. Meanwhile, societies are most likely well-off and agriculture is now far less prominent in countries that pursued a different path by breaking up large landholdings into small family plots. But men continue to rule in the workplace and at home, and pollution and resource depletion are likely to define their environmental landscape.

The four canonical land reallocation paths tend to lock in trajectories that are self-reinforcing and difficult to escape. Governments that reallocate land do not simply step aside once transfers occur. They use land to underpin national projects, win political support, and exert social control. Their chosen path determines how they structure property rights, build infrastructure, enumerate and categorize citizens, and regulate the environment. The consequences continue to mark societies long after urbanization and modernization have diminished the relative importance of agriculture.

Those consequences include some of society's most intractable problems. Land has helped to construct racial hierarchy. It has deepened gender inequity and made it more durable. Land paved the way to underdevelopment. And it exacerbated problems linked to climate change, resource depletion, and the loss of biodiversity.

To see the futures that these paths lock in, we have to set foot in the places haunted by the land reshuffles of generations past. We have to talk to those marked by the repercussions. Only then can we grapple with land's true power.

PART II

How Land Made Our Greatest Problems

CHAPTER 3

LANDS DIVIDED BY RACE

IN LATE AUGUST 1980, A SMALL BRUSH FIRE SWEPT UP THE SIDE of the San Jacinto Mountains that loom over the city of Palm Springs, California, and reignited an old battle over land. Desert winds blew the fire south, past downtown Palm Springs and then into the sacred canyons of the Agua Caliente Indian Reservation. The community's ancestral home was scorched—but this natural disaster presented an opportunity the City of Palm Springs had long awaited.

For more than fifty years, members of the Agua Caliente had been fighting off the city's attempts to take control of their lands. Among the city government's many objectives was to build a road through the middle of the reservation following the Palm Canyon Creek bed over the San Jacinto Mountains to link up with a highway on the other side. The wildfire seemed to provide the city with an excuse to kick into gear at last.

A fleet of heavy D9 bulldozers was waiting in the palm canyons before the flames were even extinguished. The workers went so far as to mark the reservation's burnt trees with blue spray paint for removal. "There was this thinking at the time that they could just go on a federal reservation and start clearing the roads and do anything they want," recalled Dr. Sean Milanovich, whose father, Richard Milanovich, was Tribal chairman for the Agua Caliente for nearly thirty years. It took members of the Agua Caliente physically interrupting the work to stop the land from being cleared and snatched away. Dr. Milanovich recalls that his father and other relatives "were up there and they were stopping these guys. They were up there all night. And they fought a couple times. My dad told the city, 'You know what, I know you want to make a road but you're not going to do it on our reservation.'"[1]

The city's attempt to use the fire as a pretext for yet another land grab formed one of Dr. Milanovich's earliest childhood memories. He recounts that his father "was completely adamant about not letting the city through. And especially to have control of the land and drive those D9s through our precious forests, through our precious palm oases and canyons, downing palm trees, downing cottonwoods, downing alders." It was just one episode among many in the long campaign to wrest land from the Agua Caliente and knock them down.

Today the city of Palm Springs is the Las Vegas of California. It is a playground for the rich and famous nestled right at the heart of the Coachella Valley. All the valley's casinos, Hollywood-style entertainment, and day spas offer a glitzy distraction from the area's troubled history. Before Palm Springs became smothered in blond hair and bright lights, it was a patchwork quilt of wealthy enclaves amid poorer areas. That pattern, set in the early to mid-1900s, mapped directly onto land ownership and use and the fate of the communities that remained there generations afterward. Who got the land, and how, made all the difference.

The story of Palm Springs is the story of how land reallocation put white settlers and entrepreneurs at the top. Incoming whites snatched land repeatedly from the Agua Caliente, tried to erase their language and traditions, and created a social and economic system that marginalized them as outsiders and dependents in their own territory. "As intelligent and as strong as we are . . . because our skin was darker, because we did not speak the same language, and we were not Christian, they [whites] felt that they could do what they want," Dr. Milanovich told me. "And so they stole our land . . . and they legitimized themselves to be . . . rulers." But the Palm Springs story is far from unique.

Land power is at the root of racial hierarchy. Select racial groups can dominate others by stealing their land and then creating political rules and economic mechanisms to entrench that dominance. As power in these societies becomes tightly linked with the racialized ownership of land and the privileges that ownership confers, a race-based social order is woven into the social fabric. How people are born, how they are raised and live, the education they receive, their work opportunities, and even when and how they die are all shaped by the color of their skin.

We have seen this script replayed time and again in societies whose lands were distributed through settler reforms. Notions of racial hierarchy are present in these societies from the start, with settlers viewing themselves as spiritually and socially superior to indigenous populations. Land power radically deepens this hierarchy and makes it even more rigid. Settlers ravage indigenous populations by appropriating their land, waging war on them, and spreading new diseases among them. That adds potent political and economic dimensions to race that put settlers in a superior position to indigenous peoples.

The story of the Coachella Valley, the Agua Caliente, and the newcomers who settled Palm Springs shows us how such a racial hierarchy between whites and indigenous peoples is built from the ground up. It also highlights the one thing that would most help to deconstruct the long-standing racial hierarchy—the land itself.

THE COACHELLA VALLEY around Palm Springs was since time immemorial the territory of the Agua Caliente Band of Cahuilla Indians. Recent excavations in downtown Palm Springs indicate that their ancestors spread into the valley and neighboring mountains and passes after migrating south to the area about 8,000 years ago.

The environmental zones of the region shaped how the Cahuilla related to the land and its resources. The Cahuilla living in the valleys relied on mesquite, a legume, as a major food source, gathering the seedpods from the flowering desert shrub that produces them between June and August. They also gathered dates from native palms;

harvested agave, both for food and for making clothing and nets; hunted small game; and used other local seeds, as well as roots, flowers, and fruits, as both food and medicine. Because of the heat, these Cahuilla lived in well-ventilated structures made from palm, willow, and arrow weed or in lean-to shelters nestled in rock formations.

The Cahuilla living in the mountains gathered and processed acorns in October and November. They also hunted deer, mountain goats, rabbits, squirrels, and other small game. They built sturdier shelters than those who lived in the valley, constructing their homes from earth, logs, and bark.

Cahuilla society was divided into ritual groups, the Wildcat and the Coyote, which were in turn divided into clans. Three of these clans later banded together to form the present-day Agua Caliente Band of the Cahuilla.[2] Villages typically had between one hundred and several hundred inhabitants. The Cahuilla occupied them year-round, though large portions of a village would move for several weeks at a time to harvest or collect food.

Trails connected villages and linked them to resources and neighbors. The Cahuilla mostly traded between east and west, linking groups from the Colorado River to coastal peoples. It was both ceremonial and economic in nature. They traded for shell beads, coastal acorns, and volcanic rock that could be used for cooking and in exchange offered arrowheads, food staples, and other materials.[3]

Although it is hard to date the origins of their agriculture precisely, the Agua Caliente were clearly growing some crops in the early 1800s. They dug irrigation ditches from nearby streams to grow corn, pumpkins, and melons. The hot springs, located in today's Palm Springs, provided a focal point for ceremonial activity, healing rituals, and other gatherings. For the Cahuilla, according to Dr. Milanovich, "everything is inside the land. Everything. Our heart comes from the land. All of our traditional stories come from the land. How we came on the land, how we move on the land, how we gathered different plants, how we hunted. All of our stories and songs are from the land. The land heals us, protects us, takes care of us."[4]

The Cahuilla's first contact with Europeans did not come from British colonizers to the American colonies, but from Mexico. At first, the Spanish began setting up trade routes along the West Coast between their northern missions in California and their Mexican possessions to the south. But serious disturbances for the Cahuilla did not arrive until after Mexico wrested independence from Spain in the early 1800s. Eager to make the break definitive, and under pressure from northern elites, the new Mexican government started doling out enormous land grants to ranchers in its California territories. This included the western range of Cahuilla land, though the Agua Caliente managed to avoid having their land appropriated, even if temporarily, at that time. Probably owing to the rugged terrain and harsh landscape of eastern Cahuilla territory where the Agua Caliente resided, their land was not yet deemed a prime target of settlement.[5]

This brief period of history is known as Mexico's "ranchero" period. It lasted only a few decades, and it was Mexico's version of a Wild West. This era produced the first recorded history of the Agua Caliente area, courtesy of the diary of a Mexican lieutenant on an exploratory expedition. He was part of a group sent by the Mexican government to find an overland route linking Sonora to California. The lieutenant's writings indicate that there was previous knowledge of the existence of the area. The Cahuilla called the area *Séc-he* (boiling water), but early Spanish explorers, and the Mexicans who followed them, translated it as *Agua Caliente* (hot water). The new name stuck.

Meanwhile, a far more grave threat to the Cahuilla was building thousands of miles to the east. Settlers on the Eastern Seaboard were gobbling up land from Native Americans and laying the foundations for an inexorable march to the Pacific. This march would eventually swallow up the Cahuilla.

EARLY SETTLERS IN colonial America lived a difficult and precarious life. They arrived after a long journey at sea from Europe to outposts perched on the Atlantic Seaboard. Many were deposited on the shores still ill or malnourished from their ocean voyage. Unfamiliar with local land, resources, and weather, they suffered hunger and cold on arrival. Lifespans were short and mortality was high in the early years.

Native Americans helped to ease the transition. The Mashpee Wampanoag Tribe of coastal Massachusetts and Rhode Island, for instance, shared food and local knowledge with Pilgrims who arrived on the *Mayflower* in 1620.[6] And they shared in feasts at the time of the Pilgrims' early harvests, which some trace as the root of the modern Thanksgiving holiday.

Before long the new colonies started to flourish, and the trickle of immigrants became a stream, then a river. The absence of religious persecution was part of the attraction. Colonists could practice their beliefs openly in the New World without the shadow of punishment and violence hanging over their heads.

But the biggest prize was land. The British Crown fostered the growth of the colonies through enormous land charters. Unlike in Europe, where rigid class structures and land pressure precluded land ownership for all but the most privileged upper strata of society, settlers had the real promise of lands of their own if they could simply make it to the frontier. This was particularly the case in the northern colonies.

Take, for instance, the area then known as the Province of Pennsylvania. King Charles II granted an enormous tract of land spanning contemporary Pennsylvania and Delaware to William Penn. In a stroke this grant turned him into the largest private landowner in the world—but now he had to settle it. Penn set about attracting colonists to the land to raise money and embarked on ambitious settlement programs, most notably an enormous schooling program that was unparalleled elsewhere in the world in terms of its broad access. Penn saw education as a key to religious literacy and enlightenment. His experiment turned parts of the northern United States into some of the most literate early societies on earth.

There was, of course, a catch. The land that the British Crown was doling out to white settlers was already inhabited by Native Americans. There is no consensus on the size of the precolonial population in what is now the continental United States, but estimates range from about 1 million to 10 million.[7]

It didn't take long for relations between settlers and Native Americans to get testy. Colonists brought new diseases with them to the New World. Smallpox and measles ravaged local populations. The settlers' march inland from the coast posed an unmistakable threat to Native American homelands. And their behavior didn't help. A number of early European explorers, traders, and settlers abducted indigenous peoples and sold them into slavery, or tried to kill or capture indigenous leaders and other community members. And settlers did not hide their beliefs in their racial and religious superiority over Native Americans, which they used to justify land grabs.

Colonial American policy toward Native American lands settled into an uneasy mix of treaty-making and violent Indian removal, often in tandem. Peaceful coexistence rarely lasted more than a couple of decades before there would be another aggressive push toward frontier settlement, resulting in pitched battles between settlers and militiamen on the one hand and Native Americans on the other.

Spanish explorers and missionaries on the West Coast closer to the Cahuilla did not behave any better. The Spanish supported the ambitious Catholic missionary Junípero Serra in setting up a string of missions in the mid- to late 1700s, spanning from San Diego to Sonoma. The goal was to civilize and Christianize local indigenous populations. They reached into the Cahuilla and other local populations and brought their members to the missions for baptism and conversion.

These missions doubled as labor and death camps. Those who were corralled at the missions were forced to work without pay, and those who escaped were often hunted down by the Spanish missionaries, who regarded indigenous populations as inferior. As Serra, sainted by Pope Francis in 2015, wrote in 1780, "That spiritual fathers should punish their sons, the Indians, with blows appears to be as old as the conquest of [the Americas]; so general in fact that the saints do not seem to be any exception to the rule." The missions also sought to stamp out local customs and culture.

European diseases decimated local populations here too, and, in the end, more Native Americans died in the missions than were born there.[8] Fortunately for the Agua Caliente, who lived at the eastern fringes of the Cahuilla people farthest from California's coast, they were too far from the missions to become their prey.

Back East, land settlement took a turn with American independence. The land chartering system came to an end, and newer, more rapacious systems took its place. One popular new policy was to designate large tracts of frontier land as military bounty land. With federal revenues running low, volunteer and ill-paid war veterans could instead receive bounty land grants in government-created military tracts. The government deliberately placed these as buffer zones between settled areas and frontier areas where Native Americans resided.

In creating a military tract in Ohio Territory in 1796, for instance, President George Washington argued that it "would connect our government with the frontiers, extend our settlements progressively, and plant a brave, a hardy and respectable race of people as our advanced post, who would be always ready and willing (in case of hostility) to combat the savages and check their incursions."[9]

The Great Reshuffle had arrived in America. Territorial acquisitions from Spain, France, Great Britain, and Mexico in the first half of the nineteenth century tripled all previous holdings. From the mid-1840s to the early 1850s alone, the United States wrested Texas, California, Nevada, New Mexico, Arizona, Utah, and parts of several other states from Mexico through annexations and forced purchases. That removed the last administrative and political barriers between the growing mass of white settlers in the East and western indigenous peoples, including the Cahuilla. Land settlement was about to reach a fevered pitch in the new American West.

JUST DECADES BEFORE settlers from the East arrived to Cahuilla territory, the growing swell of willing settlers, combined with the political and economic attractions of settlement—both on the western frontier and in the South in an expansion of the slave economy—drove the US government to ramp up Indian removal. President Andrew Jackson's Indian Removal Act of 1830 was one of the most brutal settlement policies of the era, sparking the infamous Trail of Tears that removed roughly 100,000 Indians from the southeast to designated "Indian Territory" west of the Mississippi River. The Chickasaw, Cherokee, Choctaw, and Muscogee Creek nations, as well as many others, suffered forced marches that cost thousands of lives. The government sold off some of these lands to settle war debts and granted others to new settlers.

But these policies created their own problems. Officials from new states that bordered Indian Territory sought a buffer against what they viewed as a dangerous security threat. The Missouri General Assembly, for instance, petitioned Congress for a more densely settled border region to protect its citizens who were "surrounded by restless hordes of native savages."[10] Congress repeatedly responded to appeals like these by providing land to armed settlers or to those who promised to ward off Indian attacks.

Westward expansion after the Mexican-American War pushed the potential for settlement all the way to the Pacific Ocean and to Cahuilla territory. The annexation of Mexican territory from Texas to California and the acquisition of Oregon Country in the 1840s, however, quickly made the prospect of Indian westward removal untenable. "Manifest destiny" would have to be accomplished another way.

As American settlers began trickling into Southern California around the time of the Gold Rush and the Mexican-American War, the Cahuilla and their lands became targets. Only narrowly avoiding Indian removal, they would now have to face the next American Indian policy tool: reservations.

The US government cordoned off indigenous communities into designated and often undesirable areas away from white settlements. The Cahuilla and hundreds of other groups met this fate. But before their fate was sealed, the Cahuilla first passed through an unsettling period of treaty-making and settler incursions on their land.

The Gold Rush and westward expansion brought American settlers to Cahuilla territory beginning in the 1850s. Land encroachment and attempts at taxation drew the ire of the Cahuilla along with the nearby Cupeño, Luiseño, and Serrano peoples. The anger boiled over in an abortive uprising and brought the communities into negotiation with US government agents. Leaders of these communities signed the Treaty of Temecula on January 5, 1852, under the threat of being executed, forcibly ceding their land base in exchange for a far smaller permanent reservation. The US Senate rejected the treaty but ordered its decision to be held in secrecy. Government policy in the region then repeatedly violated what the groups thought had been agreed upon, cutting them down in such a way that they could no longer successfully defend their interests or their land.[11]

A few years later, on May 15, 1856, the principal Cahuilla chief and twenty-four other Cahuilla leaders sent a petition to the commissioner of Indian affairs complaining about continued white land grabs: "From time immemorial we have lived upon and occupied the lands of and adjacent to the Pass of San Gorgonio. . . . Since the occupation of California by the Americans and particularly within the last two or three years we have been encroached upon by the white settlers who have taken possession of a large portion of our best farming and grazing lands and by diverting the water from our lands deprive us to a great extent of the means of irrigation." The petition went on to explain the consequences of these losses, and to ask for reprieve: "We have thus been frequently obliged to abandon portions of our improved lands greatly to the detriment and distress of our people. . . . What we particularly desire and ask of the Government is that certain public lands may be set apart for our use exclusively (which lands we have long occupied and improved) and from which we may not be forced by white settlers."[12] The petition nonetheless fell on deaf ears.

One year later a major earthquake hit the area, reducing the flow of stream water in the canyons where many Agua Caliente lived and forcing them into life on the floor of the Coachella Valley where they could take advantage of groundwater. That would bring them into even more direct conflict with settlers.

THE US GOVERNMENT'S efforts to settle the West ramped up considerably in the 1860s with the Homestead Act. The Homestead Act transformed the United States into the largest freeholder society on earth. It granted intrepid frontier settlers up to 160 acres of public land for a small fee. Settlers had to live on the land for five years and farm it, at which point they could file for a land title. Prospective settlers jumped at the opportunity, and waves of settlers rushed across the plains through progressive homesteading and laid claim to Native American lands. Some 1.6 million individuals laid claim to 270 million acres of land—an area equivalent in size to Texas and California combined—over the course of the program.

Sure enough, within a couple of decades settlers had washed over California and the areas inhabited by and surrounding the Cahuilla. But the final shape of dispossession for the Agua Caliente and several other Cahuilla bands occurred not at the hands of homesteaders but of a railroad company and the US government. The US government sought to supercharge western settlement and development by building railroads spanning thousands of miles to connect growing but far-flung population settlements. Railroad companies, however, were in their infancy and strapped for cash. The US government came up with a solution: granting the railroad companies vast free tracts of public land alongside rail tracks that companies could in turn sell or use as collateral to issue bonds in order to raise capital.[13]

Public land "checkerboarding" was born through this solution. The Public Land Survey System had already divided most western territories into an enormous grid of six-by-six-mile squares known as townships, which in turn were divided into thirty-six sections of one square mile each. The government decided to give odd-numbered sections to railroad companies and keep the remaining even-numbered sections. It did so within a fixed distance on either side of railway tracks, typically ten miles. This generated a sprawling checkerboard pattern of private-public land ownership across sections of the West.

Railroad land granting began in the Midwest and South in 1850 and extended all the way to the Pacific Ocean with the Pacific Railway Acts dating between 1862 and 1871. The grants eventually covered 170 million acres of land in the frontier. It was the Pacific Railway Acts that carved up the Agua Caliente.

Homesteading and railroad land grants worked in tandem to dispossess indigenous peoples and enshrine whiteness in the western frontier. A sea of white settlers surrounded and encroached on Native Americans. This was the birth of a new racial hierarchy in the West.

The Homestead Act on paper made all adults who were citizens or in the process of gaining citizenship eligible to claim land. But in practice, there was an overwhelming bias in favor of white settlers.

Congress sought to use the Homestead Act and other settlement policies to manufacture white majorities in lands previously occupied by non-whites.[14] Numerous nascent states on the western frontier appealed in part to their whiteness through settlement in making the case for statehood.

The economics of settlement quickened this process. Acquiring land was only a small part of the expense in moving west and starting a new life. Settlers had to finance the journey, buy farm inputs, build a house, and survive until the first harvest. Saving on a land purchase would have only represented about 10 to 30 percent of these costs.[15] The expenses involved put land claims out of reach for many minority groups that struggled with poverty or could not easily escape their circumstances.[16]

The heyday of the Homestead Act, from 1862 through the 1920s, was also the height of white European immigration to the United States. From 1870 until the 1890s, most immigrants arrived from western and northern Europe.[17] The trend then shifted to immigration from eastern and southern Europe. Immigration slowed starting in World War I. The decline accelerated with immigration restrictions in the 1920s, followed by the Great Depression. Furthermore, growing white populations on the Eastern Seaboard in the late 1800s pushed younger generations to seek new livelihoods in the West.

Railroad grants had a similar racial bent. Most grants went to politically connected private companies backed by white financiers.[18] Indeed, the corruption and cronyism involved in these grants sparked a public outcry that shut the program down to new grants in 1871. But enormous tracts of land had already been allocated and in most cases remained at the disposal of the companies.[19] The railroad companies sold large portions of these tracts to wealthy white buyers and speculators, and some of these buyers sought in turn to rent plots to newly arriving white settlers.[20] Companies sold other portions to the flood of white settlers arriving from the East as part of the homesteading trend.

IN AN UNFORTUNATE dint of fate, the Cahuilla lived at a crossroads for Gold Rush prospectors traveling between the valleys around Los Angeles and gold deposits in southern Arizona. This put them directly in the crosshairs of the Southern Pacific Railroad in the 1860s. The US government gave Southern Pacific a right-of-way to build its railroad straight through the Coachella Valley and Cahuilla territory, piggybacking off early stagecoach routes.[21]

As was common practice, the government allocated the railroad a checkerboard of one-square-mile sections of land around the railway line. That carved up Cahuilla land. By executive order in 1876, the government allocated the odd-numbered sections of the checkerboard to the railway and created a reservation comprising the even-numbered sections called the Agua Caliente Indian Reservation. It expanded the reservation in 1877 to incorporate more squares in additional adjacent townships. The government constructed nine other reservations for the Cahuilla in addition to the Agua Caliente Indian Reservation.[22] It recognized separate Cahuilla bands corresponding to each of these reservations. The government created most of these Cahuilla reservations in a checkerboard fashion like Agua Caliente at a similar time period. Several bands lived farther from the railway line and avoided this particular fate.

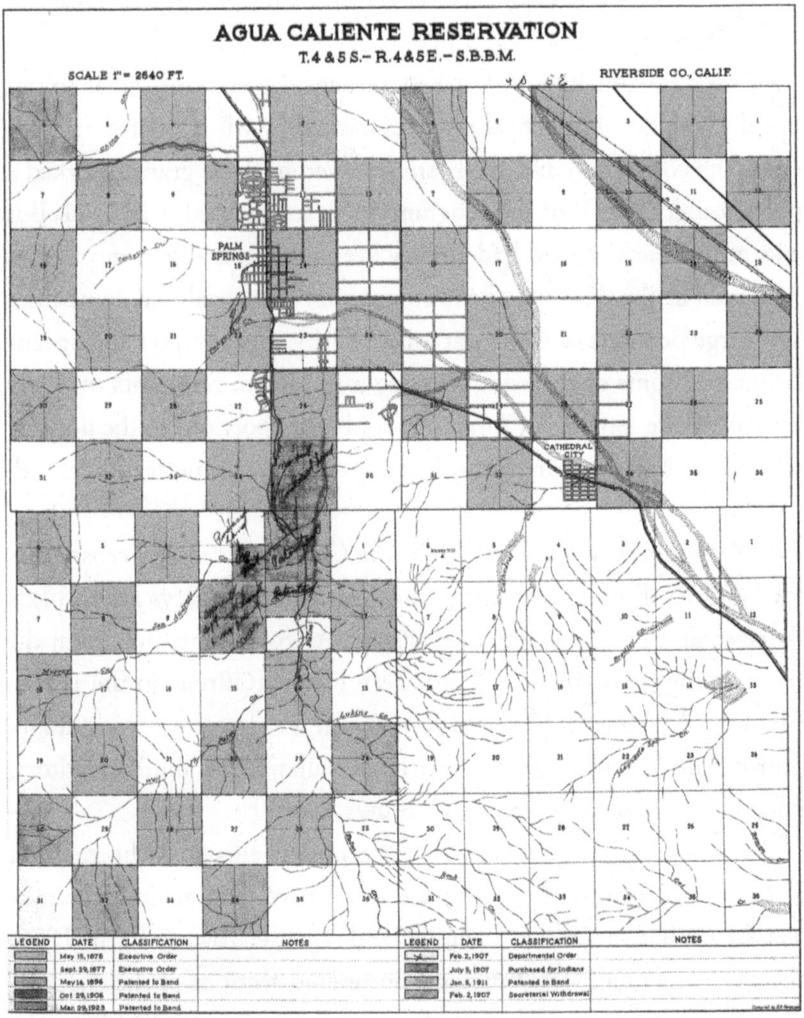

The Agua Caliente Indian Reservation, established in 1876 to 1877, is a checkerboard pattern of alternating square miles shown shaded here. (Credit: National Archives NAID: 351088153.)

These reservations marked the continued loss of land for the Cahuilla. Chief Cabazon of the Desert Cahuilla Cabazon Band told a local government Indian agent in 1898 that "when white brother come, we make glad, tell him to hunt and ride. He say, 'Give me a little for my own,' so we move little way, not hunt there. Then more come.

They say move more, and we move again. So many times. Now we are small people, we have little place."[23] Whereas Cahuilla territory previously covered most of what is now Riverside County and parts of several neighboring counties in Southern California, reservations shoehorned them into less than 5 percent of this land.

The Agua Caliente Reservation, like other Native American and Cahuilla reservations, was ostensibly an autonomous space where the Tribe would have sovereignty over its own affairs and could conduct self-governance. But that promise was a false one from the start.

Increased contact with settlers and prospectors in the years prior to the establishment of the reservation exposed the Agua Caliente to western communicable diseases. Smallpox and measles outbreaks ravaged the population and left them weakened and depleted. In an investigative report to Congress in 1883, the poet and activist Helen Hunt Jackson characterized the early reservation as "wretchedly poor."

The land grab by the US government and the railroad fractionalized the community. It frayed the community's rich link with the land and reduced it to only a small remnant of its ancestral territory. The management of resources, spiritual practices, and economic activities, all rooted in land, became strained and heavily disjointed. This experience traced those of tribes such as the Navajo Nation, the Mandan, Hidatsa, and Sahnish, and many others that had critical portions of their homelands seized from them.

The US government then repeatedly broke its agreements with the Agua Caliente and meddled in their affairs. It prohibited tribal self-governance on the reservation and instead installed the paternalistic Bureau of Indian Affairs to conduct reservation governance and manage tribal affairs. This situation continued for decades.

The government similarly held reservation land in trust rather than turning it over to the Agua Caliente. The paternalistic logic held that Native Americans would lose their land either out of stupidity or short-sightedness. One newspaper describing land use in the reservation in 1969 put it in these denigrating terms: "The government held the land in trust for the benefit of the tribe until such time as the tribe might become sufficiently sophisticated in land management as to intelligently govern the future use of their own land."[24]

Government agents adopted practices of assimilation that sought to subjugate the Agua Caliente. Starting in 1890, children from the reservation were forced to attend off-reservation boarding schools, including the St. Boniface Indian School, the Perris Indian School, and later the infamous Sherman Institute in Riverside, California. These schools taught students English and vocational skills. They forbade the practice of cultural and spiritual traditions. The idea was in keeping with the goal stated succinctly by the US general who had founded the first federal Indian boarding school: "Kill the Indian, save the man."

The Bureau of Indian Affairs replicated the suppression of cultural and spiritual practices on the reservation. It banned the culturally important mourning (*nukil*) ceremony, and it sought to promote farming in the reservation as part of the effort to "civilize" the population. In the words of the local chief engineer overseeing agriculture, this would "render this little band of Indians independent of further aid from the Government." The Bureau of Indian Affairs teamed up with the Department of Agriculture to start experimenting with farming desert crops in the area. Its agents built irrigation systems and made other improvements in the 1910s and established an experimental station on Agua Caliente land despite not receiving consent from the community.[25]

The US Indian service farmer in charge, Adrian Maxwell, whose promotion within the Bureau of Indian Affairs was linked to increasing local agricultural production, pushed ahead with planting date palms, grapefruit and apricot trees, grapevines, and alfalfa. Maxwell lamented that "the red man is the easiest man to get discouraged in the world" when he sensed caution among the Agua Caliente, who had lived through periods of drought, extreme heat, and damaging storms and had reason to believe that the government's agricultural efforts were folly.[26]

A confluence of factors led the government to later tap the brakes on agriculture in the reservation. Maxwell departed in 1916, and drought in the 1920s dealt a lasting blow to the crops. Increasing tourism in the 1920s provided alternatives to agricultural work. In 1924, a supervising engineer observed, "It is becoming more and more apparent that these Indians will secure their livelihood through working for the White settlers rather than through their efforts at farming."[27]

Yet the Agua Caliente had still only seen the tip of the iceberg. Soon the Dawes Act would breach the hull.

WHEREAS PREVIOUS POLICIES had relocated Native Americans and cordoned them off into reservations, the Dawes Act of 1887 cracked open reservations themselves to further land dispossession. Also known as the General Allotment Act, the Dawes Act accelerated and systematized dispossession at a grand scale.

Like most federally recognized tribes that had been confined to reservations, the Agua Caliente and other Cahuilla groups owned land in a communal fashion in the late 1800s.[28] Among the Agua Caliente, land access was further divided across four main clans that had distinct territorial claims. The Dawes Act aimed to break up Tribal landholdings by subdividing them into individually owned plots through a process known as land allotment.

Congress authorized land allotment within the Agua Caliente Reservation in 1891. But it did not begin until the 1920s, when increasing tourism to the hot springs increased the value of the land. When the land allotment surveyors showed up, the Tribal leadership and dozens of Tribal members pushed back in a letter to the US secretary of the interior. "We ask you to take away these allotment surveyors until we can find out just what they are going to do. Nobody notified us they were coming," the letter said. "The Indians never signed any agreement or made any petition for allotment. . . . We have patent for our land and we do not want it to be taken away without our consent. We want to keep it whole."[29]

Around the same time, the city tried to seize control of Indian Canyons, the ancestral home of the Agua Caliente at the south of the reservation. Tourists were flocking to the area to visit the stunning palm oases, and local businesses wanted a bite. The city had Tribal leaders arrested and encouraged the US government to turn the canyons into a national park. The government briefly took control of the land but then dropped it when the Agua Caliente fought back.[30]

Although the federal government left the land in Indian Canyons, the land allotment surveyors were not so easy to send home. In response to the Agua Caliente's request for the government to take them away, a dismissive reply from the commissioner of the Bureau of Indian Affairs informed them that "it is still believed it will be for the good of your people to have the allotments made."[31] Allotment was similarly imposed against resistance in several other Cahuilla reservations, such as Torres-Martinez. The start of allotment in the Agua Caliente Reservation marked a divisive moment in its history as, one by one, members of one clan began separating themselves from the Tribe and their clan to claim plots of another clan's land. Those individuals also coalesced into a political group that sought to wrest control of the Tribe from communal traditionalists.[32] A US government administrator oversaw the parceling of reservation land to individual Tribal members.

Together with forcibly sending Indian children to boarding schools, where they were compelled to speak English and dress in western clothing, land allotment sought to break down tribal cohesion and assimilate Indians into American cultural norms and capitalist economic practices. The goal was to use the power of laws to accomplish what extermination could not.

White politicians viewed the transition as a moral, economic, and cultural imperative critical to building an American national identity. In his 1901 State of the Union Address, President Teddy Roosevelt said, "In my judgment the time has arrived when we should definitely make up our minds to recognize the Indian as an individual and not as a member of a tribe. The General Allotment Act [Dawes Act] is a mighty pulverizing engine to break up the tribal mass. . . . The Indian should be treated as an individual—like the white man."

When a reservation—such as the Agua Caliente's—was opened for allotment under the Dawes Act, the Bureau of Indian Affairs, part of the US Department of the Interior, granted individual families on the reservation plots of land that it held in trust on their behalf.[33] "Excess lands" not allotted could be sold off to private citizens from outside the reservation. This policy ultimately stripped nearly 100 million acres from all reservation land, an area roughly the size of California.

As land values in Palm Springs increased with tourism, outsiders wanted a piece of the "excess" Agua Caliente Reservation lands that could be released in the wake of allotment. Clan politics also drove allotment. The Kauisik clan of the Agua Caliente controlled the land around the hot springs. In order to share tourism revenue more broadly among clans, it gave land access to other clans to set up businesses around the hot springs, provided that they shared some of their revenue to help the community as a whole. Members from other clans who wanted more security for their land claims than Kauisik promises, and more autonomy in what they did with their revenues, were the first to take up allotment.[34]

In the Agua Caliente Reservation, however, the government played games with those who sought individual plots. The Bureau of Indian Affairs authorized community members claims of forty-seven acres, divided between a two-acre lot in town, five acres of irrigated land, and forty acres of dry land.[35] Eventually over one hundred of the Agua Caliente claims were granted, and their allotments constituted about 15 percent of reservation land. But they struggled to assert ownership over these claims.

The local government agent, Harry Wadsworth, granted provisional allotment certificates to the first group of claimants in the 1920s, promising quick approval by the secretary of the interior. Some claimants started using their allotments. But government approval dragged.

Several Agua Caliente members started litigation over a decade later to have their allotments approved. In 1944, the US Supreme

Court, in *Arenas v. United States*, ruled that the secretary of the interior had to make the allotments.[36] The secretary of the interior still initially refused the allotment schedule from the 1920s and then five years later did an about-face. But by this time, the allotments varied widely in value because of population growth and development in Palm Springs. In 1954, several Kauisik clan members of the Agua Caliente sued for recognition of the Tribe's assignment of land prior to the cross-clan allotment claims. The courts ordered "equalization" to ensure fairness in allotments so that assets and revenues would be shared more broadly among the group's members.

This too sparked a land battle. The City of Palm Springs, the Bureau of Indian Affairs, and even several members of the Agua Caliente Tribal Council sought instead to sell Tribal lands off to a corporation that would in turn dispose of the land and distribute the proceeds to Tribal members.[37] Nonetheless, the Tribe ultimately sought to maintain its land base. It pursued equalization through legislation to reduce the "surplus" designation of unallotted land under the Dawes Act and prevent the mandated subsequent disposal of "surplus" Tribal land.[38] Eventually, in 1959, Congress passed the Equalization Act, and the government finalized and formalized the Agua Caliente allotments.

By the time the legal limbo had ended, the government had long since changed the rules of the game. President Franklin Delano Roosevelt's 1934 Indian Reorganization Act ended the Dawes Act's land allotment policy as part of the New Deal for Native Americans. This left a patchwork of landholding across reservation lands. Land allotment had proceeded, but in the Agua Caliente Reservation it was incomplete. A checkerboard of property rights among individual owners was now nested within the checkerboard pattern of the reservation. Some had fee simple ownership and others held land in trust. Other reservations never experienced land allotment and therefore retained communal tribal ownership.

The Indian Reorganization Act froze all individual trust lands in trusteeship into the future and ended further allotments for tribes that experienced it. The checkerboard of property rights within the Agua Caliente Reservation therefore continues today. The result is a dizzying and almost comically complex pattern of land use. The varieties of land use now range from Tribal land to privately owned fee simple land, allotted land within the reservation, off-reservation Tribal land, and other private lands. The effect of all of this complexity was unfortunately simple: a rigid racial hierarchy, reinforced by Tribal land divisions that complicate the ability to plan and flourish as a community when pressured by outside interests.

THE AGUA CALIENTE and other Cahuilla bands alike struggled economically and socially as their neighbors in Palm Springs flourished. As attempts at agriculture foundered in the 1920s, many Cahuilla took lower-status jobs in the growing white-owned tourist industry as toll collectors, campground operators, and hotel workers, while others worked as store owners, fire guards, and policemen.[39] They had fewer job opportunities, less education, and worse health care than whites in the area.

As late as the 1940s, Tribal members of the Agua Caliente could not use basic hospital services in Palm Springs. Richard Milanovich, the former Tribal chairman, who also fought the city's attempt to build a road through the reservation following the 1980 fire, was born in nearby Soboba, California, at a hospital funded by the state, because his mother was turned away from giving birth in Palm Springs. When she experienced complications during pregnancy and went to the Palm Springs hospital, the doctors told her, "We're only going to let you come in here because you're having complications. When you have your baby, you have to go to the Indian hospital. Anyone that's not white is not allowed to be born here."[40]

Community divisions deepened. Forced assimilation practices eased with the 1934 Indian Reorganization Act, but while many sought a quick return to Tribal governance, others preferred the greater political and economic independence associated with federal allotments from the Tribal land base.[41]

By the 1950s, the railroad's checkerboard sections of the Palm Springs area became wealthy and white, while the Agua Caliente's checkerboard sections on the reservation were home to comparatively poorer Tribal communities. The reservation sections also attracted other disadvantaged minorities because they were more affordable. African Americans and Latinos moved to the Palm Springs area in large numbers from the 1920s through the 1950s to work in the growing tourist economy. They settled as renters on reservation land. Many of them moved into the heart of downtown Palm Springs in one of the Agua Caliente's checkerboard squares known as Section 14, which also contains the hot springs.

Short-term limits to leases on Tribal land that were stipulated in federal law entrenched the disparity between the railroad's sections and the Agua Caliente's sections. These limits discouraged commercial development and fostered low-income housing where minorities lived segregated from the more privileged white neighborhoods of the city. The City of Palm Springs compounded these problems by refusing to provide utilities to Section 14 residents residing on reservation land. Tribal members resorted to erecting plywood and tar-paper houses, digging septic fields, running water pipelines, and burning trash in that part of the city.[42]

The Agua Caliente knew the intrinsic value of the land but could not take advantage of it. The chairman of the new all-women Agua Caliente Tribal Council, Eileen Miguel, indicated as much in a congressional hearing on land leasing in the mid-1950s. When Miguel stated to the committee chairman that she was from Palm Springs, the chairman ignorantly replied, "Then you have money running out of your ears, is that correct? We have heard how wealthy you are." Miguel replied, "No, I don't have any money running out of my ears. I'm sorry, and I slightly resent what Mr. Marshall said about us being rich. We're not rich. We have valuable land, but you can't eat dirt."[43]

That land became much more valuable starting in 1959 when individual allotments were finalized and the Agua Caliente successfully negotiated with the federal government to lease their lands for up to ninety-nine years. The wealthier white community saw growing lucrative business opportunities in Section 14. It was a game changer, triggering an explosive, racialized battle over zoning, leasing, and Tribal sovereignty.

What happened next is what happens in many growing communities where the rich live alongside the poor: gentrification and land grabs. The City of Palm Springs sought to expel the poorer inhabitants of Section 14 to clear it for business. But there was no obvious way to do so on reservation land. Land power can cut both ways, after all.

The city sharpened its elbows. It threatened to evict tenants whose homes were not up to city code. And it continued withholding utilities from the area by falsely claiming that residents on reservation land did not pay property taxes.[44] It also aggressively took advantage of a Conservatorship and Guardianship Program that the Tribal Council had agreed to as part of the land leasing deal. The program enabled local court-appointed conservators to manage the affairs of individual Tribal members. These conservators quickly turned on the Agua Caliente and their poor minority tenants in Section 14. They evicted tenants en masse and worked with the city to bulldoze portions of the downtown area. Some people had their homes bulldozed while they were at work.[45]

The city leadership invoked racist tropes in justifying its actions. Referring to the Agua Caliente who were leasing the land to largely Black and Latino populations, Mayor Frank Bogert proclaimed, "They are letting the places for flat-out moochers. . . . If you think of the value of the land and think of the kind of junk there, it's just scandalous." City Councilman Ed McCoubrey chipped in, saying, "These people are not interested in improving themselves."[46]

The city's scorched-earth tactics broke down community resistance to development. One former resident, Alfonso Mediano, recounted that, "after that, we lost track of each other. As small as that town is, the only time we saw each other was at a funeral or [when] somebody got married."[47]

The authoritarian stance of the city and the conservators only ended with state intervention in 1968. The California assistant attorney general, Loren Miller Jr., who conducted an investigation, concluded in his blistering report that "the City of Palm Springs not only disregarded the residents of Section 14 as property owners, taxpayers and voters; Palm Springs ignored that the residents of Section 14 were human beings."

Conservators also delved deep into the affairs of Tribal members unrelated to Section 14 in the decade when they operated. Their paternalism effectively stripped the ability of members to manage their own land, their finances, and their futures. One enrolled member, Moraino Patencio, related how his brother was born just weeks after the finalization of allotments and the establishment of the conservatorship program. Like any other Tribal member born after the end of allotment, his brother had no avenue for getting his own piece of Tribal land. He inherited some off-reservation land outside Palm Springs from his godmother, but a court-appointed conservator complicated his ability to receive it, and his father had to go to court to try to get access to it. "It was just an impossible situation," he told me.[48] For this "oversight," the court, conservators, and lawyers all charged exorbitant fees.

PARALLEL VERSIONS OF the Agua Caliente story played out across other Cahuilla bands in Southern California. All the Cahuilla groups lost land to white settlers and were forced onto reservations, many of them in dysfunctional checkerboard patterns like in the Agua Caliente case. European diseases ravaged their people, and the federal government sought to eliminate their customs and language through policies of forced schooling, assimilation, and outright punishment. Many Cahuilla lost further land and suffered community divisions with land allotment and government development initiatives. And some groups faced antagonistic city and local governments, though none quite as hostile, powerful, and duplicitous as Palm Springs. This broad-based subjugation gave birth to a racial hierarchy across the region that paralleled the situation in Palm Springs.

Native American displacement and settler land grabs over the course of the United States' early history manufactured a new and rigid racial order for hundreds of other Native American tribes across the United States as well. White settlers made economic, social, and political gains while indigenous groups lost on all of these fronts. This new order was entrenched at every turn with a crushing array of discriminatory policies that lasted at least through the 1960s and in some cases longer.

Behind it all were decisions about who got land, followed by decisions about how they could live on it, keep it, and preserve their lives on it—or not. Land reallocation can create prosperity, but it can also create misery and racism if we let it.

Systematic data on the welfare of Native Americans as a whole in the 1800s are unavailable. That is in part by design. The US Constitution mandated that only "taxed" Indians—those who cut relations with their tribe to live among the general population—would count toward congressional representation. The US Census Bureau therefore did not collect information on the vast majority of "non-taxed" Indians.

The blossoming of the reservation system and the growing interest in managing Native American populations, however, led Congress to appropriate funds for separate censuses of Native Americans in 1890, 1900, and 1910. Most of the detailed information from 1890 was destroyed in a fire. That makes 1900 the first clear snapshot of Native American communities.

The picture is a stark one. The Native American population in the United States had declined to around 240,000 people by 1900. This number reflected nothing short of a demographic collapse compared with pre-settlement America.

There was a wide gap in the welfare of Native Americans compared with whites that reflects the pendulum swing in land power. Life expectancy was about forty years for Native Americans against fifty years for whites.[49] This was even shorter than for the Black population, which had a life expectancy of forty-two years. There was also a considerable gap in childhood mortality, with Native American children dying at a higher rate than white children.

Native Americans themselves, of course, are widely ethnically diverse. They also have unique histories of cultural loss, forced removal, conflict, and assimilation in the face of American land settlement. And some had been on reservations longer than others as of 1900. Reflecting these differences, some nations, such as the Cherokee and Chickasaw, had relatively low mortality rates and longer lifespans. Others, such as the Dakota and Lakota, fared considerably worse. Nearly every tribe was disadvantaged compared with whites.

The early twentieth century was a period of stagnation for Native Americans. Stripped of much of their land and of control over what remained, incomes among Native Americans on reservations grew at a meager 0.25 percent annual rate from 1918 to 1942 compared with a 2.3 percent rate for the US population as a whole.[50] Income gains across the country advanced in the latter half of the twentieth century. But Native Americans remained starkly disadvantaged. US census data indicates that in 1969, one-third of Native American families lived in poverty, compared with just over 10 percent of white families.[51] Per capita income was half that of whites. And Native Americans had the lowest rates of economic mobility of any racial group in the United States.[52]

Discrimination and harmful government policies perpetuated this disparity. Starting in the 1950s, the US government sought to "terminate" remaining Native American reservations and complete its land grab. As part of this effort, the Indian Relocation Act of 1956 ended federal funding for basic services, schools, and hospitals on reservations. This drained job opportunities from reservations and drove an exodus to urban areas such as Los Angeles and Minneapolis. The federal government paid for some vocational training and relocation to cities, but many Native Americans faced a wall of workplace discrimination.[53] And it left many reservations depleted. Termination policy ended in the 1970s, but some reservations and tribes did not have their sovereignty restored.

Because the contemporary land power picture has not changed much from fifty years ago, the social picture and racial hierarchy hasn't changed much either. According to US Census Bureau data from 2018, 25 percent of Native Americans lived in poverty compared with 10 percent for whites.[54] Poverty among Native Americans who live on reservations—one-third of the Native American population—is systematically higher than poverty for Native Americans who live outside of reservations.

The persistent racial wealth gap is undergirded in part by barriers to wealth accumulation among Native Americans. Land is at the heart of the problem. The US government remains the legal steward of most tribal lands, and this prevents Native Americans from building wealth in the same way that most Americans can. Trust land status generates intergenerational problems of fractional ownership as families and land claimants grow over time. That dilutes ownership value and complicates decision-making over what to do with land. Government permission is also required in most land use decisions such as leasing, business development, and purchases. The solution is not just land privatization, which faces pushback among Native Americans themselves.[55] But there is great dissatisfaction with the current land situation. Native Americans want the opportunity to play a central role in redesigning the system in a way that is much more favorable to them.[56]

In keeping with large discrepancies in income and wealth between Native Americans and whites, there are also enormous gaps in education and health. Only 24 percent of Native American adults have a college degree, compared with 47 percent of white adults, and there is a similar gap in college enrollments.[57] Native Americans die at higher rates of diabetes, heart disease, and alcohol- and drug-related causes.[58] They have higher rates of mental health problems linked to historical traumas.[59]

Native American communities also face unique forms of neglect and discrimination within the United States. There is an epidemic of violence against Native American women. Murder is now the third most common cause of death for Native American girls and women through the age of nineteen, and the sixth most common for women in the next age group, twenty to forty-four.[60] But law enforcement has systematically neglected to engage the issue seriously, leaving Native American women vulnerable to violence.

Discrimination remains commonplace in the everyday experiences of many Native Americans. One-third of the Native American adults who participated in a recent survey reported discrimination in job applications, consideration for promotion, and wages.[61] Nearly 30 percent of the participants reported discrimination in interactions with the police, and 23 percent said they had experienced discrimination when going to a doctor or health clinic.

Indigenous lands and resources continue to be exploited, at times without due consent and consultation. Recent high-profile fights against the Dakota Access and Keystone XL pipelines illustrate widespread discontent among indigenous communities over how corporations hatch and build projects that threaten indigenous lands and tribal cultures. But there is pushback. One enrolled member of the Agua Caliente told me, for instance, that given both their history and their creation story, "we are always looking for who is coming at us, who is presently pushing us, and how do we respond to that."[62]

* * *

ON A SUNNY November morning in 2023, the Agua Caliente gathered with other Cahuilla and members of the broader community in a festive celebration to inaugurate a new cultural museum dedicated to telling their story. Located in the heart of downtown Palm Springs, the state-of-the-art museum is the culmination of a dream the Agua Caliente had decades ago. Its design reflects the traditional links to the natural springs and palm-lined canyons of their ancestral lands. At the first turn in the museum, visitors confront how the community has managed to persevere: "Our land and water were stolen, our people decimated by disease, our culture threatened and misunderstood. Determined to survive, we adapted to the new society around us."

The Agua Caliente started to close the racial wealth gap in the Palm Springs area starting around the 1970s even as many got priced out of living in the downtown area.[63] With this shift sprang green shoots for reclaiming elements of the Tribe's culture, language, and spiritual traditions that land appropriation and reservation policies had sought to stamp out.

The City of Palm Springs had its wings clipped when the State of California intervened in its land battles in the 1960s. A new dawn broke not only for Section 14 but also for the Agua Caliente as a whole. The Tribal Council struck an important land use deal with Palm Springs in the late 1970s that specified Tribal administration of its lands in the city, including Section 14. Land power began to turn again.

The new partnership came to flourish even as some tensions persisted, as shown by the city's attempt at a land grab in the context of the 1980 fire. The city and the Tribe began cooperating on economic development, benefiting them both. Favorable federal legislation such as the 1987 Indian Gaming Regulatory Act also helped. The Agua Caliente opened a set of casinos that have created revenue streams used to fund broader Tribal economic development, environmental stewardship, cultural regeneration, and educational initiatives. The Agua Caliente have become an economic success case among Native American communities in recent decades. Median income per capita among on-reservation Agua Caliente members is considerably higher than that among other racial groups in the Palm Springs area.[64] Regaining control over their land was at the root of this shift.

The Agua Caliente are now trying to use their economic gains to fuel renewed efforts to revitalize weakened elements of their community identity. In addition to building the cultural museum to teach the community and visitors about their history, they have funded archaeological excavations to learn more about their ancestors and have brought in nearby Cahuilla speakers to teach Cahuilla classes, while also supporting the broader Cahuilla community.

But recapturing heritage is not an easy task. Much has been lost, and much work remains. For instance, the Cahuilla language was almost entirely stamped out among the Agua Caliente and there are no known fluent speakers remaining. Their efforts are further complicated by prevailing fraught and racialized interactions between whites and Native Americans across the country and within their community and the state of California.

The Agua Caliente Band is one of many indigenous groups around the globe that have become victims of settler reforms. Time and again land has been a crucial tool in constructing and deepening racial hierarchies that subordinate indigenous groups to colonial populations whose members deem themselves racially superior. Because land is power, and because settler populations took the land, those racial hierarchies remain for generations and leave indelible marks on society.

One of the most effective ways for indigenous groups to recover is to retain and safeguard—and even to grow—what remains of their diminished land base. Hanging on to some portion of their land and its advantages gives them a foothold to rebuild and fight back in a system where land power has been used against them. Still, racial hierarchy—forged and hardened by decades of settler reforms—does not die easily.

CHAPTER 4

THIS LAND IS MEN'S LAND

LAND AND PROPERTY HAVE BEEN AMONG THE GREATEST ENGINES of wealth creation and power in human history. Land's value has increased exponentially over the past two centuries as population growth and nation-building heated up competition for land. With it, landowners have enhanced their well-being, improved their families' health and their children's educations, and gained social and political power. How land is reallocated matters profoundly to who receives the benefits of the Great Reshuffle and what kind of society emerges in the decades and generations that follow. Not all land reallocation is created equal—not even those reforms nominally following a similar settler model, as we will see if we turn our attention several thousand miles north of the Agua Caliente.

The vast prairies of Canada had been only lightly touched by explorers and settlers by the time the country formed as a nation in 1867. They were mainly inhabited by indigenous Canadian peoples now known as First Nations. Settlers in Canada's eastern provinces knew the area as part of "Rupert's Land," a massive fur-trading territory stretching from the Rocky Mountains in the west through much of Quebec in the east and from the border of the United States up to the Arctic Circle, all under the exclusive charter of the Hudson's Bay Company.

Canada's first prime minister, Sir John A. Macdonald, sought to expand the country's borders by annexing these territories along with British Columbia, a remaining British colonial possession on Canada's Pacific flank. Doing so would guard the new nation against encroachment from its relentlessly expanding American neighbor to the south.

To extend control over this land, the Macdonald government passed the Dominion Lands Act in 1872, a quintessential settler reform. The act opened the prairies to homesteading by eastern Canadians and European and American pioneers. It was modeled on the 1862 Homestead Act in the United States, in that it offered homesteaders 160 acres of land in exchange for a ten-dollar registration fee and a promise to farm the land and build a home on it.

But the Canadian approach to the Great Reshuffle diverged from the US model in a number of crucial ways. First, the method of actually parting indigenous populations from their lands took a slightly different course when Macdonald's government signed a series of treaties with Canada's First Nations to obtain land for immigration and settlement in the prairies. In practice, however, these agreements were sealed under duress. The increasing toll of western diseases, the decimation of bison, and the unyielding pressure of the Canadian government guaranteed that the First Nations could not easily resist. They signed in exchange for promises of government aid in the form of food and health assistance.[1] The Canadian government used the opening to try to break their cultures and links to the land by sending their children to boarding schools and attempting to force them into sedentary farming communities.

The Dominion Lands Act departed from the US Homestead Act in another crucial way as well: it prohibited women from homesteading. The law backtracked slightly in 1876 to allow women homesteaders who were the sole heads of households, typically because they were widowed or had been deserted with dependent children. The United States maintained a similar exception for married women, who were otherwise not allowed to homestead. But in the United States, single women were eligible, and in Canada they were not.[2]

Barring single women from homesteading foreclosed one of the principal economic alternatives to marriage for the vast majority of rural Canadian women—and this policy outcome was by design. Most Canadian politicians believed, as Senator Robert Poore Haythorne put it, that "the future of the country lay wrapped up in the sanctity of the marriage state," and that alternatives to marriage, or the ability to dissolve it through divorce, should be strictly avoided.[3] Progress and stability in western Canada, including through the enormous project of settlement through homesteading, could be achieved most readily by adhering to the traditional Christian conception of marriage and gender roles.[4] Allowing women to strike out on their own by homesteading land ran directly counter to these notions.

A "Homesteads for Women" movement arose in response, advocating that the prairies be opened up to women settlers. Canadian women petitioned for access to homestead land for years, but politicians repeatedly denied them. In fact, most women never had a chance to homestead, a situation that persisted throughout the duration of the program, which was largely shut down in 1930.

By the time the program ended, the Canadian government had given away over 100 million acres of land to men. It was one of the greatest wealth transfers to men in human history. Women were almost entirely shut out of the right to claim homestead land in the vast Canadian West. And it established a thick blanket of traditional, conservative gender relations from sea to shining sea in Canada.[5]

Women paid a steep price. For decades, their lack of land ownership precluded them from voting in early elections. They were dependent on men for their livelihoods and vulnerable to poverty in the case of a husband's death or departure. And they lagged men in taking advantage of costly educational opportunities as the economy of the prairies transformed. In many ways, women in Canada are still catching up.

The historic transformations that have defined the Great Reshuffle around the world have refashioned power relations, bestowed extraordinary wealth on its beneficiaries, and, when done right, fired national prosperity. They have also by and large left women out. Prevailing patriarchal gender relations in many societies prior to the reallocation of land and its appreciation in value meant that women faced discrimination in gaining land access. But it is not just that women were sidelined, as they always had been. In many cases, land reallocation entrenched and even deepened gender inequalities and the marginalization of women. This has been true across the range of land reallocation policies. Country after country has doled out land to male heads of household, and in most cases women have lost as much or more than they have gained.

Because of this pattern, the Great Reshuffle has locked in a trajectory of heightened dependence by women on their male counterparts over the course of the past two centuries. It has made everything from gender wealth gaps to domestic violence and abortion practices that favor sons even more difficult to erase than they might have been otherwise. In the majority of societies where this has occurred, it is not distant history: it came to be entrenched just a few decades or at most a century back. In some societies that are still undertaking a Great Reshuffle, this pattern is still playing out, seeding further inequality for the years ahead.

To grapple with this foundational problem for modern societies, we will explore how it has manifested in three countries from different continents, time periods, cultures, and approaches to land reallocation. In Canada, politicians prevented women from independently homesteading the country's prairies in the late 1800s and early 1900s, depriving them of a unique opportunity to gain autonomy and self-determination. In the state of West Bengal in India, a tiller reform and related programs aimed at helping sharecroppers in the 1970s ended up stoking intra-family strife and the favoritism of boys both as children and in utero. And in El Salvador, several episodes of land reallocation in the 1980s and 1990s put even more land and decision-making power into the hands of men and entrenched patriarchy.

There is no law or universal truth dictating that women will always lose out on opportunities to gain access to land or other assets that enhance their independence, autonomy, and wealth. The historical tendency in this direction is entirely socially constructed. Societies can choose a different path. And in recent decades, especially at the behest of a wide variety of powerful women's movements, many societies have done just that. But history has consequences and cannot simply be reversed. Gendered patterns of land access and ownership through policies of land allocation and reallocation in the past two centuries have placed women at a distinct disadvantage in contemporary societies that is difficult to overcome.

SETTLING THE CANADIAN PRAIRIES

Canada formed in a very different way from its neighbor to the south. The United States formed out of revolution against the British Crown and valued ideals such as liberty and equality of opportunity and social relations. By contrast, Britain hatched the formation of Canada—independence never faced a vote or movement in Canada itself. The British instead set out to forge a fundamentally conservative society that valued hierarchical class relations, religious authority, and traditional social and gender norms.[6]

Canada was not inherently a natural fit for such a project, being far from culturally and socially unified at the time of its founding. Its population comprised large groups of disparate European immigrants and indigenous Canadians in addition to eastern colonial settlers who had arrived long before the country's independence from Great Britain. Still, early conservative political leaders set out to spearhead a vision of Canadian confederation that would counteract radical egalitarian democracy and immoral and corrupting influences from the United States.[7] They would do so by entrenching traditional gender roles, and one of their chief tools was Canada's most valuable and abundant resource: land.

From the outset in Canada, land served as a gatekeeper for elite, male-dominated politics. Senators had to own considerable landed property to qualify for office, and the franchise across Canadian provinces was limited to men who met a property qualification.[8] But land was not only a useful political tool to maintain the elite and male-dominated status quo. Early government men also used land to propagate and entrench a "traditional gender order" in society.[9] The settlement of the Canadian prairies quickly became the central focus of this effort.

The most consequential policy on this front was the 1872 Dominion Lands Act—the act that cracked open the prairies to homesteading by offering settlers 160 acres of free land in exchange for a minor registration fee. With women barred from homesteading, the traditional gender order of Canadian society was locked in for decades to come.

There was no organized pushback against the gendered nature of the Dominion Lands Act at its passage.[10] Women did not have the franchise at the time, and women's rights campaigns were in their infancy in the Western world.

Women did, however, begin pressuring the government for access to homestead land outside the confines of marriage in the late nineteenth and early twentieth centuries. They penned letters to newspapers, circulated petitions, and wrote their legislators. Their demands built from campaigns for women's suffrage and efforts to win the legal recognition of land and inheritance rights for spouses not on a property title in prairie regions.[11] One early petition, published in the *Edmonton Bulletin* in 1893, bore the headline "Spinsters Want Homesteads."[12] It made the case that spinsters (single women over the age of thirty) were as deserving of homesteading as widows. But the petition sparked little considered debate over the issue.

A decade later, Georgina Binnie-Clark became a vocal advocate for women homesteading. Binnie-Clark moved near her brother in Saskatchewan in 1905 and purchased land to start a farm with her sister because her gender made her ineligible for free homestead land.[13] The sisters had great success farming. Georgina railed against government policy that favored men over women on the frontier. In her remarkable autobiography, *Wheat and Woman*, she made the case that single women could succeed as homesteaders and that the government should not disadvantage them against men.[14] A woman "may be the best farmer in Canada," she wrote. "She may buy land, work it, take prizes for seed and stock, but she is denied the right to claim from the Government the hundred and sixty acres of land held out as a bait to every man."

Some legislators began to mull over the idea of extending homestead land to women—in part because of the potential benefits for men. One example is William Roche, a Conservative legislator from Manitoba. Roche raised the idea of women homesteading in a House of Commons parliamentary session to Frank Oliver, the Canadian minister of interior, with the argument that it could help to address the increasing gender imbalance in Canada's western provinces. Men greatly outnumbered women in homesteading areas, and allowing women to homestead was viewed as a way to make it easier for these single men to find "help-meets." Perhaps more importantly, it would encourage men with daughters to move to the plains. A women's homesteading law would bring, as Roche quoted from a reverend who wrote a letter to the editor of a Winnipeg newspaper in 1910, "lovers and sweethearts that we could never get in any other way."[15]

Roche posed the question to Oliver of whether he had considered "permitting ladies . . . the privilege of homesteading" on this basis. Oliver responded that while the matter had been raised to him frequently, "the purpose . . . in giving free land to homesteaders is that the land may be made productive. . . . The idea of giving homesteads to single women would tend directly against that idea."[16]

This patriarchal and condescending position helped catalyze Canadian women to organize to petition for homestead land over the next several years. A petition circulated in 1911 called for homestead access for "all women of British birth [British-born and Canadian-born women] who have resided in Canada for six months . . . [and were] of the age twenty one years." This petition won backing from important organizations, such as the National Council of Women, the Winnipeg Board of Trade, and many women's press clubs, as well as prominent women activists, including Georgina Binnie-Clark. But when its author, *Grain Growers' Guide* editor Isabella Beaton Graham, submitted a final version to Parliament in February 1913 with over 11,000 signatures—all men, given that women could not vote—the minister of interior ignored it.[17]

World War I quieted the Homesteads for Women movement by drawing attention to other issues and generating expectations that women would support the war effort within the home. But the movement never petered out for as long as the Dominion Lands Act operated. Women wrote letters and signed petitions to expand the act to them throughout the 1920s. As late as 1929 women were continuing to press unsuccessfully for homesteading rights.[18]

While the Homesteads for Women movement simmered, Canada gave tracts of pristine prairie land to hundreds of thousands of men, doling them out like hotcakes over the course of six decades. Eventually the land distributed in this way covered over 100 million acres of land. The program came to an end when the federal government transferred public land to the provinces in 1930, closing most remaining public lands to the act.[19]

DEPRIVING WOMEN FROM homestead land in Canada had enduring consequences. The inability of women to secure homestead land in their own names prevented them from exercising the franchise in the late 1800s and early 1900s in local elections. Property qualifications screened out these potential voters and silenced their political voices.[20]

Prohibiting women from homesteading also meant that they were not afforded access to the main economic opportunity in the Canadian prairies. Together with a lack of property inheritance rights, this rendered women vulnerable to poverty and hardship in the event of their husbands' death or absence.[21] And it made rural women on the prairies easier for the government to neglect during the Great Depression as grain prices plummeted and drought ripped across the plains.[22]

The pervasive and officially reinforced notion of men as property owners and farmers and women as subordinate "homemakers" or "helpers" on the prairies also took a psychological and social toll on many women. Some farm women became grassroots feminists who sought greater recognition for their work, their own property rights to land, and a more level playing field with men on the prairies.[23] But many isolated women quietly accepted the gender status quo, in effect contributing to the perpetuation of gender inequalities in prairie society.[24]

There were also long-lasting social and economic consequences. As educational opportunities expanded on the plains in the interwar period, men pursued higher education that facilitated skilled jobs and upward mobility at much higher rates than women, and women were more likely to learn basic homemaking skills to keep their farms and families stable.[25] At the same time, women's unpaid labor on the farm freed men to participate in market wage-earning opportunities as the rural economy diversified. But women lagged.[26] Women born in the prairies prior to the end of the Land Dominions Act had the highest rates of poverty among Canadian women by the time they reached their sixties and seventies around the 1990s.[27]

At least part of women's enduring lag in status and welfare compared with men in Canada is likely due to the fact that they have never caught up with men in terms of farm ownership. In a study of Alberta farmers in the mid-1980s, only 40 percent of farm women in the province reported having any legal partnership with their husbands in the family farm enterprise.[28] Women's land ownership still lags broadly across Canada. Barely one-quarter of agricultural landholders in Canada today are women.[29]

Many other settler reforms occurring at the same time as Canada's were not much better. Although the United States and Australia at times allowed single women to claim land, married women whose husbands were alive and present typically could not acquire land. The case was similar in settler reforms throughout Latin America, where men also predominated in settlement and claimed the vast majority of land.

In Canada, the patriarchy of settler society passed into First Nations peoples. While First Nations had a wide variety of gender practices, by and large they were more egalitarian than European societies and conceived of gender mainly in terms of complementarities rather than hierarchies. Legislation such as the Indian Act of 1876 created new gender hierarchies and binaries, such as denying indigenous women the right to own land and marital property. Other practices did the same: boarding schools, for example, taught and reinforced domesticity among women. The result was that patriarchal attitudes spread widely throughout society.

As patriarchal and sexist as a society may be, it can become even more so when it sets out to use land power to stymie women.

INDIA AFTER PARTITION

Settler land reforms, as we've seen, can lock in racial and gender inequality, but it is not the only culprit. Nearly a century after Canada began its experiment in gendered homesteading, another former British colony—India—set out to reallocate land and ended up inadvertently achieving a similar outcome through very different means.

Over 80 percent of India's population was rural at the time of its independence from Great Britain in 1947. Landholding was both vastly complex and highly unequal, underpinning rigid socioeconomic inequalities in caste, wealth, and gender. This made land reallocation a pressing issue for the new democracy.

India's large population and long history of settled agriculture meant that there was very little frontier land available in the mid- to late twentieth century when the Great Reshuffle finally came to the subcontinent. Instead, India's leaders and bureaucrats took up a plan to divert small plots from the holdings of large landlords into the hands of people who worked the land, while readying several related reforms to land access and use that were similar in spirit to tiller reforms.

The reforms India pursued rested on three fundamental planks. The first was the abolition of the much-despised landlords, known as *zamindars*, and the intermediaries who collected exploitative rents from a sea of rural tenants on their behalf. This reform favored the tillers who worked under the landlords' thumbs. The second plank entailed setting maximum landholding amounts and redistributing land above those amounts from large landowners to the landless along the lines of a classic tiller reform. The third plank involved regulating land tenancy. Most Indians who worked in agriculture did so not as owners but as tenants, leasing their lands or sharecropping for an owner. Few of these farmers had secure rights or contracts, and consequently they often suffered from threats of eviction and other abuses, such as shifting payment terms from landlords. Tenancy regulations progressively shifted to their advantage, giving these farmers more autonomy and a greater share of the income they produced. The program mimicked a tiller reform in its effects but did not go so far as to actually transfer land ownership.

The legislative and administrative burden for land reallocation rested with Indian states under the constitution. States adopted a wide raft of reforms, which also varied in their extent. But it was the third plank—land tenancy reform—that would see the most action in India. The Indian state of West Bengal, wedged next to Bangladesh, pursued some of the most ambitious projects.

West Bengal seethed with peasant unrest and rural social movements in the late 1960s and 1970s. A nascent leftist insurgency advocated land occupations and land reallocation. After a period of political instability and conservative rule, the local Communist Party chapter charged into office in 1977. It promptly set to work on land reform as a defining issue and the following year announced Operation Barga: a bold effort to transform land use and agriculture in the state by bolstering the land rights and income of West Bengal's several million sharecroppers.

This flagship program was wildly popular. It fueled impressive growth in agricultural productivity and a substantial reduction in poverty. The Communists rode its legacy and retained power over the state until 2011. But Operation Barga had a dark side: it supercharged male-biased inheritance motives among the mass of sharecroppers in the state by strengthening the heritability of their land rights. The result was that it exacerbated gender discrimination within a society where social norms and practices already heavily favored men.

WITHIN INDIA, WEST Bengal is traditionally viewed, along with the state of Kerala, as a major success story for its rewiring of land use and land allocation. However, the road to reshuffling land was long and bumpy. Early land legislation in 1953 and 1955 had only mild impacts. These laws aimed at a tiller reform by setting maximum landholding sizes and reallocating land above the maximum to the landless. But because the maximum was set fairly high—and those with large landholdings were clever in evading the law, using tactics such as transferring pieces of land to family members and friends—the ultimate effect was blunted.[30] These laws also impacted land tenancy, perhaps most notably by eliminating *zamindars*—the local landholding nobles who had collected taxes for the British in the colonial era from tenant farmers on their land. Land was transferred to the state, and tenants had the state as a new landlord.[31]

West Bengal enacted another land reform act in 1971 at the end of several years of rural unrest and fractious leftist politics. It had two parts. The first part was a tiller reform, which set a strict upper limit on landholding size of five to seven hectares (twelve to seventeen acres), with additional land to be reallocated among landless families.[32] Landowner evasion and land transfers among family members watered down this portion of the law. However, it still transferred some 7 percent of the land in the state, far higher than the national average of a little over 1 percent.[33]

The second part of the law was even more consequential. This part was a tenancy registration program, which was later amended and implemented vigorously when a stable coalition of left-wing parties came into office in 1977. Known as Operation Barga, the program simulated a tiller reform in its effects on land access. A considerable portion of West Bengal's overwhelmingly rural population farmed as tenants on the properties of landlords without any formal rights or protections prior to Operation Barga. Several million were sharecroppers.[34] Landlords could evict tenants arbitrarily with no notice and without consequence, change payment terms at will, and take the bulk of the agricultural products that tenants produced. Operation Barga formalized tenancy arrangements, made tenancy rights heritable, created punishments for arbitrary eviction, and required landlords to provide proof of identity of tenants, rather than the other way around. The program also capped the portion of the harvest that landlords could claim from their sharecroppers at 25 percent.[35]

Land reform in West Bengal, and Operation Barga in particular, transformed the countryside. Farms of rice, potatoes, oilseeds, and other crops began to buzz with greater activity. Sharecroppers worked harder on their lands. They invested more in much-needed infrastructure, such as irrigation, and adopted new high-yielding seed varietals. Gradually they became wealthier.[36] And they began investing more in the education of their children.[37] Meanwhile, landlords were cut down to size, and their social and economic roles in local life were diminished. The program inscribed and registered roughly 1.5 million sharecroppers by the early 1990s.[38]

But Operation Barga intensified gender discrimination. A recent study shows that the program encouraged parents to favor sons over daughters at birth to ensure that at least one son could inherit family land rights.[39] The study uncovered increased survival rates of young boys in families without a firstborn son but not in those with a firstborn son. It also documented increased survival rates of girls with firstborn brothers but not with firstborn sisters. The sex ratio at birth reflected this pattern too, suggesting gender biases in abortion choices.

In essence, Operation Barga aggravated a preexisting bias toward passing land on to men rather than women by strengthening the ability to inherit land rights. The effects were largest for Hindu families, in which land rights were already customarily inherited and primarily passed through sons. The policy seeped into intimate choices over family planning and the gender-based treatment of young children.

Operation Barga is not the only land-related reform that has worsened the position of women within Indian society since independence. Land and tenancy reforms in the state of Uttar Pradesh also reinforced gender inequality within the families of beneficiaries. These reforms did not acknowledge the presence of women in farming, and well into the twenty-first century only male descendants were made principal heirs to land.[40]

Several studies also indicate that gender-progressive reforms to property inheritance laws from the 1970s through the 1990s had negative consequences. The Hindu Succession Act of 1956 stipulated that while sons and daughters both had rights to inheriting land that a father accumulated during his lifetime, only sons had a birthright to ancestral joint family property. Given that most land is jointly owned, this rule excluded women from land inheritance in most places.[41] A handful of southern Indian states amended this law from the 1970s through the 1990s to extend women's inheritance rights to joint property. However, these reforms did not actually increase the likelihood of women inheriting land. Instead, most families circumvented the law by "gifting" their land to their sons.[42] At the same time, these reforms raised female child mortality rates, caused an increase in female suicides, and increased the incidence of wife beating.[43] A countrywide reform to the act in 2005 brought gender equality to inheritance, but even that has not considerably enhanced women's land ownership.

Land reallocation policies in India since independence, to the extent knowable, have had little to no appreciable impact on women holding land.[44] Today women in India make up only 14 percent of landowners and own just 11 percent of agricultural land in rural households.[45] Most of these landowning women gain land through their marital families, typically as widows. Consistent with this, women are more likely to inherit land as widows than as daughters, in spite of recent legal efforts to strengthen daughters' claims to inheritance. And few women are co-owners in joint family property.

Meanwhile, by rocking the boat socially, ostensibly progressive land policies have actually backfired in certain instances as land became a more common object of dispute within traditional families and worsened gender relations. Greater land rights and ownership among the poor have raised the stakes over its control. Fathers fear losing control over their land if they cede it to married daughters, and daughters fear upsetting domestic life and damaging family relations if they claim their legal shares to land.

This situation has helped to fuel an epidemic of gender violence, discrimination, and suicide in modern Indian society, where nearly 65 percent of people still live in rural areas and depend on land for their livelihoods. One in three women report being the victim of domestic abuse.[46] The country accounts for over one-third of the world's female suicides, with family problems as the chief driver.[47] It is the most common cause of death for young women.[48] And India has long had a skewed sex ratio at birth in favor of boys as a result of male-preference sex selection—the country's approach to the Great Reshuffle only made this problem worse.[49]

Patriarchy did not originate in land reshuffles. The story of gendered inequality is much older than the shifts in land ownership that followed the Great Reshuffle. But decisions about who gets the land can sharpen a society's sexism, and land power can entrench patriarchy nearly to the point of invulnerability. India offers a stark view of how land power can exacerbate the ugliest forms of gender inequity.

EL SALVADOR'S WAR ON WOMEN

Gendered land reallocation doesn't just reflect conservative social intents and build on existing gender hierarchies. It can actually set women back by targeting them directly.

On March 4, 1980, El Salvador's ruling all-male military junta called a secret meeting. One of its members had just resigned, and a seasoned former politician who had been exiled to Venezuela joined it. The meeting agenda had one item: land reallocation. The junta gathered top personnel from the Salvadoran Institute of Agrarian

Transformation and the Ministry of Agriculture at a hotel and barred them from leaving. Over the course of the next twenty-four hours, the group designed and published a radical plan to reallocate the country's land from large landowners to peasants.[50]

The military then deployed some 10,000 members on the night of March 5 to transport an army of agronomists, land technicians, and troops to seize all large landholdings in the country by March 6. Landowners were stunned. After decades presiding at the pinnacle of El Salvador's economy and political system, they lost control of their most powerful asset.

El Salvador's large landowners were not the only losers. As in Canada and West Bengal, women lost too. Many women lost land in the broader umbrella of land reallocation policies in the subsequent decade. At the same time, women struggled to qualify as beneficiaries of the junta's land policies that wrote right around them. The government doled out land to male heads of household and repeatedly passed over women. By the end of the 1980s, a country beset by gender inequality and discrimination had managed to deepen it considerably.

Just a few decades prior, El Salvador's economy and its gender relations were stifling. As of the early 1960s, the majority of the population lived in rural areas and worked in agriculture, but nearly 40 percent of the land was held by less than 0.5 percent of the largest landholders.[51] The bottom 85 percent of landowners collectively held only 15 percent of the land. By the late 1970s, the majority of rural families were landless.[52] Many worked on the large estates of powerful and wealthy interlocking family clans.[53] The poor understood their position: the conservative government brutally repressed a mass revolt and land invasions in the early 1930s and ignored or undercut them for several more decades.

Women played traditional gender roles and faced discrimination on many fronts. Patriarchy and machismo put women in subordinate roles in the household, economy, and society.[54] Few women, aside from widows or elite women, had independent access to land or other resources that they could use to shape their livelihoods and their families.

The status quo started showing cracks in the 1970s. State repression began radicalizing civic organizations. Rural protests and land invasions of large properties increased despite government crackdowns and threats from paramilitary groups that operated on behalf of landowners.

A dissident military faction toppled the government in 1979 and set up a revolutionary junta that declared a land reform. Government turnover amid a brewing civil war in the ensuing years drove twists and turns in the policies, but there was one constant: men got the lion's share of land and women lost out. Women would only start to gain more land than they lost after civil war ended in the early 1990s and a new era of more gender-progressive—though still not gender-equal—land reallocation dawned.

THE MILITARY JUNTA'S 1980 land reallocation program envisioned three phases of reform. The first phase, implemented on those fateful few days in early March, expropriated some 470 estates larger than 1,200 acres and refashioned them as worker cooperatives.[55] The cooperatives inscribed the permanent laborers who had previously worked the land on those estates. Those new cooperative members decided key issues, such as land allocation, worker pay, and profit-sharing, among themselves.

El Salvador's cooperative reform encompassed one-fifth of the country's farmland and a similar share of its agricultural workers.[56] A second phase sought to expand the first by expropriating and reallocating medium-size landholdings, but it never got off the ground, and the government called it off in 1982.

Despite the cooperative reform's laudable immediate consequences for rural workers, it heavily disadvantaged women in practice and eroded their position within society relative to men. The reform granted cooperative access to one member per beneficiary household. Because social custom dictated that adult men served as heads of households in mixed-gender homes, men predominated heavily over women as cooperative members.[57] Even women who did serve as heads of households were underrepresented in cooperatives. Women headed 22 percent of households in rural areas of El Salvador but constituted only 12 percent of reform beneficiaries nationwide.[58]

The intrepid women who managed to win cooperative membership became second-class citizens. Cooperatives gave some members access to individual parcels of land. But whereas 82 percent of men gained access to individual land, only 65 percent of women were able to do so, and their land was typically smaller in size and of poorer quality.[59]

The minority status of women within cooperatives likely further eroded their initially tenuous position by giving them a limited role in decision-making. Although there are no comprehensive studies of how El Salvador's land cooperatives impacted women's progress, similarly constructed and gender-exclusionary cooperatives in Peru and Nicaragua from the same period show how women's wages and productivity within cooperatives came to lag behind men's, in part owing to a gendered divide in technical knowledge, access to resources, and land use patterns.[60]

The next round of reform in El Salvador was a far more gradual tiller reform, starting in April 1980. The United States played an important role in designing and advocating this reform. It had key similarities to the tiller reform that the United States had implemented in South Vietnam during the Vietnam War.[61] The goal was to convert peasants who rented their land as tenants into landowners. The government negotiated to pay landowners for their land and then attempted to pass the costs on to beneficiaries on an extended payment plan. This program suffered from poor advance planning, resistance from landowners, and administrative problems, but ultimately transferred about one-third the amount of land that was allocated through the cooperative reform.

Like the cooperative reform, the tiller reform favored men over women. Much of the land that it impacted had been farmed by small landowners who rented it out or sharecropped it. Widows and single women featured prominently within this group. Consequently, women made up 36 percent of those expropriated through the tiller reform.[62] But for reasons similar to the cooperative reform, women had a hard time becoming beneficiaries of the tiller reform. In the end, 10 percent of the beneficiaries were women, and the reform had the effect of tilting land ownership in the countryside more toward men.

El Salvador's civil war came to an end through a negotiated settlement in 1992. The peace accords sparked another round of land reallocation. This time women's organizations formed to demand fair treatment on the basis of gender. The most prominent voice was a group called Las Dignas (The Dignified), which was affiliated with the country's main guerrilla group, the Farabundo Martí National Liberation Front (known by its Spanish acronym, FMLN).[63] Many of the group's members held high-ranking positions within the FMLN and had long fought for social transformation in Salvadoran society and against the marginalization of women.[64]

Las Dignas asserted that women heads of household should have priority in land transfers. They also argued that land should be allocated to individuals rather than households so that women with partners would receive land directly. Their demands were in part met. The program that emerged from the peace accords was a tiller reform that operated based on cooperation between the government and the market. Ex-combatants from both sides and the FMLN's civilian supporters received land. Private landowners, as well as cooperatives with space for more members, willingly sold off plots to land applicants, with a new national Land Bank to serve as a broker between the parties. The program doled out land to nearly 40,000 beneficiaries in the decade after the war's conclusion, encompassing more than 10 percent of the country's agricultural land.[65]

Women fared much better in this new round of land reallocation than in the previous one, constituting 34 percent of beneficiaries. But the fact that this figure was still far from gender parity reflects the difficulties in achieving equal treatment for women. Local government functionaries and FMLN cadres who executed the land transfers still prioritized male heads of household and imposed requirements like literacy and possession of official documents, such as birth certificates or voter registration cards, which disproportionately precluded women from receiving land.[66]

This third wave of land reallocation was El Salvador's last significant attempt at such a policy. Taken together, the struggle to reallocate land in the country had served to place women at an enormous disadvantage within society by depriving them of access to a critical asset that shapes long-term well-being.

* * *

DESPITE THEIR VERY different settings and structures, a settler reform in Canada, a tiller-like reform in India, and a varied series of reforms in El Salvador all had the same ultimate effect: they discriminated against or ignored women and in doing so deepened their marginalization within society. While a patriarchal outcome was hardwired into the design of Canada's settler reform, it was not an explicit goal in India or El Salvador. Nonetheless, the men who designed the programs in India and El Salvador would not have been much perturbed by the outcomes that favored men. Their motivations and goals were far more deeply rooted in political and economic concerns. Women were an afterthought.

The power of land makes it a potent tool for change. But time and again, countries have failed to manage land reallocation in a way that yields positive transformation. Those failures are all too apparent when it comes to gender. As the Great Reshuffle swept the globe over the past two centuries, governments handed out wave after wave of land to men at the expense of women.

This tendency has cut across all types of reforms and across the political spectrum. At times it has reflected inherently patriarchal and conservative priorities, as in Spain's settler reform under General Francisco Franco, which also rewarded male heads of household, skirting women and leaving them dependent on men for their livelihoods. Italy's post–World War II tiller reform achieved much the same result. Yet cooperative and collective reforms by putatively left-wing governments have typically had similar effects. Men came to dominate decision-making and won the most lucrative and powerful positions within cooperatives and collectives, and in doing so made women second-class citizens in Peru in the 1970s, in Nicaragua in the 1980s, and in other nations. Several collective reforms, such as those in China after World War II, and in Russia after World War I, have made notable efforts to avoid this trap. But even those efforts at elevating women's access to land have foundered at the foot of both remaining gender discrimination and authoritarian politics, which prevented anyone from truly thriving off the land.

Gaining land is like riding an escalator to status and power. Land reallocation policies the world over have put men on the escalator and left women to take the stairs. But the Great Reshuffle did not stop there. It has also consigned large portions of the population, both men and women, to an unsustainable, extractive relationship to the land and its resources. Land power, after all, is not just about who gets the land, but about how it is used.

CHAPTER 5

THE DISAPPEARING WILDERNESS

THE YEAR 1958 MARKED THE END OF THE LARGEST EXPERIMENT in land reallocation and collectivization in human history. In less than a decade, the Chinese Communist Party had abolished private landholding, redistributed large landholdings among some 430 million rural peasants, and then forced those peasants into collectivized agriculture. Chairman Mao Zedong's power was at its height. He had unprecedented capacity to forge and implement policy at will. And with the lands of China thoroughly reshuffled, he had an audacious idea: an all-hands-on-deck effort at industrialization in order to catch up to Great Britain within fifteen years.

There was only one way for an agrarian economy like China's to tackle such a challenge: by squeezing the countryside. Mao believed that the key to this endeavor would be the domestic production of an enormous quantity of steel. The Communist Party declared a Great Steel Making Campaign in August 1958 that reached deep into the lives of everyone in the countryside. The goal was to produce 10.7 million tons of steel practically overnight. China's Great Leap Forward was underway, and with it, an appalling campaign of environmental destruction.

The prior reallocation of land and the organization of farmers into collectives was both a critical backdrop and an engine for the events to come. Party cadres leaned on the abolition of private property rights and collectivization to force rural peasants into melting down their rudimentary agricultural equipment, cooking utensils, and other items to forge steel in makeshift backyard furnaces.[1] The furnaces required vast quantities of fuel, forcing peasants to log their local forests for wood to feed the flames. In the southern region of Guangxi, villagers tended 190 charcoal-burning stoves, consuming large tracts of subtropical broadleaf evergreen forest.[2] And in the more central Hubei Province, mature forest area decreased by nearly 60 percent and overall forest area by 33 percent.[3] Taken together, the Great Leap Forward produced a full-scale forest resource disaster that farmers would later come to call the first of the "great cuttings."[4] More would come in due course.

The government got what it wanted, at least in part: its people produced 11 million tons of steel within four months. But Mao's goal of rapid industrialization would remain out of reach, in part as a result of other policies over the next fifteen years that similarly cut down the countryside and unleashed environmental and human havoc. These policies, made exponentially more damaging by land collectivization on a mass scale, would drive wave after wave of deforestation, land clearing, and soil degradation.

Land settlement, land reallocation, and land use and management in the era of the Great Reshuffle have been responsible for some of the world's worst episodes of environmental degradation and ecological collapse. Governments have doled out pristine land to be tilled over or clear-cut. They have organized farmers and agriculture to fuel dirty and environmentally damaging transformations to industrialization. And they have promoted land use policies that erode and drain soils, pollute watersheds, and attack biodiversity.

A full recovery in many of these cases is impossible. So comprehensive have been the changes, so systematic the campaigns that followed the reshuffling of land, that they have made permanent changes to the earth. Humans know how to clean up watersheds, reforest barren land, restore topsoils, and reintroduce species to damaged habitats. But these are expensive projects, and the resources and will to complete even these piecemeal acts of restoration are often lacking.

The repair of a whole ecosystem is another story entirely. Ecologies are delicate and they are more than the sum of their parts. When critical elements are lost, they can rarely be restored to their former status. Planting trees to recuperate a lost forest is barely a first step. Deforestation alters soils, biodiversity, and undergrowth to such a degree that they cannot be reengineered on a human timescale. To restore the rich native forests of Europe or China is now an impossible task. The same is true of restoring the American prairies.

We can see how land power has locked in environmental destruction in the story of how land reallocation has irreversibly degraded forests, soils, and watersheds over the past seventy-five years. In China, a Communist revolution followed by land collectivization and decollectivization drove massive deforestation, decimation of grasslands, soil erosion, and groundwater pollution. The country is now struggling to remediate these disasters at enormous cost and will never entirely complete the task. Half the world away, a military government in Brazil was simultaneously laying the groundwork for an environmental catastrophe. Beginning in the 1960s, the military opened up the Amazon rainforest for settlement as large landowners sought to deflate pressure from their rural workers. It is now being slashed and burned at an alarming rate and may soon cease to be the jewel of biodiversity and the carbon sink it once was. When the Great Reshuffle came to these countries, decisions over land locked in a bleak environmental fate.

The human folly and short-sightedness of these decisions unleashed unintended consequences at an incredible scale. We have to understand that reality in order to chart a different path with the world's remaining natural resources.

THE ENVIRONMENTAL COST OF CHINA'S COLLECTIVIZATION

China is one of the largest and most biodiverse countries on earth. It spans more than 50 degrees of latitude and 62 degrees of longitude and incorporates topographical regions as diverse as the arid Gobi Desert, the windswept high Tibetan Plateau, and the flat and agriculturally rich river valleys and deltas of the Yellow River in the North China Plain and the Yangtze River of Central China.

Prior to the rise and spread of agriculture around 10,000 years ago, much of modern China was covered by forests. These ranged from tropical and subtropical forests in China's south to deciduous forests in Central China and coniferous ones in China's northern region of Manchuria. These forests were home to healthy and robust ecosystems with a wide variety of thriving plant and animal life, including large species such as elephants and tigers.

Scientists have had to reconstruct this picture of former Chinese forests, however, because the natural habitats existing today are a mere fraction of those from the prior era. Natural climatic variations of the past several millennia fundamentally shaped this ecosystem.[5] But human battles over land and efforts to extract resources from it have wrought the most enduring and dramatic changes.

Serious human degradation of China's natural environment began with the transition to and expansion of agriculture some 10,000 years ago. Settled agriculture progressively sustained larger populations, more farming, and more forest clearing. Early state consolidation under the Han dynasty (202 BC–AD 220) and an associated northern China population boom drove the deforestation of most of the North China Plain as new and growing generations of settlers leveled trees to grow crops.[6] Environmental changes and pressure from invading nomadic Mongol tribes pushed the Han south over the next millennium. This expansion of farming populations led to deforestation in southern China's riverine and upland areas, with indigenous populations practicing slash-and-burn agriculture as the waves of incoming settlers pushed them deeper into the forests.

Humans had altered most of the Chinese territory by the early 1800s. The population numbered over 300 million by this time and constituted one-quarter to one-third of the world's population. The

Chinese imperial state had also reached resistance on its outer boundaries, causing it to turn inward and exploit inner frontiers: the peripheries of forestlands, vast grasslands, and previously underexploited highlands that became more economically promising with the introduction of New World crops.

Environmental degradation resulted as land settlement progressed. It advanced farthest in the north of China with the clearing of most of the remnants of native forests. This deforestation depleted soils and watersheds and drove out large mammals that had depended on healthy forest ecosystems, such as bears, tigers, and elephants. But southern forests, under considerable and growing pressure, were also shrinking.

GOVERNING CHINA IN the early twentieth century was an impossible task. Outsiders tried to pry it open for trade. The Japanese sought to dominate it and hoard the spoils for themselves. Regional warlords attempted to seize power locally. And a Communist insurgency festered in the north. The ruling Kuomintang Party did its best to centralize power, but as the Allied Powers forced the Japanese out of the country at the end of World War II, civil war metastasized and the Communists seized the advantage.

Under the leadership of Mao Zedong, by 1949 the Communists swept into power and forced the Kuomintang to flee to the island of Taiwan. Central to the Communists' immediate agenda was land reallocation on a massive scale. This program built upon local efforts to redistribute land in parts of their northern base during their decades-long insurgency. The Communists now aimed to eliminate land concentration and tenancy altogether, which were common throughout China but more prevalent in the south of the country.[7]

The Communists pursued their land agenda with revolutionary zeal. Their 1950 land reform law, which took several years to fully implement, confiscated land from landlords and rich peasants and reallocated it to poor and middle-class peasants and hired laborers. Roughly 430 million peasants, nearly 90 percent of the rural population, received land through the program.[8] It ranks as one of the largest land reshufflings in history.

The initial land reallocation spurred an opening round of deforestation before it had even begun. Most of the landowners and rich peasants living south of the Yangtze River did not have their lands seized until 1952. But, well aware that it was coming, landowners in these areas and in Yunnan and Sichuan sought to extract anything they could from their land before the reform reached them. Many turned to cutting down trees on their property and selling them for income that they could hold on to.[9]

More logging was just a few years away. Though the initial reallocation was organized as a tiller-style reform, political leaders ultimately settled on collectivization for a mix of ideological, political, and economic reasons. Deeply devoted to Communist ideas, they viewed private property and free markets as antithetical to collective aims and as fundamentally tending toward exploitation of popular classes. Collectivization emerged as the most promising way to channel common resources toward transformational national goals. And it provided tantalizing opportunities for social control on a grand scale.

After internal debate, the government ordered peasants into elementary cooperatives in the summer of 1955 and larger, "advanced cooperatives" in 1956. In the process, peasants lost their individual land claims. As this radical process of collective land reform unfolded, and peasants registered that their ownership was in peril, they turned—as the landlords and rich peasants did before them—to cutting down trees to secure income.[10] This occurred both in anticipation of the first round of collectivization and as elementary cooperatives got absorbed into larger advanced cooperatives and feared losing their collective property. And it accelerated as the government began valuing timber within cooperatives at a fraction of its cost, on the grounds that it was a product of nature rather than labor.

These environmental disruptions were just a taste of what was to come. In the coming decades, China established a damaging pattern that linked land use and management to ill-conceived grand plans that would trash the environment.

BY 1958, THE collectivization of essentially all of China's rural households cemented the Chinese Communist Party's political control over its land and people. Land use and agriculture would be the engine of any significant national change in the ensuing two decades, because the country's resources and population were overwhelmingly concentrated in rural areas. The countryside was now a piggybank that Beijing could raid at will.

As the Communists redistributed land across the country, then collectivized it and later decollectivized it, they unleashed round after round of deforestation, land clearing, and soil erosion. Three fateful periods in Communist China from the 1950s to the 1980s gravely challenged China's northern and northwestern grasslands and its remaining southern forests: the Great Leap Forward, the Cultural Revolution, and the land decollectivization of the 1980s. With the depletion of these ecosystems, natural habitats fragmented and fractionalized, placing pressure on a wide range of plant and animal populations. That pressure deepened as China sought to kick-start its sluggish agricultural sector beginning in the 1970s by blanketing the countryside with chemical fertilizers and pesticides when its economy opened to the west. Water quality plummeted as pollution leached through the soils and washed into rivers and lakes.

Healthy forests now only exist on China's margins in the far southwest and northeast. Vast areas of its grasslands are compromised and are now being further gobbled up by the Gobi Desert at an alarming rate. Watersheds are choked with poisonous fertilizers. An unprecedented number of species are in the crosshairs. Today nearly 40 percent of China's remaining mammal species are endangered, and 70 to 80 percent of plant species are also threatened.[11] Recent attempts to remedy these problems only demonstrate how thoroughly the management and mismanagement of land has compromised China's environment.

Mao's first major effort to cash in on the promise of collectivization was the Great Leap Forward, with the Great Steel Making Campaign as its linchpin. But it was hardly the only policy that forged a tight bond between land management and environmental damage. One of the strangest and most consequential policies of this period was called the Great Sparrow Campaign.

Agricultural output in China had increased from 1952 to 1958—an impressive feat that came in spite of the dislocations associated with collectivization. But the Communist Party wanted more. And it thought that collectives could achieve more if only they could control nature.

In February 1958, the government launched a campaign to rid the country of the "four pests": rats, sparrows, flies, and mosquitoes. The main thrust of the campaign was its public health and hygiene orientation. But the Great Sparrow Campaign also organized an unprecedented effort to eradicate sparrows as an agricultural pest that ate crop seeds and in doing so nibbled away at agricultural output.

Party cadres mobilized millions of people from collectives to kill as many sparrows and destroy as many sparrow eggs as possible. The campaign began in Sichuan Province. According to the *People's Daily*, the government mobilized some 2.6 million people in Wenjiang Prefecture to starve, exhaust, and capture over 1 million sparrows in the three days from March 14 to 16, 1958.[12] Another 400,000 people in Chengdu took part at the same time. People shooed sparrows from resting on any surface and scared them away from food until they dropped from the sky in exhaustion. Official reports place the number of killed sparrows at over 2 billion by the end of 1958, though it is impossible to verify these figures.[13]

The Great Sparrow Campaign radically disrupted the ecological balance in the Chinese countryside. It led to an explosion of locust populations and other crop-eating insects following the disappearance of their natural predators. These insects devoured crops with voracity. The most credible estimates suggest that sparrow killings drove an annual loss of roughly 7 million metric tons of food, which could have fed some 28 million people.[14] Coupled with several successive years of bad weather, grain output dropped 15 percent in 1959 and reached only about 70 percent of the 1958 level in both 1960 and 1961.

The result was the Great Famine: a catastrophic period from 1958 to 1961 of 30 million excess deaths and 33 million lost or postponed births.[15] Sobered by the disaster, Mao changed course. In March 1960 he issued new instructions: "Do not kill the sparrows; replace them with bedbugs as one of the four pests."

But the Communist Party's fateful effort to eradicate sparrows was not its last frontal assault on nature. In part due to the Great Famine, Mao proposed a balanced development of agriculture, forestry, and animal husbandry in 1960 while "taking grain as the key link."[16] The goal of the "Grain First" policy was food security, and it became even more imperative as relations with the Soviet Union soured in the early 1960s and the United States waged the Vietnam War on China's doorstep.[17]

This message became linked with unfettered land reclamation when the government encouraged collectives to "learn from Dazhai." Dazhai was a small and environmentally degraded village in the mountainous region of southeastern Shanxi Province. In 1963, soil erosion exacerbated a flood, which washed away houses, fields, and even fruit trees.

The secretary of the local brigade party branch, Chen Yonggui, chose not to take the state's relief funds. Instead, he mobilized villagers to build terraces on the loose loess and dig irrigation canals in the mountains. As agricultural production recuperated and rose, Communist Party cadres viewed Dazhai as a lesson in how humans could conquer and harness nature. Food could be made to grow anywhere if the natural environment was transformed.

By the time of the Cultural Revolution (1966–1976), the government was actively encouraging rural collectives to reclaim all types of land and convert it to farmland. It simultaneously cracked down on rural family side businesses and diversified operations in its zeal to prevent the resurgence of capitalism. Villages learned that the safe thing was to follow diktat and marry Grain First with Learn from Dazhai. A popular folk saying arose: "Take grain first, plant rice seedlings in all areas. Cut down trees in the mountains and deforest the whole land."

The environment again paid a heavy price. Cleared grasslands in the semiarid regions of northern and northwestern China quickly turned to desert as high winds swept away exposed soils in a manner akin to the Dust Bowl in the United States in the 1930s.[18] In Ejin Horo Banner in Inner Mongolia, for instance, desertification increased at an annual rate of 3.2 percent from the late 1950s to late 1970s. As farmers tilled over grasses and exposed large areas of virgin soils, even mild winds kicked up sandstorms and dust storms.[19] The Gobi Desert started devouring the countryside at an unprecedented rate. This in turn drove air quality in cities to the desert's east, such as Beijing, to hazardous levels.

Villagers also felled swaths of forest and tilled steep mountainous terrain in a second "great cutting." In the Yangtze and Yellow River basins, farmers logged hills and slopes that even reached more than 25 degrees vertically and planted them with crops. This broke the ability of local ecosystems to retain water and soils. Heavy rains began severely eroding soils and choking watersheds with fertilizers. Extremes in the river systems became more common as a result. The Yellow River recorded record dryness in 1997, and the Yangtze River basin suffered extensive flooding in 1998, in large part as a result of local environmental degradation.[20]

By the end of the 1970s, China's land reallocation and land use policies had desecrated the country's natural environment. Forests had been felled, the land and water polluted, and grasslands tilled over. Mao Zedong's environmental record continued smoldering long after his death in 1976.

At the end of the 1970s, the government experimented with breaking up collectives into smaller units and decollectivizing agricultural production. Within several years it introduced the Household Responsibility System, which granted families increasingly secure land use rights for cultivating particular plots of land. Families also won greater autonomy in deciding how to manage their agricultural land and any forestland they received. These policies would eventually help to reduce land degradation and sprawl within farming villages. But they brought an unintended short-term consequence: a third "great cutting" that one observer called "the most disastrous nationwide period of deforestation."[21]

The culprit this time was different. Rural people who had not previously been allowed to build their own homes in the collective era were now permitted to do so. The majority of households did just that.[22] Housing construction devoured nearly 200 million cubic meters of timber between 1981 and 1985, equivalent to roughly one year's growth from all of China's forests combined.[23] The effects were particularly severe in south and southwest China.

Two decades of land insecurity and land clearing had degraded much of China's land and left it woefully underproductive. The country's political and financial isolation compounded the problem by making it difficult to acquire productivity-enhancing fertilizers and pesticides. China had precious few fertilizer plants, and the chief tool for enhancing output for the vast majority of the farming population was to put more land under production rather than to make what they had more productive. That changed radically with a political détente with the United States in the 1970s.

The first commercial deal that China inked after President Richard Nixon went to China in 1972 was for thirteen large, advanced ammonia plants to produce nitrogen chemical fertilizers.[24] It purchased even more in the 1970s and started building its own in the 1980s. By the 1990s the country was producing nearly enough fertilizer to meet its own domestic demands.

Overcoming the lackluster productivity that had resulted from land collectivization and land degradation would not be easy. The Communist Party commandeered the fertilizer industry and heavily subsidized it. When fertilizer finally became more plentiful in the 1980s and 1990s, the government rained it down on the countryside.[25] Farmers adopted it widely. Agricultural yields leapt and rural incomes rose. But so did the pollution of watersheds.

Chemical fertilizer and pesticide runoff started to pollute groundwater to levels hazardous for human consumption, causing birth defects in babies and illness in adults.[26] It degraded water ecosystems by causing algal blooms and killed off plants and animals. It was a reprise to what was now a common theme: grand plans for land use and agriculture that cost the environment dearly.

As China razed its forests under communism, another gigantic swath of forest on the other side of the world was coming under threat: the Amazon rainforest. Land power was again the driving force, though this time it wasn't wielded by ambitious Communists or channeled through collectivization. Instead, powerful landowners in Brazil teamed up with the military to use it to win reprieve from the pressure of a growing and increasingly restive rural workforce on their estates. Their solution was to open the Amazon for land settlement. Before long, the pace of deforestation became as alarming as that in China.

SLASHING, BURNING, AND PAVING THE BRAZILIAN AMAZON

The Amazon rainforest is a remarkable jewel of the natural world and an indispensable resource in the fight to slow climate change. It contains more than 10 percent of the world's known species and reveals dozens more each year. Over 400 indigenous groups spanning several countries live in the forest. And it is a key climate regulator. It stores over 150 billion metric tons of carbon and hoovers up 5 percent of global carbon emissions annually, earning it a nickname as the "lungs of the planet."[27] The vast quantities of water vapor that it produces generate atmospheric rivers that circulate water to otherwise dry environments and impact weather patterns around the globe.

Unlike China's forests that have been shrinking for centuries, the Amazon remained largely unchanged until the twentieth century. But the Amazon rainforest is now critically endangered. Nearly two-thirds of the forest is within the borders of Brazil, a country responsible for razing, slashing and burning, and trashing the forest to a frightening degree over the past seventy-five years. Estimates are that 17 percent of the rainforest has been entirely destroyed and is irrecuperable.[28]

In 2020 alone, the amount of forest area destroyed was equivalent in size to the country of Israel.[29] And recent years have seen unprecedented wildfires threatening the forest as people who seek to expand soy farms and cattle ranching spark blazes that escape their control.[30]

Brazil's battle over land access and resources for its people has put the Amazon under increasing strain in recent decades and imperiled its future. Scientists fear that the forest may enter a "tipping point" when it reaches 20 to 25 percent deforestation.[31] At that point, the water cycle may break, locking in declining rainfall and longer dry seasons that could destine as much as half of the forest to savannah. But if deforestation continues on the current trajectory, as much as 27 percent of the forest might be destroyed by 2030.[32]

The Amazon was distant and largely impenetrable during early European and postindependence settlement in Brazil. Settlers mainly filled in coastal and nearby interior regions. But with population growth and the land pressure on large estates belonging to the wealthy coming to a head in the 1960s, the military teamed up with Brazil's economic elite to hatch an alternative to reallocating large landholdings: cracking open the Amazon for frontier land settlement.

The core of this radical effort at NIMBYism was Operation Amazonia, and the crowning jewel the Trans-Amazonian Highway. These projects opened a Pandora's box for both Brazil's environment and climate change at the global level. And they only delayed the impending pressure for land reallocation rather than shelving it.

The transition to democracy in Brazil in 1985 sped land reallocation not only on the frontier but also on private landholdings in the interior. Deforestation and land degradation have spread throughout the national territory. And with the Amazon still on the chopping block, the world continues to inch ever closer to irreversible climate change.

BRAZIL'S EARLY LAND settlement policy laid the groundwork for the recent assault on the Amazon. It spread settlers across coastal and interior regions, encircling the Amazon from the east. And it put huge tracts of land in the hands of a small number of elites, who would later resist popular pressure for land reallocation and support settling the Amazon as an alternative.

During the country's early European settlement and in the century following its independence from Portugal in 1822, successive governments adopted settler reforms favoring the powerful and well-connected. Under the Portuguese Crown, enormous tracts of indigenous land were doled out to colonizers. These tracts became sprawling plantations, which often made use of slave labor. Later, dubious land grabs by entrepreneurs were granted legal status through the right of informal possession.[33]

Given the lack of infrastructure in the interior, it was the coastal states that contained most of Brazil's early frontier lands. As cities began to grow, the frontier expanded to interior valleys and highlands. For instance, coffee cultivation spread to the Paraiba Valley between Rio de Janeiro and São Paulo by the 1850s and to the highlands northwest of Rio de Janeiro after the 1860s.[34]

Conflict at Brazil's sparsely populated southern border then drove authorities to promote European immigration to the region in the late nineteenth and early twentieth centuries.[35] Unlike much of the domestic land appropriation and enclosure, European settlement during this period cultivated a class of smallholders. But smallholding was an exception to the rule. By the mid-twentieth century, Brazil had one of the most unequal distributions of landholding in the world.[36] This was particularly consequential, as over 60 percent of the population was rural and worked in agriculture.[37]

Throughout this period, as Brazil's interior began to populate, the Amazon remained far-flung and largely impenetrable. It was agriculturally unproductive given prevailing technology and cultivation methods, and difficult to exploit for natural resources.[38]

Plans to exploit the Amazon first formed in the early twentieth century. Amid a storm of political and economic crises, many investors and entrepreneurs at the time viewed the country as an economic backwater. Its economy was heavily reliant on coffee and dairy production. The "coffee with milk" oligarchy dominated politics and throttled the country's industrialization. Worker strikes and unrest were on the rise. The economy's vulnerability to the reliance on coffee and dairy became clear at the outset of the Great Depression, which sent Brazil's economy into a tailspin. Economic and political outsiders wanted a bigger role in development.

President Getúlio Vargas saw western frontier land settlement as a cure for the nation's ills. It promised to give a shot in the arm of overall agricultural production by putting more land under cultivation and to reduce political tensions over land concentration in developed areas by shipping rural workers displaced by increasing agricultural mechanization to the frontier.[39]

The result was the "March to the West" initiative in which the government sought to colonize and develop remaining interior frontier regions. One targeted area was in the direction of the Pantanal, a natural region containing the world's largest tropical wetland area; another was at the eastern fringes of the Amazon and along the river itself.[40]

One plank of this policy was the establishment of a series of eight massive agricultural settlements constituting roughly 6.2 million acres of land.[41] From the get-go, environmental practices in the settlements were shoddy, spurred in part by government policy. For instance, in the colony of Goiás at a site named Ceres, colonists practiced slash-and-burn agriculture. When the government delayed granting them land titles, many simply moved on to new virgin land for cultivation, cutting a swath of destruction in their path.[42]

By the 1950s, it was clear that the same old formula of frontier settlement in Brazil was bound to yield diminishing returns. It helped some people scrape by, but it couldn't keep pace with the growing population. And it didn't tackle the starkly unequal agricultural heartlands where most production took place and rural workers labored.

Popular pressure was building. In the late 1950s, the Peasant Leagues movement arose among poor tenant farmers in the sugarcane region of Pernambuco. It then spread to other states. Another movement arose in Rio Grande do Sul. These groups called for radical plans to reallocate land and threatened violence if the government didn't follow through.[43]

Against this backdrop a left-leaning populist deftly tapped into the discontent to win the presidency: João Goulart. Goulart's political agenda incorporated land reallocation but shifted the focus away from frontier settler reform and toward redistribution of established landholdings. His ideas electrified the imaginations of the rural poor. But Congress, which was stacked with large landowners, blocked his legislation.

Goulart tried to do an end run around Congress, but the establishment cried foul. It rallied support for its cause, and the military toppled Goulart in a 1964 coup. It would be the military government that would end up embracing the Great Reshuffle in Brazil, though, rather than taking up Goulart's brash, populist vision of reform, the regime would unleash settlement on the untapped lands of the Amazon. It was the opening note of what would become a crescendo of destruction that today seems unstoppable.

WHEN BRAZIL'S MILITARY took power in the 1960s, the land problem was unavoidable. Something had to be done, and before turning to the Amazon, the new leaders of the country took several steps to pave the way for redistributing large, underproductive private estates to the landless in a land-to-the-tiller style reform.[44] But the risks to their political alliance with elites were simply too great, and the main consequence of their efforts was a modernization of large landholdings. The government therefore launched Operation Amazonia, a project that sought to kick-start settlement in the Amazon basin through infrastructure projects twinned with fiscal and financial incentives.

The attack on the Amazon to feed Brazil's land hunger was multipronged. The government handed out cheap land, provided credit lines, and offered subsidies—all of which fostered clear-cutting and unsustainable agricultural practices, especially slash-and-burn agriculture and cattle ranching. But no single policy had as devastating long-term environmental consequences as the military's major infrastructure projects.

Road-building, in particular, pried open the forest for settlement and enabled an ever-growing flow of resource extraction and clear-cutting. One major early project was Highway BR-163, which paved the way straight along the nearly untouched and sprawling Pantanal wetlands in the south and into the gateway of the Amazon in the north. It serviced settlements created by Brazil's new Institute of Colonization and Agrarian Reform.

But the main act was the Trans-Amazonian Highway. The core idea was simple, according to the government: to connect "people with no land, to a land with no people."[45] The plan was to build a highway extending 3,000 miles from Brazil's east directly across the Amazon basin to the doorstep with Bolivia. Construction on the road began in 1970. It soon cut like a dagger straight through the forest.

The government proceeded to distribute tracts of land in neatly aligned rectangular tiles along both sides of the highway and develop larger settlements on the route as remote outposts. Settling the Amazon was nonetheless a daunting and isolating enterprise. To entice settlers, the government provided inexpensive land repayable over twenty years, six months of salary, and cheap credit.[46] No attention was paid to ecological or environmental considerations. Rather, the Amazon was treated as its very antithesis: a blank slate.

Operation Amazonia and the Trans-Amazonian Highway catalyzed a snowballing environmental catastrophe. Tens of thousands of migrants moved to the Amazon in search of government-distributed land.[47] Migrants settled along the highway, built towns, and transformed the forest, ravaging it through slash-and-burn agriculture and clear-cutting it to ranch cattle. By the 1980s, over 25 million acres of the forest had been cut down.[48]

Eventually, offshoots to the highway sprouted up, both legally and illegally. People settled along the offshoots, spurring more offshoots, more settlement, and still more offshoots, in what is known as a "fishbone" pattern. This development quickly outpaced what planners had imagined and what the government had officially sanctioned. One study of secondary roads on the southern side of the Trans-Amazonian Highway found that settlers had cleared large portions of the forest in undesignated areas, making way for others to penetrate even deeper into the jungle.[49]

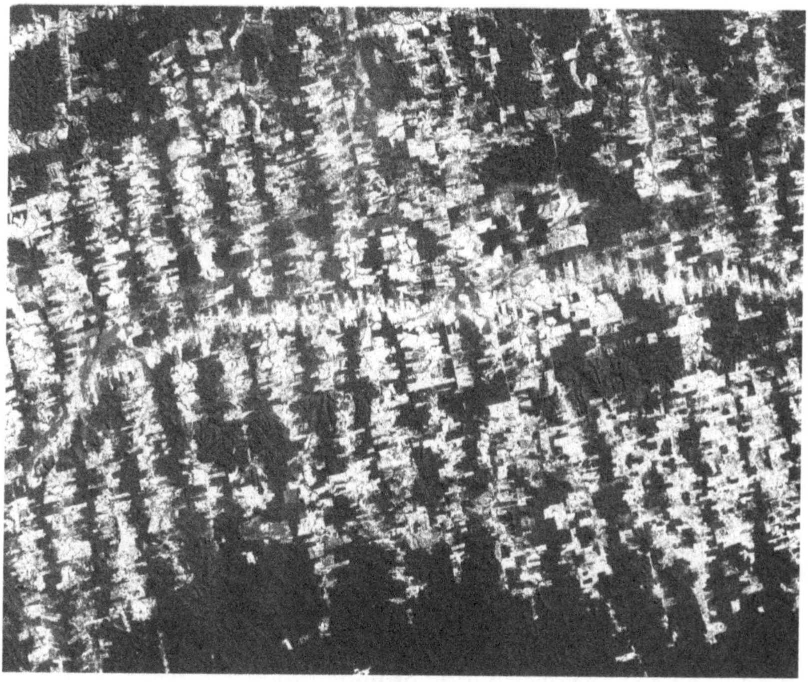

Deforestation along the Trans-Amazonian Highway. (Credit: ESA.)

The final result was environmental destruction on a massive scale. Today Brazil is a global beef-producing powerhouse, with nearly half of the country's beef raised in the Amazon. It is then shipped all over the world, mainly to China, Hong Kong, and Europe, but also to the United States as jerky and pet food.[50] Its leather exports that source from the Amazon are used in furniture and cars in the United States. Ranching introduced land practices that drain soils, pollute watersheds, and contribute to global emissions, both directly, through animal emissions, and by fueling carbon-intensive beef consumption.

Ranching is not the only unsustainable land use in the Amazon. Agriculture has not been much better: soil fertility in clear-cut areas has plummeted rapidly, encouraging farmers to simply clear more land and accelerate deforestation.

And yet for all of this destruction, Operation Amazonia did little to relieve landholding inequality in established agricultural areas in

Brazil. Rural populations continued to grow in these regions. For all of the settlement that ravaged the Amazon, most people chose not to embark on a difficult and uncertain trek into the Amazon for land. So when democracy returned to Brazil, the tensions of landless masses of rural workers seeking their fair share of land power remained to be solved.

BRAZIL'S MILITARY FOLLOWED many others in Latin America and retreated to the barracks in 1985. The country transitioned to democracy in a watershed moment for freedom in the region. But the new democracy faced many challenges. Gross economic and social inequalities collided with popular demands for inclusion and social justice. These demands were especially acute around landholding.

Brazil's new democracy quickly settled into a two-track land reallocation policy as a result: the distribution of public land through a settler reform and the distribution of underproductive privately owned land to groups of organized farmers. Both of these tracks have accelerated environmental destruction, placing the country at a point of no return on the Amazon rainforest while also degrading land and ecosystems elsewhere.

Brazil's Landless Rural Workers' Movement (known as the MST) crystallized just as the country transitioned to democracy.[51] This grassroots organization began in the waning years of military rule as small groups of farmers occupied unproductive lands in the south of the country. It quickly transformed into the region's largest and most sophisticated rural social movement, with strong internal discipline and local chapters across the country. Its goal was simple: to transfer privately held land into the hands of peasants in rural areas.

Private landowners pushed back hard. Through Brazil's constitutional assembly they won safeguards that prohibit the expropriation of productively used land and mandate market value compensation for seized property. They staved off top-down government land reallocation in favor of a more bottom-up, demand-driven process. And they pressured the government to retain a large program for distributing public frontier land to settlers. But they did not succeed in entirely barring the use of private land for reallocation. Pressure from social movements and the desire of urban elites to staunch the influx of rural people to urban areas was too great.[52]

The resulting dual policy marries a settler reform in the Amazon and on other public lands with private land reallocation to farmers, who sometimes organize themselves as private individual cultivators, but more typically as cooperatives or collectives through the MST.[53] Together these programs settled almost 1 million families on 190 million acres of land—an area larger than the state of Texas—from 1988 to 2013.[54]

The environmental damage resulting from these transfers has been extensive. Government efforts to settle landless families on remote public lands has led to the same sort of deforestation as Operation Amazonia. Recent policies to legalize the claims of rogue land grabbers on public lands have only accelerated this trend.[55] And now more stretches of the Trans-Amazonian Highway are being paved, lowering the costs of resource extraction, easing the transportation of cattle and agricultural products to outside markets, and making settlement more convenient and attractive.[56] Deforestation, resource extraction, and further development in the area are poised to accelerate.

But an equally important, underappreciated story revolves around the use of privately owned land for settlement. Because the reallocation of private property is driven by demand, rather than planned in advance by the government, it has created incentives for organized and forcible occupations of landed estates and other forms of rural conflict.[57] Forcible occupation, in turn, drives widespread property rights insecurity and encourages large landowners to show that their land is productive. They accomplish this goal by engaging in environmentally damaging practices, such as clearing more of their land and planting quick-yielding crops that damage soils.

The reason the landowners want to show their land is productive is that the MST has honed a strategy of identifying underproductive farms, gathering rural workers who want to farm it, and then staging a rapid occupation of the target farms. The government often reacts by expropriating occupied private land and granting it to the occupiers. From 1988 until the mid-2010s, several million individuals staged over 9,400 land invasions in rural areas, and some 1,200 peasants and peasant leaders were killed.[58]

Many large private landowners fear that the MST may target their land for occupation, and that the government might expropriate it in response. One recent study found that in places with more land invasions and property rights insecurity, landowners are more likely to invest in crops that have shorter times to maturity, require more natural resources, and accelerate the degradation of soils and the land.[59] In addition, landowners who perceive a high risk of expropriation are more inclined to turn to clear-cutting forested areas and introducing cattle in order to demonstrate land use.[60]

Settlers themselves often double down on deforestation and other land practices with negative environmental consequences. Like the large landowners, settlers face property rights insecurity, not only because of threats of reprisal from the landowners, but because they, too, need to demonstrate use of the land in order to retain it. They often acquire land when they have few other resources and little savings. To protect their claims and earn money quickly, they turn to deforestation.[61] In 2004, the Amazon Forest Monitoring Program found that half the land in the 1,354 rural settlements established by the government between 1970 and 2002 had been deforested.[62] This trend has continued: government-sponsored settlements are now at the center of hot spots for deforestation as original settlement areas expand.[63]

The spiraling environmental destruction in Brazil shows how the struggle for power linked to land can wreak major collateral damage that is difficult to contain. With everyone seeking to grab what they can get, the environment has nowhere to hide. It has set the country on an unavoidable collision course with nature.

* * *

CHINA'S DESTRUCTION OF its forests and grasslands and Brazil's deforestation of the Amazon rainforest are only two examples among many in which the reshuffling of land has given way to acute episodes of rapid environmental destruction. A similar pattern occurred in the decimation of North American prairies in the United States and Canada in the decades after these countries passed homestead acts.

This repeating pattern has occurred following land reforms of various stripes, but especially among collective reforms, cooperative reforms, and settler reforms. Governments have myopically focused on using land for the purposes of strengthening political control, furthering their goals for national transformation, and fulfilling ideological agendas at the expense of the natural environment.

Unwinding the damage is not easy. As land decollectivization unfolded in China, the Communist Party grew wise to the fact that the scale of environmental destruction would be unsustainable if it continued, potentially ruining both productivity and public health. Consequently, the government gradually adopted a raft of policies to rectify some of the previous excesses, particularly those linked to deforestation. The fertilizer overshot, by contrast, has still not been corrected. The country today is the world's biggest consumer of agricultural chemicals, using nearly one-third of the world's fertilizers and pesticides on only 9 percent of the world's cropland.[64] Although it has recently begun to take steps to clean up water sources, they remain badly polluted.

A new approach to land allocation and management has been key to the implementation of policies that have sought to remediate deforestation. The government never fully privatized land during decollectivization. Rural land ownership remained collectively held by villages, as it does to this day. That arrangement enabled the government to retain the ability to push villages into accepting its plans for land use, including taking land out of production.

Facing an increase in thick, paralyzing dust storms in northern China that choked Beijing and other cities, the government adopted a decades-long reforestation project in 1979. The Great Green Wall project aims to increase the forest coverage rate of northwest, north, and northeast China to 15 percent by 2050 from a mere 5 percent in 1979. The wall will eventually form a belt 2,800 miles long. The goal is to reduce the frequency and intensity of dust and sand storms, mainly from the Gobi Desert, while also promoting soil and water restoration. With over 60 billion trees planted, it is already the largest artificial forest in the world, and it continues to grow.[65]

The 1997 drought in the Yellow River and the 1998 flood in the Yangtze River were stark warnings for the Chinese Communist Party, and it adopted twin programs in response to the precarious underlying ecological conditions. The first was the Natural Forest Protection Program, which aimed to preserve most remaining natural forests. The program banned logging in southwest China, reduced tree harvest quotas in the northeast and elsewhere, and set regulations to strengthen forest management and protection. The second program was the Sloping Land Conversion Program, which aimed to convert cropland on steep slopes back to forest and grassland. Within five years, the program had forested over 7.4 million acres of land and closed off another 5.7 million acres to human activity in an effort to promote ecosystem restoration.[66]

But ecosystems are fragile. Replacing forests is not simply a matter of replanting trees. Much of China's Great Green Wall, for instance, consists of monocultured forests. The biodiversity that was lost in the initial removal of grasslands and forests has not returned. Furthermore, the lack of diversity in forests makes trees more susceptible to mass die-offs through disease. In the year 2000, a single pest infestation killed 1 billion poplar trees in the Ningxia region of northwest China, setting the project there back twenty years. It serves as a reminder that when the environment is damaged, it is very difficult to fix.

While the Great Reshuffle was etching permanent damage on the environment, it was also contributing to a more direct daily struggle among human populations to make ends meet. As we will see, politicians harnessing land power for national goals often see political predominance as within their reach, and in its pursuit wreak havoc not only on the natural world but also on economies and human well-being.

CHAPTER 6

THE UNDERDEVELOPMENT PLAYBOOK

MODERN SOCIETY DEPENDS ON PROSPERITY, AND LAND POWER can be an incredible accelerator of growth and enrichment. That's just one of the reasons why in the centuries since the beginning of the Great Reshuffle land reallocation has become such a magnet for social planners. As we have seen, it can also create racial hierarchy, bolster traditional social relations in a society, deliver to a party's political base, and produce resources or destroy them. But land reallocation done wrong also has another power—the power to chill development and retard growth for generations.

In the early 1920s, the recent Russian Revolution loomed large everywhere there was unrest, striking paranoia into the hearts of the powerful and throwing fuel on the fires of popular discontent. Mexico had only just undergone its own decade of revolutionary conflict and change, which stretched from 1910 to 1920 but still left many political questions unanswered. Fired by its own revolutionary changes and the Russian example, Mexican society entered the 1920s roiling with popular demands that land be snatched from wealthy landowners and delivered to the poor. For their part, most landowners continued to retain considerable power and influence. Political instability had become endemic, and conspiracies and assassinations proliferated, while leaders struggled to deliver economic prosperity. This toxic cocktail made politicians contemplate a surprising—and unfortunately, self-defeating—set of reforms.

The governor of the northern Mexican state of Chihuahua, Ignacio Enríquez, faced this dilemma as it played out on the local level. He had allied himself with powerful large landowners in his state. But Mexico's president, Álvaro Obregón, and his interior secretary, Plutarco Calles, pressured Enríquez to appease local groups of landless peasants by expropriating several sprawling private estates and granting the land communally to them.

Enríquez dragged his feet, then came up with an alternative. He would settle peasants on public lands and sell off select pieces of large private estates to peasants and other interested buyers who could then work the land as autonomous producers.[1] He argued that this policy would reactivate the local rural economy, catalyze land markets, attract investment, and spur modernization. Conveniently for him, it would also allow him to retain powerful landowners as local investors and avoid vesting too much autonomy in landless peasants by granting them land in common.

But President Obregón denied Enríquez's proposal. He viewed his political coalition as too fragile and the revolutionary moment as too volatile to indulge Enríquez's deviation in favor of the landlords. He also believed that turning the landless peasants into landholders would not just win their support, but put them under his control.[2] Interior Secretary Calles was even more forthright. He told Enríquez in a conversation that creating communal farming villages for the peasants would be "the best method of controlling these people by merely telling them: If you want land you have to support the government; if you are not with the government, you won't get land."[3]

A savvy political operator, Calles managed to leverage the promise of land power to win the presidency in 1924. Once he took office, the machinery of land reallocation kicked into gear across the country. For the next seven decades, Mexico's authoritarian ruling political party, the Institutional Revolutionary Party (known as the PRI), stripped large landowners of their property and social position in much of the countryside and redistributed privately held land in a communal fashion to villages called *ejidos*, which were worked by the land beneficiaries.[4] It was the Western Hemisphere's largest episode of collective land reform.

Before long, however, the critical error of Mexican land redistribution became unmistakable: the PRI had prioritized political power over economics. After some initial success, the agricultural sector lurched. Land beneficiaries reeled in the face of a dizzying array of restrictions on their land. They could not sell or rent it, could not mortgage it, could not idle it for long periods, and did not even have property titles. Banks would not loan to them. Many could not get the machinery or even the seeds they needed to farm. The land markets seized up.

If this outcome was not what Mexico's leadership had desired, it was nevertheless a predictable consequence of the system they had designed. Peasants clamored for support for their struggling farming villages, and the PRI delivered it to them, but in exchange the party demanded political fealty and crafted a system that left the *ejidatarios* (the land beneficiaries who worked the ejidos) helpless to productively use the land they had been granted. The PRI won the political control it so dearly desired, helping to underpin what Nobel laureate Mario Vargas Llosa famously dubbed "the perfect dictatorship." But it came at a steep cost: Mexico's collective reform scarred the economy deeply and left a legacy of economic dependence, emigration, and corruption that the country still struggles with today.

As for the former governor of Chihuahua who had resisted the ejidos, Ignacio Enríquez, he moved into public opposition of the government after leaving his post in the mid-1920s and sharply criticized the government's collective land reform. He argued that the government had "turned the agrarian problem into a weapon in the hands of political candidates": "Politicians prefer to preserve a state of agitation and uncertainty among ejidatarios, with respect to the possession of their parcels, in order to make them submissive to the government and to use them as weapons in their electoral battles."[5] This troubling formula long outlived Enríquez.

For all of the problems that land reallocation can bring, it is often taken for granted that it is a reliable way of achieving economic growth. Many development economists regard land reallocation as a silver bullet in the arsenal of development. Stagnation can set in when large landholders rest on their laurels and resist change. Meanwhile, the landless have strong incentives to make the most of any land they are granted. Putting a ready workforce together with fertile tracts of land can both grow the economic pie and divide it more evenly than plantation farming or a contract farming system run by absentee landlords. Places such as Taiwan, South Korea, Japan, and the Indian states of West Bengal and Kerala have followed this path to success.

But the realities of redistributing land are complex, and land reallocation is far more likely to stall economic development than to speed it up. Few of us think very often about the fact that owning land rests on a bureaucracy devoted to keeping track of who owns which tract, and a set of laws and courts and state agents devoted to protecting ownership rights to the land. Land power isn't just an idea—it is political, and if a society's protection of property rights is weak, or if its leaders hope to use it to reward their supporters and punish dissent, and thereby bolster their control over society, land ownership rights can be trumped by politics. We've seen how settler reforms can entrench racial hierarchy, gendered land reforms can entrench sexism, and extractive and unplanned land use can entrench environmental destruction. Land reallocation systems built around political carrots and sticks can be just as malignant, dooming a country to stagnation.

The tragic outcomes of the political reshuffling of land power are on clear display in the experiences of land reallocation in Mexico as well as in Venezuela, and dozens of other countries, such as China, Russia, and Zimbabwe, have fallen victim to similar problems. As we will see, the desire to maintain and consolidate political power drove governments in Mexico and Venezuela to reallocate land in economically distortionary ways and to withhold property rights from land beneficiaries so that they were easier to manipulate politically. We will also see that while Italy's land reallocation was far less disastrous than Mexico's or Venezuela's, it nevertheless illustrates how politics and mismanagement can tie up new landholders in long-term loans and a politicized bureaucracy. The way reallocation played out in Italy created a stagnant rural underclass and fueled a bloated political patronage machine as the Italian and broader European economies transformed and became more competitive.

Land power in the hands of politicians can create growth or restrain it. The economic power of land and its importance to millions means that choices over its allocation and management can set countries on generations-long development trajectories. All too often it is used to entrench political power rather than to unleash economic dynamism across society.

MEXICO SPRINGS A DEVELOPMENT TRAP

Mexico at the dawn of the twentieth century was a poor country plagued by stark inequality. From a colonial era defined by the dispossession of indigenous communities, it had inherited a lopsided distribution of land that favored the descendants of a small number of colonial administrators and Spanish colonists. These elites amassed large estates and the power to levy taxes and extract labor from indigenous communities that lived within their appropriated territory. The long dictatorship of Porfirio Díaz that spanned the turn of the twentieth century allowed elites to grab even more land.[6] Díaz kick-started a drive toward economic expansion through resource extraction, infrastructure development, and agro-exports, but the upshot was intensified land concentration, forced labor, and worsening subjugation of the indigenous groups that remained.

On the eve of the Mexican Revolution in 1910, over 75 percent of the population lived in rural areas.[7] Less than 11,000 owners of large estates, known as haciendas, controlled nearly 60 percent of the national territory and the lion's share of the fertile and irrigated land. A single landowner controlled an estate as large as the country of Costa Rica. Half the rural population worked as resident laborers on these large estates and smaller landholdings as debt peons who had access to a small plot of land but owed the landowner the bulk of their labor in exchange. Many more were landless. And rural populations at the fringes of the hacienda economy eked out a living at the agricultural periphery on fragmented lands of poor quality.[8]

This was tinder for revolution. A series of regional rebellions broke out as Díaz was forced from office in 1911, and a charismatic peasant revolutionary named Emiliano Zapata took up arms in southern Mexico. Zapata amassed a formidable following and played a foundational role in shaping the outcome of the Mexican Revolution. His demand was both simple and revolutionary: return the land to the people.

Assassinated in 1919, Zapata would not live to see the consequences of his appeal, but the centerpiece of land reallocation was Article 27 of Mexico's 1917 constitution.[9] It granted the government the authority to expropriate and reallocate large private landholdings from their owners to communities that had little or no land access. It would become the engine of a reshuffle that would level wealth and radically reallocate the country's land into the 1990s.

But in the early days, land reallocation proceeded in fits and starts. There was considerable political instability and regionalized factional fighting, as well as a debate over the form that land allocation would take, as illustrated by the debate between Ignacio Enríquez on the one hand and Presidents Obregón and Calles on the other. Matters coalesced toward the end of the 1920s alongside the formation of Mexico's dominant party, the PRI.

The government settled on a collective reform that granted large private landholdings to villages as a whole in the communal arrangement known as the ejido. Ejidos originated in a prerevolution model of indigenous rural communities rooted in self-government, local autonomy, and inalienable access to land.[10] This return to a familiar form was appealing to landless people sick of having their land taken away by the powerful. Many peasants believed that collective landholding in the ejido style would act as a safeguard against a possible return to land dispossession.

PRI leaders supported this model while also modifying it to their political advantage.[11] The traditional mode of ejido land distribution had entailed individual distribution within collectives. The PRI removed the individual claim to ownership, making the grants wholly collective in nature. They vested the government rather than communities with the responsibility of protecting ejido rights.[12] Finally, the PRI created a formidable and hierarchical bureaucratic structure to link ejidos and their members to the party.

In the new ejido system, groups of peasants had to petition for land grants from the government. When they were successful, they acquired the land collectively as villages and could use and work it individually or collectively as the village decided. But their individual rights to land were extremely limited. They did not receive title to their land or full property rights as landowners. Peasants were not permitted to leave their plots idle for more than two consecutive years, and they were not allowed to rent individualized plots. Neither villages nor individual peasants could sell the land or use it as collateral to access commercial loans.

The land power remained in the hands of the PRI, which spent most of the twentieth century seizing land from large landowners without compensation and granting it to Mexico's peasants in this fashion. The reform swallowed up huge swaths of the countryside. It eventually touched nearly half of the country's entire land area and most of its agricultural land.[13]

Land held as ejidos in Mexico. (Courtesy of the author.)

IN ITS FIRST few decades, the reform dramatically reduced land inequality.[14] In the end, however, the political utility of Mexico's collective reform came to outweigh its economic benefits. Although the PRI had a founding vision grounded in social justice that emerged from the revolution, its control over land and peasants through land allocation became a central tool for sustaining its political networks, ensuring stability, and churning out votes in sham elections.[15]

Land reallocation rose during election years and was greater in places where the threat of rural unrest was most elevated.[16] The government purposely withheld property rights from the beneficiaries, and even further distorted them, once it realized that this strategy had the politically useful effect of generating greater leverage over land beneficiaries.[17] Land beneficiaries learned that they had to toe the party line to gain assistance. If they resisted, they had to forgo benefits and face a life riddled with the troubles that stemmed from weak property rights and heavy-handed government bureaucracy.

The economic consequences of this distorted system followed a predictable pattern. Poor peasants who took control of land quickly set to farming it with a focus on immediate production. Because the land seized from large landholders had often been neglected, these bursts of productivity manifested in localized waves of short-term economic growth. These efforts drove improvements in economic equality for a brief period after the revolution.[18] But Mexico's development trajectory eventually came to sag under the weight of its politicized version of collective land reform. Problems and stagnation among the growing masses of longtime beneficiaries came to outweigh the fleeting gains of new waves of beneficiaries. The deep inefficiencies and distortions inherent in the system spilled over to the broader economy and brought a return to inequality.

The PRI's decision to imbue the ejidos with weak property rights was central to the reform's economic failure. Stifling restrictions on land sales, leasing, and mortgaging smothered rural land markets. Banks would not touch ejidos, starving them of access to private credit. Peasants had nowhere to turn but the government for subsidies and credits for seeds, insurance, fertilizer, and other basic necessities for farming. The government proliferated federal agencies to grant agricultural credits, purchase harvests, distribute fertilizer, and settle land use conflicts and boundary disputes.[19] But the price of all of this was political control. Agencies could threaten to deny communities the basic necessities for farming if they failed to support the party at election times.

Decreasing state investment over time compounded peasant dependence on the government and production inefficiency.[20] Declining access to credit meant that most ejidos were unable to afford new farming technologies as they became available.[21] The lack of investment caused productivity to stagnate and the broader economy to underperform.

Ejidos also suffered from a tragedy of the commons. Uncertainty over property rights and poverty fueled people to overuse commonly held community resources and underinvest in community infrastructure. Overgrazing, deforestation, and soil degradation were widespread, placing stress on core resources.[22] The overexploitation of land within ejidos deepened as rural populations grew, driving down yields.

The government tried to breathe new life into agriculture by handing out subsidized fertilizers and pesticides, including a tsunami of the toxic chemical fertilizer DDT. This decision had some of its intended consequences for production in the short term. But it widely polluted watersheds, degraded soils, and unleashed a wave of health hazards, from outright poisoning among farming families to physical and mental developmental problems in babies.[23]

Peasant communities bridled under the thumb of government control and property restrictions as well as their damaging consequences. As populations grew and the first generation born into the newly formed ejidos came of age, there was a great deal of conflict within households, between households, and against ejido bosses who had been bought off by the PRI, generating a push for changing the system to improve land access and secure greater protections.[24] Some peasants organized to demand greater legal security to their landholdings.[25] Several business interest groups similarly advocated for clearer and more secure property rights for ejidos and their members.[26] Many more peasants sought to skirt property rights restrictions and turned to informally renting or selling their plots despite the risks.[27]

Meanwhile, cognizant of the economic problems they were creating among ejidos and seeking to limit the damage, the government ring-fenced certain private farms by creating a parallel, secure property rights track in the countryside. It began issuing private landowners formal guarantees against expropriation so that agricultural production as a whole would not crater. Private farms enjoyed increasing access to credit and greater productivity, while ejidos foundered.[28]

The government also invested heavily in industrialization through business subsidies, tariffs, and urban infrastructure as it deprioritized the countryside.[29] Growth in industry and private-sector agriculture helped to fuel robust overall economic growth on a national scale from the 1940s through the 1970s. This growth period became known as the Mexican economic miracle.

But as Mexico's collective reform advanced throughout the twentieth century, inefficiencies in agriculture spilled over into the broader economy. Facing marginal profits and precarious land security, many land beneficiary families could not afford for younger generations to leave the farm. This stunted migration into urban areas at a time when cities provided the most attractive opportunities for upward mobility.[30] Meanwhile, some families took a risk and encouraged grown children to emigrate, at least while the head of household held on to rights within the ejido.[31]

By the 1960s, economic inequality between urban and rural areas had spiked to levels not seen since before the Mexican Revolution.[32] The collective reform had become an Achilles' heel for the broader economy. Mexican states where land reform had gone furthest suffered lower rates of economic growth over the course of decades.[33]

The death spiral of Mexican agriculture came into sharp focus as a series of debt and financial crises sparked external intervention in the

1980s and 1990s. Mexico became a repeat customer of the International Monetary Fund (IMF) and the World Bank. In exchange, these international agencies demanded structural economic reforms. Mexico also entered into negotiations for the North American Free Trade Agreement (NAFTA) in the early 1990s, which brought pressure for economic liberalization and raised the specter of agricultural competition with a flood of food imports from the United States and Canada.

One critical reform entailed extending and strengthening rural property rights. As the PRI scrambled to patch up glaring economic problems and stoke growth, it ended its collective reform and worked with the World Bank on a plan to finally grant land beneficiaries property rights to their land. The vast majority of ejidos took them up on the offer by the mid-2000s. The government did not ask ejidos to break up, though it gave them that option. Most ejidos elected layered property rights that gave members separate titles to common resources, individually farmed land, and houses. Ejido members also won rights to sell land within ejidos and lease land within ejidos or to outside members.

Decades of mismanagement in agriculture could not be reversed overnight. Mexico is still grappling with the economic distortions of its collective reform. But there are signs that reforms to the core problems, including inadequate property rights, have started to pay off. Agricultural productivity has increased and poverty has declined considerably among rural families. Many of them inherited reform land and continue to live within ejidos.[34] But just as Mexico was winding down its program of land reallocation that prioritized political obedience over individual welfare, Venezuela was ramping up its own version.

VENEZUELA'S CRASH LANDING

On December 10, 2001, at the historic battlefield of Santa Inés in the sweltering southern Venezuelan state of Barinas, President Hugo Chávez convened a crowd of government functionaries and farmers. The date was laden with symbolism. On that same day in 1859, the famous general and advocate for peasant rights Ezequiel Zamora had triumphed over the powerful conservative landed oligarchy in a battle at Santa Inés. Chávez had returned to the battlefield to symbolically take up Zamora's mantle in celebration of the newly passed Law of Land and Agrarian Development, which promised to reallocate large and underproductive private landholdings to the poor.

In characteristic fashion, Chávez's rhetoric soared: "The revolution goes to the counterattack, against the reaction of the oligarchy that threatens, conspires, and undermines it," he declared. "From Santa Inés de Barinas and shouting 'Long Live Zamora!,' beginning today, I declare the revolutionary Law of Land and Agrarian Development to be in effect."[35]

In stark contrast to the pomp and celebration in Barinas, the rest of the country had ground to a halt. Venezuela's largest business association had joined with a major workers' union, several political parties, and a mass of everyday people to stage rallies, massive street marches, and strikes across Venezuela. The timing was not coincidental. The general strike was a response to a sweeping package of laws passed by presidential decree weeks earlier, with Chávez's Land Law as one of its central and most controversial elements.[36]

Protesters sought to repeal the new laws. Many wanted Chávez sacked. The business sector and media ramped up pressure on Chávez in the subsequent months with unrelenting criticism and an ongoing series of demonstrations and strikes. A raucous and unruly set of demonstrations and counterdemonstrations culminated in a coup in April 2002. The military turned on Chávez and ferried him to a Caribbean island off the coast of Venezuela. They installed the strike leader and head of the national business association as president.

But Chávez had the last laugh. Machinations among the presidential guard returned him to the national palace just two days later, and his supporters flooded the streets to give him a hero's welcome back. Now aware of what his recalcitrant opposition was capable of, Chávez played political hardball in the following years. When the Supreme Tribunal of Justice, Venezuela's supreme court, struck down core elements of the Land Law in November 2002, Chávez packed the court with his allies and passed an amended version of the law.

Much like the land reallocation policies of Mexico decades earlier, the Venezuelan law proved to be a political boon for Chávez and his handpicked successor, Nicolás Maduro. It served as a partisan weapon to dispense patronage to government allies and punish political opponents. The government used the law to harass and cut down prominent political challengers by seizing their assets, to deny benefits to opposition voters, and to churn out supportive votes by selectively doling out land.

Yet much in line with Mexico's experience, the economy paid a steep price for land reallocation in Venezuela that prioritized political incentives above all else. Venezuela's Land Law destroyed property rights. Investment in land and agricultural production dropped, plunging the country into a devastating hunger crisis as the broader economy sharply contracted in the 2010s. The country has now traced one of the biggest economic collapses during peacetime in recorded history.

FROM A PURELY economic perspective, Venezuela at the turn of the twenty-first century stands out as a somewhat unusual country to opt for a massive program of land reallocation. The Great Reshuffle had already come to Venezuela, with a round of land reallocation spanning from 1960 through the 1980s. Some 20 million acres of land had changed hands. Three-fourths of this was state-owned land doled out as a settler-style reform, and the remainder was privately owned land granted to rural workers and farmers through a tiller-style reform.[37] By the early 1990s, 85 percent of the country's population lived in urban areas. Oil production made up around half of the government's revenue and the lion's share of the nation's export revenue.[38] It was hardly a country teeming with oppressed or restive landless workers, like Russia in the 1910s, Mexico in the 1920s, or China in the 1940s.

But that didn't matter. The political backdrop was ripe for populist land reshuffling. A major economic crisis hammered the country in the late 1980s and early 1990s. Venezuela's political party system crumbled after more than three decades of stability. The government weathered two coup attempts in 1992 alone, one of them spearheaded by a young and charismatic military officer by the name of Hugo Chávez. He landed in jail but walked free several years later. After winning the presidency in 1999 on an anti-corruption and anti-poverty populist platform, Chávez quickly began dismantling the country's checks and balances. Chávez forged a new constitution, strengthened the presidency, and eliminated the upper house of the legislature.

Empowered by these institutional reforms, Chávez next set out to destroy his political rivals. These rivals included Venezuela's media, the business sector, and large landowners. The first major salvo was the package of decree laws passed in late 2001 with the Law of Land and Agrarian Development as its cornerstone. In just a few years, the Land Law would transform the country into an economic basket case.

Early legal battles limited the initial implementation of the Land Law. Land grants came strictly from state-owned land in the first several years. The reform proceeded as a blend of a settler reform and a simple property rights reform that legalized existing informal land settlements on state-owned land.[39]

But as the government further consolidated its power, Chávez succeeded in pushing through an amended, more muscular version of the law in 2005. The government called it a "war to the death against large landowners." Private landowners had nowhere to hide. The law redefined property rights across the country, demanding that landowners trace an uninterrupted lineage of land titles to their property back to 1848 in order to support a valid legal claim to their land and protect against government expropriation. Shoddy recordkeeping, illegal land grabs, and a commonplace historical practice of selling land without keeping track of the title relegated over 90 percent of landowners to informal or insecure status overnight.[40]

The law also mandated that property serve a vaguely defined social function. It flagged large and underproductive properties for potential expropriation regardless of whether landowners could meet the rigid new standards for proving the legality of their land titles.[41]

The implementation of the law could only be described as Kafkaesque. The government did not have complete land registers or any way to estimate adequate productivity, so they called on people to take enforcement into their own hands. The government empowered any Venezuelan citizen to apply to provisionally occupy private property that they suspected to be incompliant with the new law. This set off an epidemic of land squatting across the country.[42]

Flying blind, government bureaucrats came up with crude rules of thumb to try to make sense of the law's provisions. In doing so, they generated perplexing catch-22s. For instance, they told cattle ranchers in southern plains states who had fewer than one head of cattle per hectare of land (about 2.5 acres) to increase the size of their herds, partition their land and sell parts of it, or face expropriation. The government then turned around and commenced expropriating ranches with more than one head of cattle per hectare on the grounds that these ranchers were mishandling natural land resources by depleting the soil through overgrazing. In another example, the government mandated that large corn producers sell their products at below production cost in order to keep popular corn-based food products cheap. Those that complied went broke; those that did not faced expropriation.[43]

The land that was reallocated was granted inconsistently. Bits and pieces of thousands of private properties were granted to individual tillers, typically on a provisional basis without circling back to confer clear and definitive land titles. At the same time, the government expropriated a host of large landowners, many of them political opponents, and converted their estates into collective or cooperative farms. Collective farms are typically run by local rural laborers in collaboration with the state. Cooperative farms are formed by groups of landless applicants who apply to access and work land as a cooperative. Millions of acres of formerly privately owned land have transferred hands through these varied channels.[44]

AS IN MEXICO, Venezuela's blended reform was a political triumph even if it was an economic nightmare. The system created an environment of deliberate legal vulnerability, enabling the government to attack political opponents who spoke out and to scare others into submission. Perhaps the most high-profile case was the National Guard's occupation and seizure of the property of Manuel Rosales, a former governor who stood as the chief opposition candidate to Chávez in the 2006 presidential election. Rosales was soon after hit with trumped-up corruption charges. He fled to Peru before eventually returning to Venezuela.

The reform also created an army of politically reliable land beneficiaries. Beneficiaries were screened and received land without solid property rights.[45] The government used its largesse and the legal vulnerability of beneficiaries to mobilize support in increasingly unfair elections that kept first Chávez and then Maduro in power for decades.

This political win came at an exorbitant cost. Pervasive property rights insecurity and politicized land seizures drove widespread disinvestment in rural and urban areas alike. Many established farms and agribusinesses scaled back on their plans or entirely shut down. Beneficiaries were similarly wary of investment as a result of property insecurity. Agricultural production suffered major disruptions against these headwinds. Meanwhile, urban real estate developers and large property owners also faced increasing property rights insecurity as the government expropriated businesses and granted cover to urban squatters in residential and commercial real estate.

The government was able to paper over many of these problems in the 2000s as a massive oil boom filled state coffers and fueled a government spending spree. It spent heavily on subsidizing basic food staples and running or supporting farms that had been seized from private landowners. Spending on these and other policies lifted millions of people out of poverty and considerably reduced inequality. But the economic fundamentals were rotten. The economy cratered when sky-high oil prices went bust in the 2010s.[46]

Draconian exchange rate and import controls sparked hyperinflation and widespread food shortages, given that domestic agricultural production was woefully insufficient. Debt ballooned and creditors clamored to be repaid. The health-care system collapsed and hunger spread. By the late 2010s, one-third of the population was skipping meals daily, in many cases to help feed their children. The poverty rate spiked to above 80 percent, and economic output cratered by three-quarters.[47] The decline drove over 7 million people to flee the country.[48] For all practical purposes, the country dove into a tailspin, and it will take generations for it to recover.

Venezuela revolutionized who holds the land but neglected everything else about the process in the meantime. Simply by creating a functional bureaucracy to carefully track land and assess need, it could have won political support, enhanced equality, and fueled economic growth in the process. But the inability to put petty political calculations aside is all too often the downfall of revolutions in who holds the land.

POSTWAR ITALY AND THE WOUNDS OF REFORM

Even countries that avoid the extremes that Mexico and Venezuela took can still end up in the development trap. The lure of political advantage has derailed the positive transformative potential of land power and ensnared economies all over the world.

In late October 1949, as Mexico was still in the midst of its radical land reallocation and Venezuela was in the throes of a stifling episode of military dictatorship, a group of some 14,000 peasants from villages in the southern Italian region of Calabria mobilized to settle scores with a local landowner. Whole villages of peasants, including men, women, and children, were on the march. Some carried Communist banners next to portraits of the patron saint of their village. Their target was the Berlingieri family in the town of Melissa.[49]

The peasants laid claim to land that was part of a Berlingieri estate called Fragalà, which had been set aside for the peasants' use in an 1811 grant under Napoleonic legislation. But following a common playbook in the region, the Berlingieri family had gradually pushed the peasants off the land and taken it as their own. When local peasants briefly occupied Fragalà in 1946–1947, the Berlingieri family offered them a smaller piece of the property, but the peasants had refused to accept it. They were again pushed off the estate.

As the procession arrived at the disputed land, they staked it out, divided it into portions, and immediately set about plowing and sowing it. A set of local deputies affiliated with the ruling Christian Democracy (Democrazia Cristiana) party quickly traveled to Rome to summon police intervention. Local police and units from neighboring regions flooded into the area and began arresting peasants and union leaders, which only inflamed tensions. The movement grew. Rome then sent in the riot police, who spent the night at the home of the Berlingieri family when they first arrived. The next morning, the riot police tried to expel the peasants from Fragalà, but the peasants again resisted. The police fired into the crowd.

Salvatore Filosa, one of the peasants in the crowd, recalled the horror of the event: "The marshal fired a pistol shot, and as if was an agreed-upon signal, the police charged us with machine guns, hand grenades, and truncheons. The crowd fled in chaos and in a few seconds there was smoke everywhere. Most of the police fired from positions above us. Among the crowd there was confusion: some ran, others fell to the ground wounded, and others screamed."[50] Three people were killed and another fifteen were wounded. The police fled the scene back to the Berlingieris' home without even providing aid to the wounded.

The police brutality at Melissa set off a shock wave in the country. It quickly became national news. And it fueled a wave of rural unrest across southern Italy that lasted into early 1950 and resulted in more peasant killings and arrests at the hands of the police. All the while, the Communist Party was working behind the scenes, assisting villagers in organizing more land occupations and demonstrations.

The ruling Christian Democrats had their backs against a wall. Although they counted many important northern and southern landowners among their supporters, growing social and political grievances in the countryside threatened national political stability and their own skins. The potential of the ongoing unrest to benefit their political archenemy, the Communists, posed the greatest threat of all. If the Communists managed to forge an alliance between rural and urban workers, they might seriously contest the Christian Democrats' grip on power. The Christian Democrats were determined not to lose the fight.

The most obvious solution was to give the people some version of what they were asking for: land reallocation. In 1950, the Christian Democrats navigated resistance from within their own party and passed a momentous series of three land laws that would transform the Italian countryside and mark its economy for decades. The reform undercut the appeal of the Communists and helped the Christian Democrats continue to dominate Italy's political landscape for nearly forty years.

But the reform's economic legacy was far more mixed. While the country's economy took off with urbanization and industrialization, the areas targeted for land reallocation slowly fell further and further behind. The peasants at Melissa got their land. But many of their children and grandchildren would not take part in Italy's economic transformation. The outcome had similarities to what transpired in Mexico and Venezuela, but Italy's particular political backdrop provided a twist.

ITALY BETWEEN THE two world wars had been a heavily agricultural and poor country much like its southern European counterparts of Spain and Portugal. The country had only unified in 1871 as Italy's more economically advanced northern Piedmont region finished a decades-long campaign to gobble up rival northern provinces, the economically backward southern Kingdom of the Two Sicilies, and the papal states centered in Rome. Large portions of the south were plagued by malaria.

Slightly over half of the labor force worked in agriculture in the mid-1930s, and millions of rural workers toiled as wage laborers on large estates. This scenario predominated not only in southern Italy, where large estates dominated the economy, but also in pockets of central and even northern Italy. The fascist dictator Benito Mussolini had the support of large landowners and did little to alleviate the problem despite his efforts to open up more land for cultivation by draining swampland areas. The situation became untenable as population growth further strained rural poverty. Many workers emigrated to the United States, parts of Latin America, and elsewhere.

This toxic atmosphere exploded in the aftermath of World War II when soldiers returned home to find their meager lot unimproved. The countryside roiled with discontent. A wave of rural unrest and occupations of large estates shook the country from 1944 to 1947 and fueled the meteoric rise of the Italian Communist Party (Partito Comunista Italiano). The Communists won a growing following as they organized workers to occupy and farm large, often uncultivated estates.

After a brief lull, the massacre of peasants at Melissa in 1949 sparked a massive new wave of unrest. The Christian Democrats that governed the country had to respond. If they took no action, social and political grievances in the countryside could boil over and threaten national political stability. The Communists loomed particularly large as a political threat. The Christian Democrats were not the only ones worried. The United States and other Allied governments thought that large land ownership in Italy was a destabilizing force that had underpinned support for fascism and then served as a rallying cry for a snowballing workers' movement.[51]

Their solution was a tiller reform. Politics played in its fashioning. If done right, the tiller reform could undercut the appeal of the Communists and bolster the Christian Democrats, restore stability, and even stem a potential flood of migrants to the industrializing north, where the Christian Democrats had their initial stronghold. And it could be part of the broader restructuring of the Italian economy. There was precedent in other tiller reforms, such as the Irish reform of more than a half century prior. And tiller reforms were in the air:

the United States was simultaneously helping to advise and fund several major tiller reforms in East Asia.

A trio of land laws in 1950 targeted eight different geographic areas for reshuffling land ownership.[52] These areas spanned the country and covered one-third of its territory but focused mainly on southern and central Italy. The aim was to expropriate large and underproductive estates and turn them over to rural workers while breaking them up into individual family plots. The laws exempted small, productive farms. Unlike in Mexico or Venezuela, in Italy the government gained a degree of buy-in from landowners, core to the Christian Democrat coalition, by compensating them for their land. They were allowed to retain up to one-third of their holdings if they used the land in accordance with government stipulations regarding production and labor laws.[53]

The Ministry of Agriculture generously funded the reform. It spent the equivalent of around $10 billion in today's US dollars in a little over a decade, or around $100,000 per family.[54] A government development fund known as the Cassa per il Mezzogiorno (Fund for the South) complemented this effort in order to accelerate economic and rural development in the region. The United States also supported the reform through Marshall Plan funds.[55]

Rural workers lined up to receive land. Over three-quarters of them were landless farmworkers or tenants, mostly from the same local towns where land was targeted for expropriation.[56] Successful applicants to Italy's tiller reform received either a small plot of land, about twelve to fifteen acres in size on average, ostensibly intended to be a self-sufficient farm, or a smaller plot intended to merely supplement income from other sources.[57] The demand for land far outpaced its availability.

Regional reform boards quickly set to work on implementing the laws and reallocated most land within five years.[58] They ultimately reallocated nearly 2 million acres of land to some 115,000 families. Slightly more than half of these families received just a tiny plot of land to supplement their income; less than half received enough land for a full farm.[59]

Given the opportunity to pick and choose among land applicants, the government reform boards became patronage juggernauts that worked to build a loyal political clientele for the Christian Democrats.[60] The government also required beneficiaries to join a cooperative association to assist with tasks such as accessing credit and insurance and selling products. The tight control over the process gave the Christian Democrats the ability to wield powerful threats against crossing them and to use precious resources as rewards for supporters in order to pump their political support. Politics once again prevailed.

In contrast to Mexico's collective reform and Venezuela's blended reform, Italy's land beneficiaries received clearly delineated, individual plots with land titles. But they did face some consequential property rights restrictions. Beneficiaries purchased plots with thirty-year government loans and could not sell them until they had paid off their debts. Nor could they clear the debt in advance. These features of the reform helped to stem a rising and worrisome tide of internal immigration to Italy's northern industrial zones. And they kept land beneficiaries in limbo, tethered to the reform boards and the looming shadow of the Christian Democrats for decades.

The problems were predictable and stacked up over time. In part due to the Christian Democrats' attempts to build ties with as many farmers as possible to increase their support and deflate unrest, land grants turned out to be too small in size to enable a single family to support itself. Spending on infrastructure and subsidized credit was uneven, and many of the poorest farmers received the least support. And the requirement to hold the land for thirty years tied people to the land. Though many viewed land and agriculture as a "safe bet" in an otherwise risky job market, agriculture simply was not very lucrative. The inability to change course made it harder for the land's beneficiaries to participate in more dynamic parts of the economy. This problem continued into the next generation, as beneficiaries typically passed their land on to firstborn sons, while other family members had few other options than to leave.

Italy's tiller reform dragged down local development even as the broader economy rapidly transformed in subsequent decades. The country has industrialized and urbanized in the time since its tiller reform, especially in the north, and it became far more prosperous as it became tethered to the European Union. But prosperity has been uneven. A series of economically stagnant and poorer rural areas have lagged behind the country as a whole. Many of these areas conspicuously map onto the areas associated with Italy's land reshuffle.

The reform in Calabria and the area around Melissa is a microcosm of what went wrong. There the reform ended in economic failure. And it fell short of the expectations held by peasants like the ones who had marched on Melissa in 1949.

The Calabria reform board reallocated about 15 percent of the land in its zone, mostly in interior areas where soils were poor and there was insufficient water for farming. Many influential local landowners evaded reform and helped to craft land policy. The backdrop of social unrest encouraged the board to spread land grants widely to reduce social tension.[61] "Self-sufficient" farm plots averaged just over twelve acres in size, hardly enough to support a family given the poor quality of the land. The board spent considerable sums on housing and roads but far less on irrigation, especially in places that desperately needed it, including Melissa.

The reform board initially doled out generous credits to farmers, but then tightened credit in 1957–1958. By this time, the Christian Democrats had clearly established their ability to keep the Communists at bay. Beneficiaries foundered throughout the region. Even so, 90 percent of them retained their farms as of 1969.[62] Beneficiaries stuck to the land and gained skills in independent farming as the broader Italian economy passed them by. Family members who fared better either emigrated or worked in the local building industry in Cosenza. Melissa was destined to be forgotten in the new Italy.

Calabria's reform took place against its own locally specific backdrop of social conflict, powerful landowners, and a half-hearted reform board. But it is not an isolated case. The reform backfired even in more promising areas. A quintessential example is the Maremma region on Italy's central western coast.[63] Here, a more dedicated and thorough reform board reallocated considerable land without nearly as much social tension as in Calabria. But even in Maremma, areas that saw reallocation experienced less development in subsequent years than neighboring areas that did not, and even today they suffer from higher rates of poverty.[64]

Most of the beneficiaries in the Maremma region could only earn enough to survive rather than to thrive, owing to small farm sizes and the steep learning curve in independent farming.[65] Because initial land beneficiaries had to repay their long-term loans before they would have full land ownership, the overwhelming majority remained where their land was located.[66] Those who remain and work locally face fewer and lower-paying job opportunities than people who have been willing to work elsewhere and can access broader regional job markets with more diverse employment and educational opportunities. And with farms too small to be subdivided, the inability to inherit drains young talent and innovation from these locales, skewing demographics toward a higher ratio of older to younger generations than in areas just outside of the zone.[67] These were among the slow-motion series of economic and demographic wounds inflicted by Italy's reform that dragged down local development for generations. And much of it was due to the narrow political calculations of the reform's architects.

As the Italian economy modernized and grew after World War II, land reallocation modified the local effects of development and the reaction to the major northern economic pull by adding significant drag. The poor economic performance of Maremma, Calabria, and other reform zones in Italy does not mean, however, that Italy as a whole would have been better off without its tiller reform. Many expropriated landowners used their compensation to invest in industrial expansion.[68] And the reform spurred demand for building materials and agricultural machinery.[69] Compared with Mexico or Venezuela, where land reallocation clearly came to undercut the economy as a whole, it is harder to know whether Italy's reform contributed overall to national development. What is more certain is that it left behind precisely the areas it aimed to uplift.

As with Mexico and Venezuela, land power in the hands of politicians was where the Italian experiment went awry. The Christian Democrats constructed and used Italy's tiller reform in considerable part to cement a political monopoly and bolster the existing political system. Indeed, as the party landscape shifted over decades in Italy, the Christian Democrats were able to lean more heavily on their ties in southern land reform zones to remain the country's most powerful party into the 1990s. Land's power to shape national politics and derail growth in this way is precisely why getting land reshuffles right is so important. Otherwise, a society will pay the consequences for decades.

* * *

COUNTRIES THAT WANT to use land for development today, or those trying to redress problems from prior programs, have to thread a difficult needle to master the political imperatives while not sacrificing the economy. The power in land provides an abundance of distracting political temptations during land reallocation. Leaders in Mexico, Venezuela, and Italy all fell prey to these temptations, though Italian leaders were sobered to a degree by rising concerns over communism and restricted by the uncompromising geopolitical environment in Europe in the aftermath of World War II. They managed to generate plenty of wiggle room for politics, but might have gone even further without any guardrails. Mexico and Venezuela paid an especially dear economic price for using land for cynical political gain.

Taming political distractions is not enough in itself to ensure that land reallocation works for development. Beneficiaries must be given enough land and consistent support for at least a decade until they are thriving on their own. In an increasingly populated world with shrinking frontiers and government turnover, that is no small feat. And countries have to work with markets and the current geopolitical environment rather than against it. That means paying attention to property rights and market incentives. Some countries are still learning this very basic lesson.

But there are more lessons to learn.

We've seen how land reallocation can encourage racial hierarchy, patriarchy, environmental degradation, and economic stagnation. These Four Horsemen of modern social maladies are all inextricably tied to land. But once you see, and can follow, the long history of land, power, and the making of society, you also begin to see that land itself can play a role in solutions. Land can be shared with women to improve gender equity. It can be distributed to marginalized communities that lost it or that were never given an opportunity to access it. Land can be registered and regulated by the state in ways that benefit its owners and society to a greater degree. It can be restored and rejuvenated in order to repair damaged ecosystems and capture more carbon. And it can serve as the symbolic referent for reparations where populations have been denied land access and will not reasonably return to owning and managing it at a large scale.

Just as land reshuffles can doom a society, they can also invert the problems inherited from the last reshuffle. In a world where appeals for reparations and revolutionary change are once again beginning to be heard, there are lessons that we can learn about how to respond in order to avoid the worst outcomes of mishandled land reallocation and instead create a more just and sustainable world.

PART III

Land as a Solution

CHAPTER 7

THE ARC OF HISTORY IS LONG, BUT IT BENDS TOWARD DEVELOPMENT

IN THE EASTERN FOLDS OF THE PERUVIAN ANDES WHERE THE warm air and lush vegetation of the Amazon basin lap at the sides of the rugged and windswept mountains, Wilber Vivanco's grandparents spent most of their lifetimes working and living at a sprawling hacienda named Pintobamba. In the early twentieth century, Pintobamba's 42,000 acres were planted with cacao trees and coca, a traditional plant with great significance to the lives and customs of highlands communities.[1] Like other haciendas in Peru's highlands, Pintobamba, located in the Cusco region, relied on peasant labor for its operations. Several hundred families lived on the estate, where they picked coca leaves and harvested and processed the cacao. In exchange for providing fifteen days' worth of labor to the landowner each month, each peasant family received a small plot of land within the hacienda for its own use. If a family could not fulfill its work obligation, it could be removed from the land.

The working conditions were harsh, but some workers at Pintobamba managed to eke out a living and even brought desperately poor landless migrants down from higher in the Andes to help fulfill their work obligations. Still, many fell into debt and struggled with the endless labor. Life on the hacienda, and on those surrounding it, had much in common with life under serfdom in earlier European history. In these suffocating conditions, peasants on the haciendas in the area around Pintobamba eventually revolted. A social movement simmered even as the government sought to repress rebellious elements in the region in the early 1960s.

Pintobamba soon changed forever. A 1968 military coup ushered in a radical new government. Peru's new military leaders decreed a massive land reallocation aimed at shattering the hacienda system and untethering peasant workers from servile labor for large landowners. It expropriated what was by then a smaller but still substantial version of the Pintobamba estate from its landowners in 1971 and turned it over to its workers. Wilber Vivanco's grandparents were freed from the hacienda. They finally had direct access to land and even a government document with their names as land beneficiaries. But there was an important hitch: their access was not spelled out in the form of a clearly delineated plot of land and it was not recorded in public registries.

The government created a new system of cooperatives from most of the properties it seized from landowners. But the system was doomed from the start, because its failure to secure land rights meant that most of the country's peasants were now shackled to the cooperatives, just as they had been to the large landowners that preceded them. Within a decade, peasants were fed up. Agricultural production stagnated and the economy teetered. The military retreated to the barracks, but no one in the Peruvian government that succeeded the military regime dealt seriously with the frustration boiling over in the countryside. Cooperatives collapsed like dominoes, and people divvied up the land informally among themselves. When Wilber's grandparents left the Pintobamba area in the 1980s and his parents bought the land, there was no longer even a link between the government document for their land that they left behind and Wilber's parents as landholders. His parents may have held the land, but they did not own it.

A deep economic crisis and growing guerrilla insurgency finally spurred the country to action. In the 1990s Peru passed legislation to systematically document landholding, provide clear land titles to legitimate landholders, and register those rights in the public land registry. Government bureaucrats fanned out across both rural and urban areas in a massive effort to blanket landholders with property rights. Wilber was still in school, going back and forth on breaks to help his parents farm coffee and coca on their small farm, but found his own calling in the effort to make right the errors of the previous reshuffle. He began training in Peru's prosecutor's office, got a legal degree, and took a job with Peru's new land titling agency in 1998. It was not just a livelihood: for him it was "a social service," he told me. "The state didn't come out into the countryside much to help people in need, and I trained to help these people formalize their legal status on the land."[2]

When the government's land titling initiative came to the Cusco region in the early 2000s, Wilber's parents received a secure and verifiable land title in their own names for the first time. "They became more protected," Wilber said, "because the title was entered into the public registry. And at the same time they got more legal security. They could be sure that the land belonged to them and that no one could challenge that. And now they could access loans, more easily sell the land if they chose to, and leave a will that covered the land."[3]

It was just the beginning of a broad transformation that would soon become visible across the area where Wilber's parents held land. Wilber, who has spent his career working for several Peruvian agencies dedicated to land titling and formalization, recognized that the change was linked to property rights: "Now with their land titles in hand, people learned how to take out loans from small lending agencies like mutual credit associations, cooperatives, and municipal and rural savings and credit associations," he told me. "Public investment in the countryside is now more secure. Now the government invests in improvements in coffee production, corn production, and all that because they know who they are working with. And people feel more empowered, because they have means of producing that resides in their own name and that they can easily leave to their children without fear that someone will take it from them. And that also gives the land value. Because you can sell if you want for a better price, and because of a title, not only is the state more likely to invest in your land but also NGOs [nongovernmental organizations]."

Wilber hopes one day to retire to the land his parents now own. There are thousands of stories like the Vivancos' across Peru, which has become a poster child for property rights. Its economy is booming and investors have flooded it with cash for the past two decades. The country joined the ranks of upper-middle-income countries, and it recently began discussions to join the much-vaunted Organisation for Economic Co-operation and Development (OECD), the exclusive club of the world's most advanced capitalist economies. Despite glaring inequality, Peru's development trajectory is the object of envy among many lower-income countries.

Correcting the mistakes of a self-destructive land reallocation effort was not easy. Peru careened from one crisis to another in the late 1980s and 1990s. The country threw open its doors to international financial and development agencies, becoming a laboratory for the World Bank and International Monetary Fund (IMF). Yet the transformation it needed finally took hold with its efforts to secure property rights over land and liberalize its economy. The road has been rocky and contentious. While property titling has enjoyed broad popular support, it has also fractionalized some indigenous communities and eroded traditional ties to the land, spurring pockets of justifiable resistance. But the project on the whole has set the country on much firmer footing to escape its underdevelopment trap, and it points to land power's ability not just to entrench economic distortions, but to root them out as well.

Time and again, countries have reallocated land and rewired their economies only to see those economies sputter and stagnate. Cooperative and collective reforms in particular have driven hundreds of millions of people into the depths of hunger and poverty and many more into lives of mediocrity and disappointment. The twentieth century has witnessed these reforms poisoning economies again and again, and they have left enduring legacies of stagnation all over the world.

The failure to secure property rights over land is at the heart of the problem. Whether for ideological reasons, to ensure political pliancy, or out of simple incompetence, most governments that have reallocated land on a massive scale have failed to grant secure property rights to the recipients of that land. Holding land without property rights is like having a job without any contract. The landholder is trapped in a state of constant uncertainty and vulnerability. That weighs on every decision about how to use the land and whether to invest in it, deprives the landholder of credit, and renders the landholder helpless in the face of abuse and exploitation, whether from private parties or the state itself. Landholders who lack property rights have few avenues for recourse to protect themselves.

But although it's clear that land reallocation can entrench a bad outcome, it's also clear that doing reform correctly can reverse that outcome. The malign consequences of the Great Reshuffle are not irreversible, and the lessons from the mistakes show us what it takes to repair the structural flaws in how a society deals with land power.

Delivering, tracking, and enforcing property rights can help to counteract the disappointing development outcomes linked to many land reallocation episodes. That entails delineating who owns what land; giving people predictability in what they can do with their land, along with a sense of trust that the law will treat them fairly; and protecting people against land theft. Secure property rights can in turn increase land value, foster markets, and encourage investment in the land and productivity. Over time that changes economies as people invest more in the future. These investments can include things like sending their children to school rather than to the fields—and training them for upwardly mobile jobs in emerging sectors of the economy.

The story of Peru's restoration of property rights in land provides insights into how it can be done.

PERU WAS STILL saddled with the baggage of Spanish colonialism 150 years after it gained independence. As of 1960, land remained at the center of its economy. Half the population worked in agriculture, while the wealthiest 1 percent of large landowners controlled 80 percent of the land.[4] The country's deeply rooted system of hacienda landholding meant that many of these large landowners could trace their family holdings all the way back to the colonial era. But the clock was ticking on this arrangement. Peru was on the cusp of its own Great Reshuffle.

Labor unions and worker protections had started to take root on the coast by the 1960s, driven by worker organizing and the tighter incorporation of coastal enterprises into international markets. But working for a large landowner was fundamentally exploitative in the highlands where most people lived. Many peasants, such as Wilber's grandparents at Pintobamba, had to labor on large estates with little or no pay. Some, especially women, did menial work in the owner's house. Peasants could not easily leave, and many suffered physical and emotional abuse.

One woman I spoke with, Justina López, had been born into a tiny settlement at the upper parts of a large hacienda in the Cusco region's Sacred Valley. She told me that in those days she had walked several miles daily between her home and the hacienda's fields in the valley where she worked all day long, "week after week after week after week."[5] Villagers did not have running water or toilets, and the grassland was so spare that there wasn't enough dirt to make an adobe house. The chilly Andean wind at almost 15,000 feet above sea level slipped right through the walls of the settlement's stacked stone houses. During the corn harvest, the hacienda's workers carried corn out of the fields on their backs "like a donkey." Her parents and grandparents had done the same. "Everything belonged to the landowner," she told me while sitting next to the courtyard of the now abandoned hacienda owner's house, waving her hand up toward the mountain peaks across the valley floor. "There was nowhere for anyone to live freely. . . . The landowners were like kings." There was no school and everyone lived and died illiterate. "The landowner didn't want us to study," she told me. "If we studied, people would have left."

A military coup in 1968 spelled the end of these arrangements. The country's young democratic government was struggling to overcome its own fecklessness in the face of an obstinate conservative opposition, corruption and foreign influence, and outbreaks of unrest. The military thought it could do better and took the reins.

Military rulers embarked on a massive cooperative reform. They seized half of the country's privately owned land between 1968 and 1980, mostly during the rule of General Juan Velasco, converted this land into large cooperatives, and then inscribed peasants in these cooperatives. The state retained formal ownership over the land and had a heavy hand in overseeing cooperatives. Peasants were thrilled to receive more direct land access. When I visited Justina López's community in 2014, it still had General Velasco's portrait hanging at the entrance to the former hacienda that had been turned over to its workers.[6] A small number of peasants got lucky and had land adjudicated to them directly rather than through cooperatives. That is what happened to Wilber's grandparents. But even these peasants lacked secure land titles.

Landowners across the board were shocked by the reform. Some resigned themselves to it while others became recalcitrant and sought compensation. One former senator of Peru whose family had owned enormous swaths of land in the coastal region of Ica, as well as in the highlands that the government seized in the 1970s, railed against the reform to me in a meeting at Lima's exclusive country club in 2018. He told me that he intended to use his office to force the country to make amends. His abortive plan sought to reroute water that naturally flowed east off the Andes into the Amazon instead to the west to irrigate arid coastal lands the family had repurchased, netting them a windfall that he felt they were owed.

People in the cooperatives in turn quickly got fed up with their flaws. They wanted their own land and autonomy and recognized that the government was using the system to play favorites with compliant groups. The link between work and pay was fuzzy, and work quotas were often tied to quantity rather than quality, which generated internal conflicts over profit-sharing and labor and a sense of unfairness. There were also tensions over cooperative leadership and corruption.[7]

Agricultural production stagnated as a result and the country fell into a trap of underdevelopment.

Protests grew in the late 1970s and Peru's economy teetered. The military got skittish. It stage-managed a transition to democracy and retreated from the responsibility of day-to-day rule as the troubles escalated. The country elected the same president whom the military had ousted in its 1968 coup, Fernando Belaúnde.

Once in office, Belaúnde got the message from the countryside that people would no longer tolerate the cooperatives. But he was also distracted by a growing drumbeat of problems exacerbated by Peru's underdevelopment. The country he came to lead a second time was radically different from the one it had been in his first term.

The economy suffered a series of further blows as the Latin American debt crisis blew up in 1982, spreading inflation and divestment across the region. Political parties and politicians were trying to rebuild themselves after a long episode of dictatorship during which parties and elections had been banned. There was also a Maoist-style guerrilla insurgency building in the Andes driven by the rebel group Shining Path (Sendero Luminoso). Shining Path sought to topple Peru's government and construct a form of agrarian communism with roots in indigenous peasant communities. It formed in the neglected and foundering Ayacucho region and subsequently spread to rural areas, particularly those where local authorities were ineffective and the military response was either weak or marked by indiscriminate violence. The insurgency also lodged in places where Peru's land reallocation was more limited and remnants of the hacienda system persisted, fueling support in the countryside for deeper and even more radical reform.[8]

In the face of these headwinds, Belaúnde took a practical step: he tapped the brakes on cooperatives. His government passed several pieces of legislation that enabled cooperatives to begin to disband and break up their lands among their members. But, to the frustration of many people in the countryside, the government stopped there. It did not create an agency to help dissolve cooperatives, parcel land among members, secure newly defined landholdings, or help new small peasant proprietors to get their footing in a refashioned economy.

The result was a free-for-all. Cooperatives themselves decided whether to disband, and if so, how. They grappled with a raft of contentious issues, such as who should get what land, how infrastructure and farm equipment should be managed, how any debts would be settled, and how landless cooperative members who joined as workers should be treated.

Government agents no longer played a role as overseers. Nor did the government track this enormous transformation. A thick fog of murky property rights settled in. Property ownership and property rights in the countryside became essentially undecipherable. The vast majority of landholders did not have documents or records indicating proof of ownership.

The fog only grew thicker throughout the 1980s. A new government in 1985, led by the charismatic new president Alan García, at first equivocated on continuing the breakup of cooperatives and then supported it. But there was little direct government involvement. Meanwhile, economic change and urbanization accelerated. Land transferred hands in the countryside. But no one knew exactly where or to what effect.

On January 2, 1989, Peru's National Statistics Agency released a dire figure in the midst of a snowballing economic crisis: inflation in the country during the prior year had reached 1,722 percent. Everyone expected it to climb still higher. Peru's mountain of foreign debt was piling up, and investors clamored for the government to liberalize the country's economy and take a plain vanilla approach to capitalism. That included clarifying and strengthening property rights. The IMF stood at the ready to shovel cash into Peru's economy in exchange for structural economic adjustment and secure property rights.

President García had other plans. He had already thumbed his nose at the IMF and nationalized private banks in order to "democratize credit" and foster state-led economic development. Peru's most famous novelist, the eventual Nobel laureate Mario Vargas Llosa, led a popular movement to oppose the "totalitarian" controls linked to nationalization.[9] But García carried the day. And in doing so, he drove Peru's economy into the ground. Inflation ballooned to 3,000 percent and the economy shriveled. García's popularity took a nosedive.

Sadly, this wasn't even Peru's worst problem. The guerrilla insurgency that had simmered in the early 1980s had now boiled over. Murders, kidnappings, and extortion spread across the central Andes. The violence started to spill into Peru's coastal cities. Bombings intruded on even the chic neighborhoods of the capital, Lima.

Like so many other countries that reshuffled land by adopting collective or cooperative land reforms, Peru had gotten stuck in an underdevelopment trap. Poverty, weak property rights, and a lack of investment reinforced the country's economic stagnation and political instability. But the crisis that rocked Peru in the late 1980s set the stage for an inflection point that finally set it on a path to securing property rights in land.

PERU'S PRESIDENTIAL ELECTION in 1990 pitted its national author, Mario Vargas Llosa, against a political novice and agricultural engineer, Alberto Fujimori. Fujimori ran on the vague platform of "Change," in an effort to capitalize on García's unpopularity during his waning days in office. Although Fujimori was a virtual unknown until shortly before the first round of the presidential election, he eked out second place in a fractionalized field and advanced to a runoff against Vargas Llosa.

In light of Peru's runaway inflation and deep recession, the race between Vargas Llosa and Fujimori boiled down to two possible approaches to economic management: "shock" or "no shock." Vargas Llosa advocated an immediate and painful "shock" to the economy through price increases, the removal of subsidies, and currency devaluation followed by a program of shrinking the size of government and its role in the economy. One of his controversial campaign television ads presented a monkey behind a desk, symbolizing a government bureaucrat, gobbling fruit, accepting a bribe, and then defecating on the desk. Vargas Llosa's own campaign slogan is a cautionary tale in political messaging: "It will cost us . . . but together we will make Big Change."

Fujimori staked out a more centrist position as the "no shock" candidate. Instead, he advocated a more sequential approach to stabilization that would minimize job losses and avert a steeper economic recession. He promised to trim government fat rather than privatize it across the board. And he targeted the messages and language of his campaign at the middle and lower classes.

The result was a stunning rebuke. Fueled by popular queasiness with Vargas Llosa's proposals for economic reform, disdain with his links to the political establishment, and mistrust of his upper-class origins, Fujimori trounced Vargas Llosa by over twenty percentage points.

Despite his resounding win, Fujimori was in an unenviable position. He inherited an economy in free-fall. Time was not on the side of a cautious, sequential economic fix.

Fujimori made a bold gambit: he simply adopted the "shock" approach. It would become a recurring pattern reflecting Fujimori's cunning and ruthless political instincts. Less than two weeks after his inauguration, he rolled out the tanks in Lima and announced radical price increases in fuel, medicine, food, and other goods and services across the economy. "Fujishock" had arrived.

The next step was structural economic adjustment. Fujimori's reforms cynically followed the outline of Vargas Llosa's proposals.[10] This was no mere coincidence: Fujimori turned to part of Vargas Llosa's economic advisory team to resolve the economic crisis.

The most prominent figure was the renowned economist Hernando de Soto. De Soto's influential book *The Other Path* argued that the government's poor property rights provision and enforcement had given rise to its enormous informal sector and deprived citizens of the support they needed in order to thrive economically. The implication was that Peru's endemic social and political instability could not be overcome absent major property rights reforms. The fog of murky property rights was choking the country.

De Soto's ideas were in keeping with a new strain of "neoliberal" economic thinking. Adherents to this school of thought believe that property rights are important for development because they encourage accumulation and production. People can confidently make productive investments when property rights are secure because they do not have to worry that their property or investments might be arbitrarily seized. The transparent and enforceable nature of ownership and interests also enables people to use their property as collateral to obtain loans in order to improve their assets or invest in productive activities such as sending their children to school. And secure property rights support the functioning of property markets by making it easier to value, sell, purchase, lease, and mortgage property.

Incomplete and insecure property rights do just the opposite. They depress the value of land and make it difficult to sell, lease, or use as collateral. They encourage short-term thinking and short-term investments, because owners are worried about counterclaims or appropriation. Those threats encourage people to remain on their property more than they otherwise would in order to protect it, suppressing seasonal migration and working outside the home for long periods. Unless communities are tight-knit and customary law is strong, a widespread lack of property rights can scare off investors and capital.

Property rights have to include a degree of tradability to have any real meaning. You can have a property title, but if the government prohibits you from selling, leasing, or using your property as collateral under any circumstances then it is not much of a "right" at all so much as an obligation. Property rights allow holders to transform their property or use it to get other things they want. If you can't do that, you are stuck, and so are the markets.

Excludability is another inherent aspect of property rights. You have to be able to prevent other people from using your property or infringing on your property rights. If everyone can use a resource and no one can exclude others from it, then everyone has an incentive to use as much as they can. But that depletes the resource and makes everyone worse off.

De Soto's ideas were powerful. Many of them had not been rigorously tested. But that didn't matter much in the environment at the time, especially because de Soto had deep international connections. This was crucial for setting the course of Fujimori's economic policies.

De Soto had encouraged Fujimori to take a trip to the United States and Japan before he assumed the presidency. Through his brother, who was an assistant to the United Nations secretary general, Javier Pérez de Cuellar, a Peruvian, de Soto arranged a meeting for Fujimori in New York with the president of the World Bank, the managing director of the IMF, and the president of the Inter-American Development Bank. These kingmakers of the international financial world presented Fujimori with a stark choice: take the "no shock" path and end up isolated and unpopular like outgoing president García, or take the "shock" path and receive a windfall of international financial support and assistance.[11]

The prime minister and emperor of Japan reinforced the same message. His input had a personally outsized impact on Fujimori, given his Japanese ancestry. Noting Fujimori's receptivity to the "shock" approach, the leaders of his transition team quit shortly thereafter and before Fujimori took office.

Fujimori's initial shock therapy delivered the anticipated pain to the population. Worker salaries plummeted in real terms. Official estimates indicate that the move plunged one-quarter of the population into extreme poverty. They joined another one-third of Peruvians who already suffered extreme poverty.

The economy as a whole then staged a remarkable turnaround, notwithstanding stubbornly high poverty and inequality. Within a year, the government checked hyperinflation, returned the economy to growth, and reduced unemployment.[12]

The government then set to work on structural economic reform under the guidance of international financial institutions. Fujimori appointed de Soto as a personal representative to liaise with these institutions and guide reforms. The reform package included ambitious efforts to liberalize the economy to trade, privatize state industries, and strengthen property rights.

One of the projects that de Soto spearheaded was a massive urban land titling program. With support from the World Bank, the government registered and gave property titles to hundreds of thousands of people living in informal housing in Peru's urban peripheries.[13]

At the same time, the government started to deal more systematically with the fog of murky property rights in the countryside, which had notably thickened in the wake of the country's land reallocation program and the subsequent breakup of cooperatives. The opening salvo came in 1992 with a large-scale land titling program known as the Special Land Titling and Cadaster Project (known as PETT).[14] Its goal was to formalize rural land rights across the country. That included mapping property boundaries, creating a land cadaster (a comprehensive, official register of property ownership and boundaries), and distributing and registering land titles centrally. The Inter-American Development Bank stepped in with financial assistance to help as the program tested pilot projects and got up and running in its first few years. The government then passed legislation that promised to distribute land titles to beneficiaries of Peru's land reform in particular. And it took steps to meet the demands of indigenous communities that had become increasingly organized and vocal and wanted state recognition of their status and land rights.

PERU'S COOPERATIVE REFORM had been a nightmare from the perspective of neoliberal thinkers. It suffocated land markets and private investment and it failed to channel worker initiative and work incentives. The government leaned on state agencies to stoke productivity by picking winners and losers, which became infused with political calculations and meddling. When the lackluster results became apparent, the government made it worse by putting cooperative management more directly under its own bureaucratic control. The free-for-all that followed the cooperative era was not much better.

International financial institutions were so keen on economic reform in Peru that they largely turned a blind eye toward Fujimori's authoritarian tendencies, including when he shut down the opposition-led Congress in 1992 and centralized power. And they ignored rampant human rights abuses as Fujimori unleashed a brutal counterinsurgency campaign that crushed the metastasizing violence from Shining Path and returned security to the country. Fujimori's luck eventually ran out in 2000 as evidence of abuse of power and corruption mounted. He fled to Japan and resigned.

But by then the tide was beginning to turn. Rural land titling accelerated in the 2000s with Peru's return to democracy. The government began blanketing areas with massive land titling efforts. People marched for land titles. Politicians campaigned on doling them out. The government put up enormous billboards in the countryside advertising the country's land titling agency and the progress it had been making.

Property rights in Peru became something much greater than a neoliberal recipe for marketization. They became a political goal for peasants across the country. One former official I spoke with, who worked on land titling first in the Cusco region and then at the national level in the 2000s, recounted that "people organized and went to the land titling offices in the rural areas and in regional capitals." He underscored, "Both people from indigenous communities and people from the towns, they came intensely, clamoring, 'We want land titling from the state.'"[15] Rapid economic growth and development during this period further spurred those demands as it came to impact and encroach on undocumented traditional landholders. Those landholders, the official told me, "wanted a way to regularize all of this." To document and register landholdings, "people mobilized and organized and set up meetings with municipalities supported by COFOPRI and PETT." The Commission for the Formalization of Informal Property (known as COFOPRI), like PETT, was a land titling agency.[16]

By the end of the decade the government had issued over 2 million titles to rural plots of land, covering former land reform beneficiaries and other rural inhabitants alike.[17] This constituted half of all rural plots. Property titling extended still further in the 2010s.

Like Wilber Vivanco's family, many people who received property titles benefited in ways large and small. Juan de Dios Condori, who works for an NGO in Cusco on land issues in indigenous communities, told me how his parents were impacted by receiving a secure land title from the government in 2002 for over 1,200 acres of pastureland. His parents were living in an indigenous community named Sallani in the Canchis province of Cusco, and most people within part of the community informally held land that had been passed down through private transactions. With community backing, they wanted to separate those lands from communal lands, and Peru's land titling agency assisted in the process. For Juan de Dios's parents, it helped resolve a complicated family issue. His parents managed a herd of llamas and alpacas and had land as one of three lines of kinship from the prior generation. But without clear property delineations and titles among those lines, they could not be certain where they could pasture their animals permanently, and they didn't want to invest in their house and in infrastructure without more clarity.

Having their land titled gave them relief and the clarity they needed. "It gave them legal security," Juan told me, "and gave them the security to know that they could stay in one place. They improved their house. And they started to invest in infrastructure that would help with productivity, like ranching and production systems, irrigation, and other things."[18]

The property titling programs did not just stick to the one-size-fits-all neoliberal playbook of granting complete property rights to individuals. While some indigenous communities, including Sallani, wanted to split up their land among families, others wanted property rights of a different stripe. Indigenous communities had received about one-third of the land distributed through Peru's land reallocation program.[19] Bits and pieces of these communities, and sometimes more than one at a time, had been pulled into the cooperatives that the government had formed.

Indigenous communities wanted legal recognition of their communities as well as rights over both communal lands and the lands that community members worked as households. They made the case that property rights do not have to be go-it-alone individual rights in order to be complete, and that collective groups could hold property rights just as private individuals do. That called for a different organization of rights, including inalienable rights to traditional indigenous community land and the recognition of communally held lands within communities that chose to organize themselves in part with communal resources.

The government responded by formally recognizing and titling thousands of indigenous communities, returning to and refining a policy it had started in the 1920s. One of the foremost observers of this process called it a "renaissance of Andean social groupings."[20] By 1998, the government had recognized 5,700 separate communities, and 4,000 of these had received land titles. Community land titling and more sophisticated and precise mapping proceeded in the 2000s. Over 5,100 communities had received titles by 2016, and the government now recognizes nearly 6,200 communities.[21]

This process has been rocky at times. Given the high stakes of land titling, many communities have engaged in boundary disputes with their neighbors. Others have been embroiled in contentious internal debates about how to manage land ownership. Still others have resisted property rights reforms, whether because they at times encroach on community lands or because some perceive them as a threat to traditional ways or as a hook that draws them into deeper obligations to the state. In part in response to discontents like these, indigenous communities in recent years have won other protections to their lands and a greater political voice, such as the legal requirement that the government engage in dialogue with them and take their viewpoints and interests into account in advance of development initiatives or administrative processes that may affect them.

Favorable external conditions in the 2000s, combined with Peru's internal economic reforms beginning in the 1990s, put the country on a path to robust economic growth. The country's gross domestic product grew at an average rate of 5 percent annually in the first two decades of the new millennium.[22] This is considerably above the growth rate of many of its Latin American peers. Peru entered into the group of upper-middle-income countries by 2010.

Peru got slammed harder than most by the COVID-19 pandemic, however, suffering a steep economic contraction and the highest recorded death toll per capita in the world eighteen months into the pandemic.[23] But its economy quickly regained its footing, and the OECD entered discussions with Peru in January 2022 regarding its accession to the club of advanced economies. The only other Latin American countries in the club are Chile, Costa Rica, Colombia, and Mexico.

This success story is a multifaceted one. Peru's mining-oriented economy benefited from the enormous commodities boom in the 2000s. Its favorable trade policies, light regulatory environment for foreign capital, and stable economy have made it attractive for investment.

Greater property rights protection is also an important part of the equation. Peru rectified one of the most glaring problems of its land reallocation program by securing property rights in land to a greater degree. It simultaneously shored up property rights over urban land and in the business sector.

Extending property rights delivered a boost to land reform beneficiaries that long lacked them. By the early 2010s, poverty, illiteracy, and inequality dropped in these populations while agricultural productivity went up.[24]

"The impact that the process of land titling and plot regularizing has had in both urban areas and rural areas is enormous," the former official who worked on land titling for most of the 2000s told me emphatically. "Formalizing property helps to incorporate people into economic activity. With a property title, a person can access credit. . . . And once someone has their land in the public registry, they can mortgage their property and they can make legal transfers." He pointed to credit as especially important in sparking economic dynamism. "The banks have been creating facilities for giving credits and loans. That has sparked entrepreneurship among people [who received a property title]. Accessing credits and loans has helped a lot in starting small businesses and initiatives."

PERU'S REFORMS BEGINNING in the 1990s transformed the country into a model for property rights in the developing world. And as a real-world laboratory, the country began influencing international development trends.[25] But property rights reforms are complicated. They take time, money, and dedication to show results. Governments have to invest in registering and tracking property as it changes hands and transforms. People have to see value in property rights or they will not go through all the legal steps to transfer and register their property. And where governments are weak, corrupt, or unresponsive, a property title is not enough. Property rights have to be defensible and well-enforced. If someone tries to take your property, but law enforcement or the courts do not do anything about it, the title is not worth the paper it's printed on.

Capturing the benefits of land reallocation becomes ever more difficult as time passes. The cracks in an existing property rights system grow wider if people sell their land informally and there is no paper trail. That makes it more difficult to reap economic returns from prior episodes of land reallocation through property rights reforms alone.

A dense fog of property rights in Peru had blanketed the countryside for decades. By the time property rights reforms began to lift the fog, informal land sales and transfers had transformed some areas. Mining companies had elbowed their way into some communities. A brutal El Niño year in 1998 ruined a swath of farmers. And Peru's guerrilla insurgency had displaced people in many rural communities and put their property up for grabs. All of this reshuffled Peru's rural population. A considerable number of people who had finally received their own land as cooperatives disbanded had lost it.

The Peruvian government also failed to provide the comprehensive support necessary for small farmers to thrive and to compete against larger competitors. While the government was shoring up property rights, its economic reforms simultaneously made other aspects of farming more difficult. Currency and trade reforms raised competition from agricultural imports. Fujimori shuttered the Agrarian Bank, which had been a source of cheap agricultural credit. Private lenders were hesitant to fill the gap. And he gutted the Ministry of Agriculture by firing more than three-quarters of its employees.[26] Many of its programs came to a screeching halt. These shortcomings help to explain why Peru's work to secure property rights over land and put them in the service of development paid off, but not as spectacularly as might have been possible.

Japan, South Korea, and Taiwan offer a benchmark for a best-case scenario. All three countries created a thriving small farming sector by reallocating high-quality land from large landowners to tillers; they then showered the new beneficiaries with generous agricultural inputs and credits while limiting property rights restrictions. Within a generation, land beneficiaries were sending their children to school rather than having them work on the farm. Governments used this early growth to transform their economies toward export-oriented manufacturing, further advancing development. The circumstances of reform in these three countries were unique. Nonetheless, if Peru had reshuffled differently, in a manner more akin to that of Japan, South Korea, and Taiwan, its path might have been different.

Peru continues to suffer from government weakness and turnover, bureaucratic red tape, and corruption. Outright discrimination against its indigenous population also continues. These problems make it hard for property rights reforms and broader development initiatives to fully blossom. For instance, there remain too many hoops and costs to registering land and clearing property titles. Government milestones and agencies shift frequently with political instability, offices are difficult to access for many people in the countryside, and bureaucratic training is uneven.[27] Land in parts of the countryside is falling back into informality as it changes hands outside of public registries. And some people prefer to hold land informally to avoid assuming obligations toward the state, such as paying property taxes. Taken together, these problems risk unwinding some of Peru's progress.

In part because of government weakness and neglect, rural areas turned out heavily to elect the populist president Pedro Castillo in a stunning 2021 election. Castillo promised to return the favor through a "second agrarian reform" that would provide farmers with loans, tax breaks, and technical support.

But just over a year later, Castillo landed in jail after he tried to dissolve Congress in a bungled attempt to grab more power. This is nothing new in Peru. All but one of its former elected presidents since the mid-1980s have been charged with or jailed for corruption or abuse of power. Members of Congress often come under investigation for corruption as well.[28] It is a stifling backdrop for carrying out complex and long-term reforms.

Nevertheless, Peru's example is instructive: it teaches us that although the underdevelopment trap is difficult, it is not terminal.

* * *

FOR COUNTRIES STRUGGLING with underdevelopment as a consequence of their land reallocation policies of the past, discerning a path to prosperity entails paying attention to property rights in land rather than ignoring them. Property rights alone are not a silver bullet for development. They require other complementary reforms, such as making investments in administration and recordkeeping, and strengthening the rule of law. And there is no one-size-fits-all type of property rights. They are most effective and garner greatest support when they are adapted to on-the-ground cultural and social practices.

For Peru, the first step was to recognize and codify the remaining on-the-ground practices of informal land tenure and rights locally before more was lost to the remaining pockets of murky property rights. Documenting current land tenure and land occupancy is a critical step toward eventually securing property rights and has to be followed by systematic tracking of land rights and transfers. Next comes the hard work of government reform. That includes strengthening the government, putting property registries in order, reducing corruption, and working to incorporate and respect the rights of both individuals and indigenous communities.

The treatment of indigenous communities and lands is particularly important in Peru. In many ways, the long-term development problems of the country are linked to the dispossession and exploitation of these groups both during the time of Spanish colonization and since independence. They have been forced into labor for others and stolen from. And their second-class status and unprotected land claims have made them vulnerable to exploitation.

This situation has only recently started to change with the legal recognition of indigenous communities, new laws strengthening their property rights, and policies giving them a right to prior consultation before their land is impacted by outsiders such as multinational mining companies. Outsiders can no longer count on easily pushing these communities around. The pendulum has started to swing in the other direction: outsiders are beginning to recognize that it is better to have clearly delineated communities and rights, so that they can predict what will happen if they want to extract resources from an area, than to risk sparking social resistance and protest. This change in attitude is part and parcel of how property rights can facilitate development.

Creating and maintaining property rights in land is far easier said than done. Governments that reallocate land at a massive scale often also seek to influence and control beneficiaries for political and social reasons, and are therefore hostile to the notion of secure property rights.

As a result, episodes of land reallocation that derail development rarely right themselves. They require one of two types of major bumps to set them on a different path. The first is a turn to democracy. Authoritarian governments have been the chief advocates of the most economically disastrous collective and cooperative reforms. A turn to democracy often spells a new dawn. Policy tends to get better when people have a say—and when politicians have more incentives to listen to them. When democracies replace authoritarian regimes that have put such reforms in place, few people want to continue life in the government-imposed collectives and cooperatives. So democracies born with them have typically folded them and broken up the land for private forms of ownership. They have granted land to families or communities, depending on people's demands, and secured the new owners' property rights over the land. Much of Eastern Europe after the fall of the Berlin Wall pursued this route.

Peru started along this path but fizzled out. Its democratic leaders in the 1980s facilitated the breakup of cooperatives, but they did not provide a real solution to the people who had been part of the cooperatives. Rather than setting them up on a path to success, the government simply stepped aside. That approach failed.

The second bump to breaking free of the underdevelopment trap involves economic crisis. Some governments face crises so severe that they are forced to call in a lifeline from international financial agencies. Since the 1980s, these agencies have made their aid conditional on economic reform. One common condition is to strengthen the weak or absent property rights that land reallocation programs have left in their wake. International donor agencies and financial institutions, such as the World Bank and the IMF, sweep in when countries are in the throes of crises and compel them to reform how they manage the countryside.

International financial agencies have placed pride of place on property rights reforms. They have helped to design and implement large-scale land titling and land formalization programs to people lacking formal rights. The argument is simple: as property rights advance, so does development.

This second bump was the one that jolted Peru. It has also shaken other countries, including Mexico and Vietnam. Both Mexico and Vietnam adopted radical collective reforms in the twentieth century that endured for decades and that came to stifle their economies. In Mexico, a collective reform in the wake of the Mexican Revolution broke up a hacienda system and delivered land to communities as a whole. In Vietnam, a new Communist government in the North cut down landlords and imposed collectives a few years after the end of World War II. Following the Vietnam War and unification, it sought to collectivize agriculture in the South as well, but it had far less success there than in the North, in light of the tiller reform that the US government had implemented there in the early 1970s. A debt crisis followed by a financial crisis in Mexico in the 1980s and 1990s forced the country to turn to the World Bank and the IMF for help. An economic crisis in the mid- to late 1980s did the same for Vietnam. Within several years of engagement, both countries were on a path to providing property rights in land to the beneficiaries of land reallocation that had lived without them for decades.

As in Peru, the property rights reforms in Mexico and Vietnam were controversial, costly, and even paternalistic in many ways. But they mostly paid off in the long term. All of these countries have attracted investment and seen domestic shifts in behavior that have supported economic development and transformation.

Land reallocation can be a disease afflicting the body politic with social maladies such as underdevelopment. But under the right conditions it can also become a cure. Land reshuffling and land power can be harnessed to advance development as much as they can to disrupt it. They can also be trained on fixing even more insidious social problems.

CHAPTER 8

ONE SMALL STEP FOR WOMEN

ELENA ANTONIA PARODIS MEDINA WAS BORN AND RAISED IN THE countryside of northern Colombia. Her story is a typically complex one in a society that has been rent by land strife and conflict for the better part of a century, but it also has a simple through line: for generations, men in her family worked the land, mostly as hired help or as renters, while women raised the children and hustled to help make ends meet.

Elena came of age working on nearby farms to help her parents put bread on the table for her and her nine younger siblings. She met her husband on one of these farms and together they moved to work at a large ranch nearby named Tranquilandia. The ranch owners let them live on a small plot, where they raised six children together and grew food for their own consumption. But they longed to have land of their own.

They were not alone. When the ranch owners sought to sell the property, the farmworkers at Tranquilandia formed an association and petitioned the Colombian government to buy the estate and turn it over to them. They succeeded. In 1996, Colombia's national land agency purchased the property and handed it over to its workers to divide among themselves.

This reshuffle represented a pivotal moment in Colombia's history of land reallocation. After decades of doling out land to men and privileging men in land ownership, women began organizing and advocating for their fair share. International and domestic women's rights movements worked together, and in the 1980s they convinced the Colombian government to shift to jointly granting land to both partners of couples.

Elena and her husband provisionally received a plot of eighty acres where they grew corn, cassava, plantains, and bananas, raised pigs, and had three cows for milking. It was a modest life. But Elena's land was not quite hers; she and her husband had to make monthly payments to the government in order to eventually be granted full ownership with a clear title. Just a few years later, war would shatter the dream of land ownership.

Leftist guerrilla groups had formed in Colombia's countryside in the mid-1960s to contest large landholding and the elite-dominated political system. One of their central demands was land reallocation in favor of landless peasants. By the 1990s, the country's civil war was metastasizing and had drawn in drug cartels and paramilitary groups.

In 2001, paramilitaries entered the farms at Tranquilandia and targeted the farming association. They brutally killed many of its leaders and several members, burnt their homes, and committed a host of unspeakable human rights abuses. The danger escalated so quickly that Elena's family had no time to even gather their belongings before they were forced to flee. She and her husband lost everything, including one of their sons, to the violence and chaos. Their family was now homeless, living and begging in the streets of the nearby town of Fundación. Her children slept on park benches. "That was really hard," she recalls. "We suffered a lot."[1]

Meanwhile, along with a number of their neighbors who also fled from their homes, they began the process of registering their property for restitution. The group, driven mainly by women who had survived the forced displacement, eventually got in touch with a legal nonprofit called the Yira Castro Legal Corporation (Corporación Jurídica Yira Castro). Named after the prominent activist and leader for women's rights and student demands Yira Castro, the nonprofit helped families displaced by Colombia's conflict in their effort to recover their land and livelihoods. It worked with the land agency to find the legal documents on the prior land transfer and verify that Elena and her husband and the other families had faithfully made their monthly land payments to the agency prior to their displacement.

In 2019, after the land agency and the courts had sifted through a heap of subsequent land transactions at Tranquilandia and associated land claims in the aftermath of the paramilitary incursion, the land agency called a meeting in a local school to deliver land back to the remaining members of the original community.[2] Elena went there on a typically hot and humid day on November 14 along with other beneficiaries, officials from the land agency, and the members of the legal team that had provided aid for the petition. Recalling the feeling she'd had when the agency handed over the title for the land, she told me, "I was so happy after so many years to know that we got the land we had so wished for."[3] It was an appropriate ending for someone who lived near the childhood home of Gabriel García Márquez, Colombia's most famed author, known for his fantastical novels full of twists and turns.

Elena is one of the first women in her extended family to own land. It has changed her life. "When you know how to work, it makes you feel proud. And when you have your own land to work, well, it feels really good," she said.[4] She now works the farm with her husband and two of her children. Together with her daughter, who serves as secretary of the association of restituted families at Tranquilandia, she is active in pushing for development and better infrastructure in the area.

Elena is one of many thousands of Colombian women who have come to own land for the first time since the government pivoted to be more inclusive of them at the behest of women's organizations. This historic shift, which started in the 1980s, has advanced the position of women in society and is part of a broader shift away from male dominance over both public and private affairs in the country. It reveals land power's capacity to give women opportunities that their mothers and grandmothers could not have conceived.

As we have seen, land plays a foundational role in the creation of wealth and power, so when it changes hands, the beneficiaries make gains in both respects. The transformations of the past two centuries across the globe have largely left women out, deepening gender inequities, sometimes through inattention, and sometimes by design. But these dynamics, much like the underdevelopment trap, are not intractable. Prodded by increasingly organized women's movements and changing sensibilities about traditional gender roles and norms, some societies have embraced a different approach to land and gender.

Land ownership is an object of change as well as an accelerator of it. When men dominate landholding, it can tighten the grip of patriarchy by giving them greater control over household decisions and inheritance. But land also has the power to loosen men's hold. Putting land into the hands of women can empower them to own their own destiny, gain wealth and influence, and improve the welfare of their families. The effects trickle into every gendered aspect of society.

Reversing patriarchy is never a fast and uncontroversial process. In most places, there is a long-standing edifice of male-owned property that cannot be easily dismantled, especially if property rights are strong. Progress toward gender equity in land ownership struggles with this potent legacy. Gender-based reforms to property ownership can also unsettle relationships between husbands and wives, parents and children, and citizens and rulers. It is sensitive terrain. But it can be done.

Changing gender relations through land is easiest to do in places where there is land readily available to reallocate or in places where property rights are poorly defined and can be rewritten. Two particularly notable paths toward advancing gender equity with land run through Colombia and Bolivia.

Colombia revised its male-biased land reallocation laws in the late 1980s to be more inclusive of women. As more women began to directly gain land, the gender gap in the ownership of land began to close, and bit by bit Colombian society started becoming fairer for women.

In Bolivia, an enormous program of land reallocation in the second half of the twentieth century largely overlooked women and entrenched gender disparities. But property rights were weak across the board. As economic crisis and foreign intervention pushed property rights to the fore, women had a chance for a redo. Fueled by powerful women's movements and a reformist government, Bolivia has put women on the map over the past twenty years by granting them ownership of land along with men. Although rural women continue to struggle, many of them now have opportunities and a voice that their mothers and grandmothers could not have dreamed of.

COLOMBIA CHANGES COURSE

Colombia has struggled with land strife, political instability, and gender inequality for most of its history. It has a long, unhappy tradition of private land grabs from the public domain and from those too weak to resist. Spanish colonial settlement stripped indigenous communities of their land and created a system of large landholdings—haciendas—dominated by local patriarchs. The haciendas, the Catholic Church, and municipal governments accelerated indigenous dispossession in the first century of the country's independence on the back of indigenous population decline. Ideological goals and conflict between Colombia's two main political parties, the Liberals and Conservatives, drove the Liberals to turn on the church and seize its extensive landholdings in the 1860s and 1870s. Some of these lands were auctioned off to wealthy landowners, and others entered the public domain. The only real way for women to hold land during this time was to be widowed and take control of the property of their deceased husbands.

As the twentieth century began, commercial agriculture underwent dramatic expansion in Colombia, with growing international trade and demand for coffee, sugar, bananas, cacao, and tobacco. Large landowners snatched up land from the public domain and peasants alike. Disputes between rural workers on one side, and landowners or the government on the other, boiled over repeatedly, generating land invasions, repression, and at times regionalized efforts at land reallocation.

These problems became particularly acute in the mid-twentieth century as they were grafted onto growing partisan conflict between Liberals and Conservatives. Partisan attacks, mixed with land conflict and a state too weak to contain it, resulted in a brutal civil war from 1946 to 1960 that killed over 200,000 people.[5] More than half of the population worked in agriculture at the time, and inequality was severe. In 1960, the largest 2 percent of landowners collectively held over 55 percent of the country's land, whereas the smallest 63 percent of landowners held less than 5 percent of land.[6]

Women were sidelined from accessing even the meager resources held by the majority of the population. Married women did not gain legal capacity and the ability to manage their own property until 1932. And it would not be until 1974 that they gained legal footing to share in representing and managing the household and its assets.[7] Widowed and single women stood apart in managing their property. Patriarchal gender norms further smothered women's limited rights under the law, particularly in rural areas.

Following the country's transition to democracy, a new round of civil war began in the mid-1960s that cast a pall over the decades that followed. On the back of the 1959 Cuban Revolution, which resulted in a Communist government and massive land reallocation, new Communist guerrilla groups, such as the Revolutionary Armed Forces of Colombia (known as the FARC), began forming.[8] As in Cuba, they rooted themselves in rural areas, promising to take land from large landowners and give it to landless peasants. Landowners fought back, hiring paramilitaries to protect their properties as insurgents took control of whole areas and began declaring peasant "independent republics." Politicians tried to get ahead of the problem in 1961 by adopting a serious and sustained effort at land reallocation.

Colombia embarked mainly on a settler reform, and to a far lesser extent a tiller reform, in order to relieve land pressure from the landless. Large landowners seeking to keep their property levied immense pressure on the government to forestall any considerable reallocation of privately owned land. The government made nearly 350,000 land settlement grants covering nearly 32 million acres of land between 1961 and the early 1990s.[9]

The result was an enormous giveaway of public lands to men. The land settlement process only designated one beneficiary per household. This approach overwhelmingly advantaged men in accordance with the prevailing family civil code, which charged husbands with representing households. A point system that favored education and farming experience further advantaged men. Women made up only 11 percent of the beneficiaries of these grants.[10] This stands in contrast to the 17 percent of rural households headed by women during this period.[11] The reforms managed to further entrench the already deep gender divide in the countryside.

GROWING INTERNATIONAL AND Colombian women's rights movements, however, would eventually help to reverse what the reforms had aggravated. Countries across Latin America ratified the landmark 1979 UN Convention on the Elimination of All Forms of Discrimination Against Women during the 1980s, with Colombia signing on in 1982. The convention's section on property emphasized the need to recognize the right of women to own, inherit, and administer property in their own name. It also specified equal treatment for women during land reallocation programs in particular.

Colombia's homegrown women's associations and organizations had started to form around professions in the late 1960s and 1970s and looked something like a blend between unions and advocacy organizations. The country's first national association of rural women formed in 1984. It had local branches across the nation that merged local considerations with national-level goals. That association played a critical role in a watershed moment for gender equality: the explicit recognition of women's land rights through Law 30 in 1988.

The backdrop of the new law was a spiraling insurgency. Illegal armed groups proliferated as the drug trade boomed. Guerrilla groups increasingly grabbed land both for drug production and to expand their territorial control. Large landowners pushed back, funding paramilitary groups that attacked guerrillas and civilians alike.

The government viewed land allocation as a way to deflate rural support for guerrillas and stabilize the countryside. Giving land to peasants could ensure their loyalty to political parties rather than to rebels and give them a stake in the status quo rather than casting their lot with insurgent movements that threatened property rights.

One of the law's most important legacies, however, is how it reshaped the playing field for rural women. Reflecting the pressure that women's associations and organizations had put on lawmakers, it stipulated that subsequent land grants and land titles to partnered households had to be issued to couples jointly, regardless of their marital status.[12] The law also created special provisions to grant priority access to settlement land for women heads of household.

Joint titling benefited partnered women in several ways. They gained a say in making critical household decisions regarding whether to sell, lease, or mortgage their property, and more broadly in administering their property. It gave them greater protection against losing their greatest asset in the case that they separated from their partner. And women could no longer be entirely cut out of a will if their partner died.[13]

Things did not change overnight for women. It took several years and a few more nudges. In a country where many bureaucrats, themselves men, favored giving land to men, the land reallocation agency still had to overcome gender bias within its own ranks before it could use land power to target bias in the country at large. The executive committee of the land agency issued a directive in 1989 that its staff had to comply with requests from couples to add women on land titles.[14] And in 1991 it began giving the increasing number of women who were widowed or abandoned as a result of the rising violence in the country preferential treatment in land applications.

By the mid-1990s, women were finally getting more direct access to land distributed through the settlement reform. Close to half of all settlement grants in the late 1990s directly benefited women.[15] For the first time in many decades, women started to close the gender gap in land.

Meanwhile, Colombia partnered with the World Bank to launch a separate experimental program of land reallocation in 1994. With civil war raging and drawing fuel from rural discontent, the idea was to acquire and dole out privately owned land through a market-based tiller reform. The government would purchase land offered voluntarily by private landowners at market rates and then turn around and sell it in a subsidized fashion to small and landless farmers. This was the program that transformed the Tranquilandia estate and provisionally gave land to Elena and her husband.

The new program mandated joint titling to couples and prioritized women at risk owing to the conflict regardless of their marital status. It only lasted a few years and benefited roughly 20,000 families.[16] But it reflected the newfound gender progressivity of the tiller reform. Nearly 70 percent of land grants went jointly to couples. Another 12 percent went to individual women, and the remainder went to men.[17]

The new policies were crucial to promoting greater gender equality in the countryside, but they faced myriad obstacles. The program was expensive because it required paying large landowners up front in cash for the property that would then be used for reallocation. The land agency bureaucracy was also bloated and inefficient, spending more than twice as much on administration as it allocated to beneficiaries.[18]

Equally problematic was the precarious position of the country as a whole as it entered the 2000s. The political system and bureaucracy teetered as guerrilla groups and paramilitaries took control of large swaths of territory and started encroaching on the capital and other urban centers. Elena and her community were caught up in this wave of violence. The land reallocation agency briefly shuttered.

The government of President Álvaro Uribe raised funds to beef up the military and brutally cracked down on insurgents. Security forces committed a raft of human rights abuses as they reasserted control over territory. But by the 2010s, the government had gained enough breathing room to consider how to address the violence and displacement in the country, problems that affected millions of Colombians. Land took a central position in the scheme of restitution and reconciliation that lay ahead.

COLOMBIANS WENT TO the polls in 2010 in the safest environment the country had experienced in years. They elected Uribe's protégé, Juan Manuel Santos, to the presidency in a landslide. Santos staked his early administration on restitution to conflict victims. His government passed the pathbreaking Victims Law in 2011. It promised reparations for victims of the armed conflict and their families. A centerpiece of the law was a land restitution mechanism for people like Elena whose land had been stolen from them or who were forced to abandon it.[19] The law explicitly took into account the unique ways in which women experienced victimization and provided resources to help them overcome gender-based barriers in seeking restitution. On signing the law, Santos declared, "If I accomplish nothing else, this will have made my presidency worthwhile."

The Victims Law took women into special account in two main ways. First, it made partners of victims of land displacement eligible for land restitution. Since men held most of the land and were far more likely than women to be killed in the conflict, this component of the law ensured that partnered women would have access to land restitution even if they were not on the initial land title.[20] Second, the law created a special access program for women in land restitution to make sure they were not left out of the process in the face of ongoing gender discrimination. That component included training land restitution agents in gender issues, identifying and resolving restitution barriers unique to women, and informing and training women in how to claim benefits.

In its first decade of operation, over 9 million people registered as conflict victims, and half of these were women.[21] Of these, 127,000 victims of land dispossession or forced abandonment petitioned for land restitution.[22] Many of these claims are still in progress; Elena's land petition was on the leading edge. But by mid-2019, women had been party to half of the roughly 10,000 cases in which the courts had ruled in favor of land restitution.[23] Many victims have requested other forms of compensation, such as housing subsidies. Of the nearly 80,000 housing subsidies granted to victims, women represented 30 percent of the heads of households. And women make up 37 percent of the small private agricultural enterprises supported by the government.[24]

The Victims Law faced new challenges of its own. Sifting through land claims proved exceptionally complex. And the country's conflict again flared up in the ensuing years with a spate of kidnappings and confrontations between armed groups, civilians, and the state. Against this backdrop of violence, it was difficult to provide security and resettlement for women and men alike seeking land restitution. What the country needed was peace.

The year after passage of the Victims Law, the government began peace talks with the country's largest guerrilla group, the FARC. Negotiators for both sides met in Havana, Cuba, to discuss the conflict's most sensitive issues: rural reform, political participation for the FARC, drug policy, reparations to conflict victims, and the logistical steps to enact a settlement, including FARC demobilization, disarmament, and reintegration into society. At the start of the talks, it was essentially a men's affair; women had very little representation.

But with support from the United Nations and other international advocates, women's organizations, feminists, LGBTQ groups, and conflict victims' organizations protested and organized to get women a seat at the table. Women knew what was at stake and refused to be sidelined. Both negotiating teams agreed to include women directly in the talks. And they agreed to create a Gender Subcommittee tasked with committing each side to affirmative gender-based actions. When the final peace agreement was inked and approved by Congress in 2016 after four tough years of negotiation, it contained more than

130 provisions on gender and women's rights that spanned all of the major issues contained in the deal.

The first plank of the agreement centered on Colombia's thorniest issue: land. Everyone knew the conflict had its origins in land and that it would not end without taking rural reforms seriously. As in many late twentieth-century compromises ending drawn-out insurgencies, land was central to peace. At the behest of Colombian and international women's organizations, and with the hard work of women negotiators, special care was taken to include and prioritize women in reallocating and restituting land, formalizing property rights, purchasing new land, and providing legal services, rights protection, and dispute resolution around land. For instance, land petitioners received extra points in their evaluation score for being a woman and even more for being a member of a women's organization.

These efforts bore fruit. In the five years following the peace agreement, 20,000 women won access to nearly 1 million acres of land, constituting 30 percent of the land granted by the state for settlement through various programs. Several thousand more had their property rights secured over their land. Half of the families that received subsidies for land purchases were headed by women. And nearly 50,000 women—more than half of all cases—accessed special land dispute resolution courts.[25]

Colombia's initiatives to close the gender gap in land access have paid real dividends. The position of women like Elena in rural areas has improved notably over the past several decades. And there is far more organization and awareness among women regarding their rights to land ownership and the tools available to them to make those rights a reality. The legal nonprofit that Elena's community turned to for assistance with restitution and similar organizations have helped both to spread awareness and to facilitate land restitution for what are typically disadvantaged claimants.

But gender equity is still a long way off. The most recent agricultural census, conducted on the eve of the peace agreement in 2014, shows that women hold 26 percent of rural land, men hold

61 percent, and the remaining 13 percent is jointly held. This represents a considerable shift in favor of women since the 1980s. And it is an important one, given that a quarter of the population still lives in rural areas. But it also shows how stubborn the gender disparity has proven to be. Relatedly, women hold smaller plots of land than men on average and have less access to mechanized equipment and credit.[26]

There are explanations for the persistent gender divide. Although the government has sought to move the gender dial in land ownership through land reallocation, those programs still only represent a minority of land transactions in any given year. Most land still transfers hands through sales and purchases in the private sector or inheritance rather than land reallocation.[27] The government has been far less hands-on in regulating how that land is owned or controlled across genders. Patriarchal gender norms persist in much of the countryside, and especially in areas untouched by reforms.

The slow pace of land reallocation has compounded this issue. Social pushback and bureaucratic constraints are both to blame. A number of prominent land and women's activists have been murdered by counterreform criminal bands.[28] Many women are rightfully fearful of being restituted land in far-flung rural areas without adequate protection and support against a backdrop of continued violence. Land agencies are also struggling to advance land restitution, land formalization, and ongoing tiller and settler reforms. They are sitting on a backlog of unresolved land disputes, many of which pit claimants against criminal bands or powerful large landowners. And they have clashed with other government ministries and local judges and politicians, who have sometimes resisted cooperating in resolving land disputes.

What's more, though the reforms are more gender progressive than in the past, they remain stymied by gender biases of their own. Many women are constrained for social reasons in seeking land access or prefer to work partly or entirely out of agriculture. And many bureaucrats, while now trained to be sensitive to gender biases, nonetheless continue to hold them. Women are still less likely to receive land than men through most programs, and the plots they receive tend to be smaller.[29]

The government has also come under increasing criticism for treating women in monolithic terms and gender as a simple dichotomy. The treatment of women as a homogeneous category ignores critical differences among women in factors such as race and ethnicity, class, regional identity, marital status, and lived experiences that fundamentally shape how different groups make claims on the government and the policies that would be most effective in terms of government response.[30] Along similar lines, there is little attention or capacity to address claims from individuals who do not identify along traditional gender lines.[31]

Nevertheless, there is more being done and plenty more land slated for reallocation. Colombia stands as an example to the world that land has the power to catalyze gender equality. When put in the right hands, land can reverse long-standing social injustice. And Colombia isn't the only example.

SHAKING BOLIVIA'S PATRIARCHY

On August 7, 2006, Silvia Lazarte stood before Bolivia's newly created constitutional assembly as its president. Wearing traditional Quechuan clothing that demarcated her rural indigenous heritage, she introduced herself to the assembly: "I come from a very poor family and did not have the economic support to carry on with school. Many people ask me if I have the professional credentials to lead the Constituent Assembly and I proudly reply that I do not, because I was marginalized and because in my childhood my father told me that as a woman and oldest daughter I should give opportunity to my brothers."[32]

Lazarte's rise from a humble farming family to the leadership of the deliberative body charged with forging a new social contract in

Bolivia was a stunning development in a country that had long been run by mestizo men. But although she had little formal schooling and faced discrimination both for her gender and for her indigenous background, her experience as an activist and trade union organizer was nearly unmatched. Only her most prominent political backer, Bolivian president Evo Morales, was comparable.

In 1980, when Lazarte was sixteen, a group of indigenous women formed what would become the country's most powerful women's organization, known popularly as the Bartolina Sisas, or Bartolinas.[33] That same year, Lazarte's father, who was sick at the time, presented her to the local farming union in Chapare to represent him, because her brothers had moved elsewhere. She bitterly recalls being rejected as both a woman and a minor. But with Evo Morales's support in 1982, she started a local women's union of her own. Her path soon crossed with the Bartolinas, and she rose to lead the organization from 1999 to 2001.

As the Constituent Assembly got to work under Lazarte, members of the Bartolinas took important positions in committees working on land and on women's issues. They fought to bar discrimination against women in access to and inheritance of land and to guarantee their rights to land in both land titling and land reallocation initiatives. Once Lazarte's job was done and the assembly had drafted a new constitution, she returned to her hometown to dedicate herself to farming on her own land and to activism. The new constitution that emerged from the Constituent Assembly, and that the Bolivian public overwhelmingly approved in a nationwide referendum, would go on to radically change the lot of rural women in a traditionally conservative society.

Few women had legal rights to land in Bolivia when Morales was elected president in 2006. And there were weak property rights covering the country's vast majority of land. Under a land reallocation program that began in the 1950s and lasted for several decades, large landholdings were seized and distributed mainly to peasant men. But the government did not confer on the recipients verifiable or secure legal titles to their land. Men held the lion's share of land in the country but had no paper trail to back it up.

The government started cleaning up the mess in the late 1990s by giving out land titles. Women realized they had a chance to become the legal owners of a far larger share of Bolivia's land, and with Morales's election and the Bartolinas' rising star, they finally had influential political allies. Powered forward by the new constitution and a political majority, Morales increased the pace of land titling. In line with the new constitution that Lazarte had shepherded along as well as the demands of the Bartolinas and other women's organizations, his government shifted to titling land to both men and women.

Women became major property owners in Bolivia within a decade. The country began a transformation from one of the most gender-unequal societies within Latin America to one of the more gender-progressive ones. Indigenous women like Lazarte took positions of unprecedented political power alongside men and gained a stronger voice in community governance and affairs. Discrimination against women, particularly in rural areas, remains considerable in the country. Many are consigned to the domestic sphere and struggle to be heard. But respect for women, their ability to have a say in household affairs, and their ability to work alongside men in positions of power and authority have advanced in ways that would have been hard to imagine as recently as the early 2000s. Land is a cornerstone of this historic shift.

BOLIVIA WAS A feudal society from the time of Spanish colonization until the 1950s. Indigenous groups progressively lost their land and independence with the expansion of haciendas. The wealthiest few percent of landowners, typically of European or mixed descent, came to control over 90 percent of the country's farmland.[34] Most people in rural areas, which meant the overwhelming majority of the population, lived on the estates of large landowners and labored for them in the fields and in their homes. That was the case for Silvia Lazarte's grandparents and for her mother.[35] Women managed domestic affairs in their meager households, helped in the fields, and performed crafts such as weaving, and some served as maids for the landowners. Landowners tied resident workers to their estates through perpetual indebtedness and sold them with the land. Workers faced abuse and exploitation, and many women faced arranged marriages.

A revolution in 1952 toppled the teetering and brutal status quo at a time when Colombia was mired in internecine civil war. The new government passed a collective reform that reallocated large and underused landholdings to peasants. Groups of peasants in the well-populated highlands region organized and petitioned to obtain land.[36] By the 1980s, the government had guided the transfer of nearly 42 million acres of land from large landowners to peasant groups.[37] Alongside this reform, to reduce population pressure in the highlands the government also handed out frontier and state-owned land through a settler reform.

This radical transformation in land ownership and freedom did not extend to women. The reform stipulated only one parcel of land per beneficiary household and heavily favored male heads of households. Married women did not gain the legal ability to administer and manage their property or represent their households until 1972.[38] Only widowed and single women had those capacities. In practice, however, customary norms of male dominance over land and household assets meant that few women even exercised their limited legal rights.

Men also monopolized the government-linked peasant unions that emerged from the revolution. These unions were critical local organizations with political ties to the government. They assisted with communal governance that is the lifeblood of rural Bolivia, made critical decisions about land use, channeled goods and services, and held what limited land titles the peasants received with their new property.[39]

The main union split in 1979 as peasant beneficiaries of land reallocation sought to forge their own path with greater autonomy. The Bartolinas formed in the aftermath of this split in 1980 as a women-only branch of the countrywide union for land reallocation beneficiaries, the Unified Syndical Confederation of Peasant Workers of

Bolivia.[40] The Bartolinas took their name from the national heroine Bartolina Sisa, an Aymaran woman who in the 1700s had helped lead a series of indigenous rebellions against Spanish colonizers in what is now Bolivia. Most famously, together with her husband Túpac Katari and several other indigenous leaders, she successfully laid siege to a major site of Spanish colonial authority in La Paz for six months in 1781. The Spanish caught and brutally executed her a year later, on September 5, a day now commemorated as the International Day of Indigenous Women.

The founders of the Bartolinas emphasized the overlapping layers of discrimination peasant women faced for being indigenous, peasants, and women simultaneously. The layered nature of the discrimination had generated deep social marginalization, economic exploitation, and gender oppression.[41] In recognition of this multilayered identity, the Bartolinas did not form as explicitly feminist, in contrast to some of the middle-class mestiza women's organizations that started to form in cities in the 1980s. The Bartolinas' views on gender, while diverse, mostly derived from indigenous concepts of complementarity between men and women, as opposed to Western liberal concepts of individual equality. The notion of complementarity does not imply carving out different public versus domestic spheres with associated gender roles, but rather sharing each sphere and performing tasks and duties in gendered ways.[42]

In that vein, the Bartolinas sought to "accompany" men in the struggle for land, community autonomy, and democracy and to amplify women's voices in union politics and community decision-making.[43] As a powerful indigenous movement began gathering steam, the Bartolinas became the main women's organization within that movement and by far the largest women's organization in the country.

Lazarte's early life in organizing began at this same time. After struggling with gender discrimination in the local union that her father had participated in and helped to found, she struck out with the support of Evo Morales to found and lead several local women's unions. Morales by that time was actively organizing coca farmers in

Chapare and other local farmers, whose ranks grew rapidly with the closure of important mines.

By the time Lazarte came to lead the Bartolinas in 1999, women had largely missed out on land reallocation. Bolivia's collective and settler reforms wound down in the mid- to late 1980s as the county was buffeted by economic crisis and government instability. Women headed 22 percent of rural households in the early 1990s but made up only 17 percent of the beneficiaries of land reallocation up until that point. Even this figure overstates how women fared in land reallocation. Very few women received land in the 1950s and 1960s. Although more women became direct land beneficiaries starting in the 1970s, a considerable portion of this gain appears to be linked to corruption under a 1970s military dictatorship that sought to hide the extent of frontier land it doled out to male allies through its settler reform.[44]

BOLIVIA WAS ROCKED by crisis and social upheaval in the 1990s that ultimately created space for the kind of change for women Lazarte was fighting to achieve. The country's new democracy was still reeling from major economic problems in the 1980s. Hyperinflation caused the country to call in the International Monetary Fund for help in the mid-1980s. But it fell into an economic slump and had to invite the IMF back in along with the World Bank in 1993. These organizations wanted the country to take property rights seriously as part of structural economic reforms. Meanwhile, beneficiaries of the country's collective reform of the previous decades, along with lowland indigenous groups, also clamored for stronger property rights. Giving them land had given them power and enabled them to press harder for their demands. These groups held enormous swaths of land in the legal shadows and sought greater land security to protect against encroachment—and they wanted to be treated more fairly within society.

The result was a new law in 1996 that aimed to make land access more secure by clearly delineating and providing titles to land that was informally held.[45] In practice, that meant cementing the control of those who held the land. At the behest of donors, NGOs, and women's organizations, the law promised equity for women in access to and the administration of land. It was an unparalleled opportunity for women to get a greater share of ownership in the land they lived on. Colombia, by comparison, had more established and stable property rights throughout most of the country when it first introduced gender-progressive, forward-looking laws. That meant there was a large preexisting bias in landholding favoring men that could not simply be erased under Colombia's gender-based laws that guided new land transactions. Bolivia, by contrast, effectively had a chance at a rerun. From a gender perspective, at least in the majority of households run by couples, property rights were far closer to a blank slate.

But as the new land agency, the National Institute for Agrarian Reform (known as INRA), proceeded with land titling, it did not take steps to make women aware of their legal rights or to encourage their participation in the process.[46] And INRA bureaucrats were overwhelmingly men that had no training in administering land rights to women. Several NGOs, along with the Bartolinas under the leadership of Silvia Lazarte and other groups, realized that women had a hard time claiming land rights from INRA and were being left out of the process. The new window of opportunity for women to get their share of ownership over land would eventually close, and unless women organized quickly, they might again be shut out of their share of land.

The NGOs began working with INRA in the early 2000s to reform its procedures to be more inclusive of women.[47] Meanwhile, the Bartolinas turned to an international partner known as La Vía Campesina (lit.,"the peasant way") for help.[48] La Vía Campesina is a prominent international association of peasant, indigenous, rural worker, and women's organizations that advocate around land-related issues. The Bartolinas invited La Vía Campesina on a mission to investigate gender bias in the reform and then hosted a seminar with this group on women's land rights. The discussion revolved around improving the position of women within communities and rural organizations while also supporting collective land rights and territory.[49]

The Bartolinas began advocating strongly for the titling of land to women either individually or jointly with their partners. They successfully lobbied Congress to provide rural women with free birth certificates and identification cards, documents that many women did not have but that are required to receive a land title. Now under the public microscope, INRA began supporting joint titling of land to couples.

But all of this was a warm-up act to the main event. Land titling in the most populated highlands region of the country initially proceeded slowly. That would change with the election of Bolivia's first indigenous president. The interest in land titling would get a big boost, and women would be able to capitalize on the new energy by bending the curve away from sexism.

The Bartolinas formed a central part of the political coalition called the Movement Toward Socialism that brought Evo Morales to power in 2006. The coalition had its roots in peasant and indigenous unions and social movements, including the Bartolinas, that had been stirred by land reallocation and its deficiencies. Those unions and movements coincided in the 1990s on the need for a political project that would advance their interests on the national stage. Their leader, Evo Morales, was a longtime supporter of the Bartolinas and had honed himself into an activist and organizer in Chapare alongside Silvia Lazarte.[50]

The Movement Toward Socialism coalition, which in an unprecedented move put women in nearly half of its congressional seats, quickly revamped land laws to mandate joint titling of land to both women and men for couples. It then worked with Lazarte to forge a new, more inclusive and progressive constitution for Bolivia. The Bartolinas took important positions in committees in the Constituent Assembly working on land and on women's issues. When the new constitution was promulgated in 2009, it barred discrimination against women in access to and inheritance of land and guaranteed their rights in both further land titling and land reallocation initiatives.

That same year, Morales won another mandate in office. Women, including several of the Bartolinas, made more gains in parliament. Morales named women to half of his cabinet posts. Most were indigenous women activists. Land titling sped forward. As of 2014, Morales had presided over 94 percent of the nearly 400,000 land titles issued since 1996 and nearly 70 percent of the land titled.[51] This covered most of the privately owned land in the country.

Women finally won the direct access to land power they had been fighting for. Outside of communal landholdings, 82 percent of the beneficiaries under Morales were couples and 7 percent were women, with the remaining 11 percent of titles going to men. The result is that since 1996, some 46 percent of beneficiaries have been women and 53 percent men, with the remaining share constituting communal grants.[52]

This process has empowered women and is opening up new social spaces for them. One important setting where this is occurring is in community governance. Political rights in community governance are often connected to land ownership.[53] Women are using their new share in land ownership to have their voices heard in community affairs. As one woman testified regarding speaking at community meetings, "Now, even if they [men] kick us out, we [women] stay and participate. I am an owner and I have a right to speak and participate, I tell them."[54]

A married woman who has a share in the ownership of her land is also more secure in the case of separation or the death of her husband. As one woman put it, "Before, when a woman became a widow, or she got separated or divorced, the community would expel us from the place. Now men cannot expel us, because before everything was theirs, now it is in our name. As women we should have rights, including after our marriage. They cannot expel us from our houses. For example, before when our husbands died, our in-laws would expel us from our houses; now it is not like that."[55] Relatedly, as men migrate temporarily to seek better work opportunities, women who remain and who have a share in land ownership are more likely to stand for them in decision-making.

The rapid pace of social change around gender has also stirred resistance from men. When asked in 2009 what obstacles women confront to their progress in Bolivia, the well-known activist Domitila Chúngara stated, "Machismo, mainly. Not long ago, after finishing one of the literacy programs, a woman came up to me. She was sad and told me that she hadn't participated in the course because her husband didn't want her to go. He told her that if her parents had 'raised a donkey, that's how she should stay.' That's why I think that the first battle Bolivian women need to win is in the home."[56]

This type of patriarchy remains prevalent, and perhaps especially so in communities that are governed internally by traditional practices.[57] Men both inside and outside these communities have ignored or sought to evade requirements to include women on land titles. And some communities continue to reject requests by single women to own land individually.[58] There remain other considerable inequities as well. Land titled to men as individuals in the first several years of Morales's tenure tended to be considerably larger in extent than land titled to women.[59]

Social change on the scale it is occurring in Bolivia is never completed rapidly or without pushback. But when it finally comes, this type of change is also hard to reverse. Women are now major owners of Bolivia's land. Through that land they are gaining visibility, inclusion, and more comprehensive citizenship rights.

* * *

IMPROVING THE POSITION of women in society by giving them a greater share of land is a long journey that many societies have not even begun. As in Colombia and Bolivia, it requires pressure from women and a political opening. Sometimes it even comes out of disruption, tragedy, and war. The fastest way to move the dial is through changing property rights and property law as Bolivia did rather than through land reallocation. Extending property titles to women within couples and changing inheritance laws to eliminate or reduce favoritism for sons are two examples. These policies can give women opportunities and independence that they would not have otherwise. Countries as different as Ecuador, India, Ireland, Nepal, and Vietnam have pursued these paths.

Changing customs and traditions is difficult. There is often pushback by men who protest or ignore these changes. That pushback can overwhelm reform efforts. And sometimes reforms are too timid to have major effects, as in Vietnam. But the experiences of Colombia and Bolivia show that real progress can be made. Modernization and urbanization can accelerate that progress. Modernization changes social values and gives women a greater voice that they can use to effect change. It is also linked to shrinking birth rates, which sharply decreases gendered competition for property inheritance and opportunity among children. Urbanization reduces population pressure on land and, like modernization, can lead to value changes and facilitate women's movements.

Most of the countries that have tried to empower women through land reallocation efforts, as Colombia has done, have failed to make much progress. Some notorious examples include the Soviet Union and China, where women were sidelined from decision-making within collectives. Even well-intentioned contemporary efforts have foundered. South Africa's land restitution and reallocation programs aimed to include women, but because of the persistence of customary practices and prevailing gender biases, and because they neglected to take the unique needs of women into consideration, women have still been left on the sidelines.

Given the social barriers to change, it is not surprising that landholding across most of the world continues to favor men and that this gap fuels further gender inequity. But those barriers are slowly breaking under women's pressure. To be sure, it has been the countries facing the darkest national circumstances where the most progress has been made. In times of catastrophe, disruption, and even war, it can become possible to graft women's empowerment onto other necessary state projects to heal national wounds. But regardless of how these openings have come about, where women have won property, they have won far greater equity with men.

CHAPTER 9

RECLAIMING NATURE

ON A COOL, SUNNY AFTERNOON IN LATE JANUARY 2018, A PRESIdent and a philanthropist met in Chile's southern Patagonia region to sign into existence a massive new network of national parks.

The signing ceremony took place on the recovering grasslands of the windswept Chacabuco Valley, which the American philanthropist Kristine Tompkins's conservation nonprofit had worked to restore after purchasing the land from a private landowner in 2004. Over the past century, the Chilean government had granted the enormous valley for initial settlement to a company that promised to exploit it, taken it back and handed it to local workers in a cooperative reform, and then taken it back once again to auction it off to a private landowner. Through the twists and turns, eighty years of ranching and reshuffle after reshuffle had left the valley's natural ecosystems and wildlife damaged and struggling. But the same land power that had painted a target on this environment could also be used to protect it from harm.

With the stroke of a pen, Chilean president Michelle Bachelet accepted Tompkins Conservation's donation of some 200,000 acres of land spanning the Chacabuco Valley and several other smaller properties. The Bachelet government agreed to combine these lands with two adjacent publicly owned protected areas to form Patagonia National Park, with a size of over 700,000 acres of land. At the same ceremony, Bachelet expanded two other national parks and created two more. Kris Tompkins, a former CEO of the outdoor apparel company Patagonia, and her late husband, North Face founder and philanthropist Doug Tompkins, had played a role in fostering all of these natural spaces through strategic land purchases and conservation efforts.

"This is not only an unprecedented effort of preservation," Bachelet remarked to the gathering of government officials, conservationists, and philanthropists as a group of guanacos (an animal closely related to alpacas) grazed in the valley behind her. "It is an invitation to imagine other forms to use our land. To create other economic activities. To use natural resources in a way that does not exhaust them. To have sustainable development—the only stable economic development in the long term. . . . The path to creating the network of national parks shows us what we have, who we are, and what we can achieve."

Kris Tompkins declared that the creation of the parks affirmed "the conviction that it is possible to leave future generations a world where they can prosper and where all species have the space and security to prosper." It marked the fulfillment of a dream she first had in April 1994 as she was lying in a tent in the eastern Chacabuco Valley for the first time. When I spoke with her in 2023, she recalled the conversation she and Doug had had then as they puzzled over how to restore the natural landscape in what they saw as "one of the jewels of the country."[1]

The parks deal was the culmination of decades of involvement in land conservation in Chile for Doug and Kris Tompkins. They had begun purchasing land in southern Chile for the purpose of conservation in the early 1990s. Initially, they kept their intentions to themselves, but gradually they began talking about their goals in a more public fashion. Their approach was reminiscent of what John D. Rockefeller Jr. had done in Wyoming when he had set about helping to create and expand the Grand Teton National Park, purchasing and patching together a disparate set of ranchlands surrounding the region's iconic mountains. With the support of several other donors, the couple and their nonprofits, later combined into Tompkins Conservation, acquired roughly 1 million acres over several decades. The aim was to piece together contiguous lands that could be stitched into bigger protected parklands. Some of these lands were lightly used or nearly abandoned, leaving their ecosystems nearly intact. Others, including the Chacabuco Valley, had suffered extensive degradation.

Tompkins Conservation donated its massive collection of properties to Chile in several rounds. One month after the January ceremony, they handed over 700,000 acres of land to form Pumalín Douglas Tompkins National Park. "National parks, monuments and other public lands," Kris wrote just after the first donation, "remind us that regardless of race, economic standing or citizenship, we all depend on a healthy planet for our survival."[2]

It was the largest public-private partnership in land restoration and conservation that the world has ever seen. By working together, the philanthropists and Chile's government accomplished a conservation feat that neither could have accomplished alone. Marcelo Mena, the minister of the environment who had worked to convert the land deal into law, called it "the most important ecological act of this century" and told me that "it changes the destiny and identity of Chile moving forward toward one of conservation."[3]

It has enormous consequences for the environment. From 2014 to 2018, Chile went from protecting just 4 percent of its land and sea area to protecting 36 percent.[4] Vast areas of pristine land are now destined for preservation. An estimated 900 million tons of carbon will remain naturally sequestered in the soils and plant life of these parks. And expansive landscapes that had been degraded through land settlement policy and heavy human use are now recovering, embracing the return of nature and its wild beauty.

Population growth and the increasing demand for land and food over the past several centuries have driven human societies to eliminate large swaths of wilderness and replace them with farmland, housing, and urban developments.

Evidence of the harm this has caused is all around us. Consider the western plains of the United States. In the span of a few decades beginning in the late 1800s, a tidal wave of homesteaders seeking land in the prairies uprooted one of the largest grasslands on earth, home to millions of buffalo, antelope, birds, and other species. Many species were driven to near extinction, and the American West today is now a heavily fertilized blanket of monocropped fields crisscrossed by roads and dotted by mere pockets of native habitats. Settlers seeking land for ranching and logging in Brazil have likewise gnawed away at the Amazon rainforest. Millions of acres of virgin rainforest have been clear-cut in the past half century, destroying ecosystems and severely damaging the forest's ability to serve as a carbon trap for the world. There are hundreds of similar stories spanning countries across the world.

As societies around the globe now struggle against climate change, the enormity of reckoning with past harms can boggle the mind. Entirely reversing resource and biodiversity losses in the American prairies or Brazilian Amazon seems wholly unrealistic, and the human population is far larger than it was a century ago, making land reclamation impractical. Rural poverty and the desire for a comfortable life in developing countries makes sustainable environmental practices difficult to enact and maintain when they are bound to conflict with much-needed short-term economic growth.

At the same time, there is an explosion of creativity and investment in attempts to conserve and protect land and remaining resources and to improve them for future generations. Some of these efforts are proving more promising than initially anticipated. This chapter tells the story of how two countries, Chile and Spain, have managed to make advances in protecting and even restoring the environment through land conservation. They have done so by flipping the polarity of land power to achieve completely different goals from those pursued in the past. Land power has in a sense been used against itself, to return the land to its natural state of simply land.

In Chile, two American philanthropists, Doug and Kris Tompkins, started by buying up large swaths of land for preservation in the

1990s. They then struck an unprecedented land deal with the Chilean government to turn that land into national parks if Chile would contribute more land and protect it. The partnership forged a sprawling new series of national parks that are protecting natural habitats and restoring damaged ecosystems on formerly settled lands at a large scale through a program of "rewilding."

Decades earlier, in Spain, an ambitious government program of land settlement after the country's civil war began converting arid and swampy areas into farmland through irrigation and drainage projects. As the program crept into one of Europe's largest marshlands, threatening bird and marine habitats, environmental activists organized to halt the damage and reverse some of it. The World Wildlife Fund and Spain's Doñana National Park were born out of these efforts, and they left a legacy of environmental activism both in Spain and abroad.

Land conservation efforts in this vein are a different kind of land reshuffling than the settler, tiller, cooperative, and collective reforms that dominated over the past several centuries. If anything, they are like a reverse settler reform in that they take humans off the land or encourage them to tread far more lightly on it. However, as in Chile and Spain, they do not necessarily hand these lands back to indigenous communities that previously inhabited them. Those communities may have been entirely destroyed or removed elsewhere, and if they still exist, they are at most invited as partners to steward the land rather than to physically return to it.

Reclaiming and restoring the natural environment through land conservation requires overwhelming any local land power. Existing landowners have to be coaxed, bought, or badgered out. In their place a new conception of that power is installed, fused with state power and the notion of landholding vested in the nation as collective patrimony. The environmental ills of personalized land power are substituted for the broader environmental and climate interests of society as a whole. Like all types of land reshuffling, these reforms lock in a new trajectory far different from the extractive, environmentally disruptive path of the past.

CHILE'S CONSERVATION TURN

Chile's Patagonia region is a stunning natural gem, studded by volcanoes and fjords, vast primary forests and grasslands, and a wealth of unique animal and plant species, all crowned by rugged snow-tipped mountains. Spanning the southern third of the country, it is home to dozens of unique forest and grassland ecosystems. And it contains some of the richest land in South America in terms of carbon storage, making it a critical resource in the fight against global climate change.[5]

Central Patagonia, home to many of the new national parks the Tompkinses were involved in, remained largely unexplored and unsettled by outsiders into the late 1800s owing to its remote and rugged nature. Within the Chacabuco Valley of what is now Patagonia National Park and the surrounding areas, the indigenous Tehuelche (Aónikenk) people had lived for millennia as hunter-gatherers, following the movement of guanacos and transiting the dry, cold, windy valley.

Outsider interest in the area increased when Chile almost went to war with Argentina in 1902 over a border dispute in Patagonia. At issue was the dividing line between the two countries, which had been described in an 1881 border treaty but remained ambiguous: interpretations diverged in central Patagonia over whether it was the line of highest mountains dividing the Atlantic and Pacific watersheds, or instead the drainage basins, that marked the delimitation.

The dispute and fears over cross-border encroachment drove the Chilean government to craft a policy of land settlement aimed at the area in order to populate and secure the Chilean side. It also viewed the region as a new frontier for resource extraction and production. The government began doling out enormous ranching and logging concessions over publicly owned lands on attractive leasing terms to entrepreneurs who in return promised to encourage broader settlement, build infrastructure, and produce for growing domestic markets.[6]

One of the largest land concessions in the Patagonia region went to a business association known as the Sociedad Explotadora del

Baker in 1904. It incorporated the entire Baker River basin, spanning some ninety miles from north to south and running from the southern shore of Lake General Carrera, which saddles the border between Chile and Argentina, out to the Pacific Ocean. The Chacabuco Valley is one of the offshoots of the Baker River within the broader river basin.

One of the earliest descriptions of the area before it became a target of settlement comes from the diary of William Norris, whom the Baker business had hired to scout the area for suitability to logging and ranching. On his first sojourn to the region in 1905, Norris called it "beautiful country covered with forests and grasslands." "When we first entered the Baker country," he wrote, "we saw plenty of guanaco and ostrich in the open valleys. . . . Of pumas there must have been plenty when we first arrived. . . . There is a very fine specimen of mountain deer called 'huemul,' but as there is so much cover they are seldom seen."[7] Over the next few years Norris drove thousands of sheep and cattle into the area through a pass in the Andes Mountains leading from Argentina. Norris did not encounter Tehuelches, and there are no historical accounts of European explorers meeting Tehuelches in the valley. By the early 1900s most of them lived farther south, perhaps because of dwindling numbers from earlier European contact.

The Sociedad Explotadora del Baker foundered in subsequent years and another business group, the Sociedad Hobbs y Compañía, organized to explore ranching possibilities in the concession area. As Hobbs sought to draw in more participants to develop different areas of the concession, it reached out to a business group called Bridges and Reynolds, whose associates had successfully managed large land concessions at the southern tip of Chile's Tierra del Fuego. The group nominated Lucas Bridges to explore the Chacabuco Valley area. Bridges's father was a British immigrant who had founded an Anglican mission in Tierra del Fuego.

Lucas Bridges traveled on horseback and on foot through arduous and lawless parts of Patagonia for several weeks to the Chacabuco Valley in 1916. He recounted in his journal from the trip that he thought it would be "very difficult and expensive" to fulfill the government's mandate to open up a new route to a port through the valley or along the Baker River. "Nonetheless," he wrote, "that place with its abundant streams, sheltered and verdant valleys, and pleasant climate and my passion for adventures, were irresistible to me."[8]

Bridges set up an initial ranching operation in the north of the valley and built houses for the workers and administrators at the valley's windswept eastern entrance in the steppe, close to the border with Argentina. But he quickly moved on before it was well established, first to fight in World War I for Great Britain and then to settle in Rhodesia. Hobbs's company struggled with personnel turnover and financial difficulties in the intervening years. In 1921, it again reached out to Bridges, and he returned to the Chacabuco Valley.

Reenergized on the project, Bridges attracted Chilean and European settlers to the area to work at the property. At a frenetic pace and with a daring that shocked even his workers, he surveyed local rivers, dynamited mountainsides to build bridges, and forged a route to transport and warehouse products. Then in the course of the 1920s he ramped up the size of the sheep herd in Chacabuco to 70,000 animals.[9] The sheep were used for wool for domestic and foreign markets as well as for domestic meat consumption. Eventually, a small neighboring town called Cochrane sprouted up with most of its inhabitants working for Bridges. Bridges had successfully driven settlement in the area and established new economic activity on the land that settlers took part in.

Bridges did not carefully keep track of the local environment and ecology. But it is evident from the size of his operation as well as his descriptions of some of the ranch's activities that the local environment paid a toll. Bridges tore up native steppe grasslands to plant hay for the sheep, exposing the young, thin glacial soils of the valley to erosion and the riverbeds and wetlands to heaps of silt. He fenced in what had previously been open natural areas, carving up habitats of species such as guanacos, rheas, foxes, deer, and pumas. And he ordered workers to cut down primary old growth forest to harvest wood for building bridges, housing, and barns and to serve as fuel for heat. The massive herds of sheep trampled native bunch grasses; eroded soils that take thousands of years to build up in the cold, dry climate; and crowded out endemic animal life. The only way to turn a profit on land characterized by poor soils for agriculture and limitations on the regrowth of grasses for grazing animals was with large-scale ranching. Within a decade, Bridges's myopic campaign to develop a massive ranch to serve Chilean markets had severely compromised the rich natural environment. By the time of the 1943 census, the Chacabuco Valley estate, run by the refashioned business association Sociedad Valle Chacabuco under the name Lago Bertrand, was divided up into forty-eight fenced sections and had nearly 75,000 sheep and 400 cattle.[10]

The Chilean government's encouragement of land settlement and economic development in the area also extended beyond Bridges's operation, with similar consequences for the natural environment.

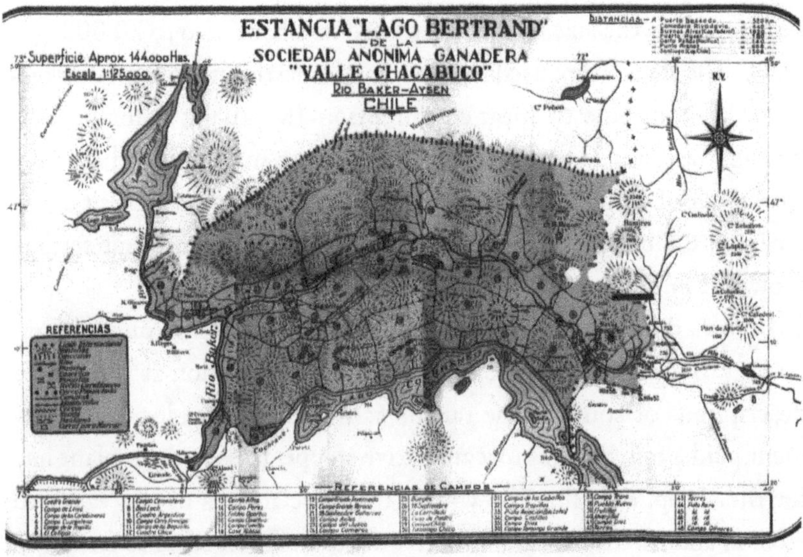

The Chacabuco Valley land concession, the basis of today's Patagonia National Park, 1945. (Credit: Rewilding Chile.)

Other independent land settlers came to the area both within the Chacabuco Valley and outside it, in part with the promise of gaining ownership over land through a settler-type reform. They dedicated themselves to ranching, exploiting the forests, and engaging in small-scale agriculture.[11]

Many settlers clear-cut or burned the forests to open up their land and, in accordance with government guidelines, to assert ownership through use. "The culture [of settlers] was never one oriented toward protecting the environment," one inhabitant of the town of Cochrane, just outside the Chacabuco Valley, recently put it. "In the past there was a very aggressive relationship [with nature] because they had to adapt and survive."[12] The soils of the region eroded and desertified, eliminating wildlife, altering plant communities, and even changing the course of rivers. One town at the base of the Aysén River, Puerto Aysén, had to be moved three times as the river changed course as a result of environmental interruptions.

Bridges hired some settlers but at times battled with others and with politicians over control of the land within his state concession. Consequently, the land he managed waxed and waned in size, at times reaching nearly half a million acres, but always centered on roughly 200,000 acres spanning all of the Chacabuco Valley and some of its immediate surroundings.[13]

THE BROADER CHILEAN economy shifted dramatically in the late 1800s and early 1900s over the course of the Chacabuco's settlement and conversion into extensive ranchland. Expanding international trade and growing urban centers increased agricultural demand. The amount of land used for agriculture doubled from 1875 to 1930 as the farming frontier expanded.[14] But access to that land was starkly unequal. In 1928, less than 3 percent of the largest landholders in the country controlled 80 percent of the arable land.[15] A landlord-peasant system of landholding prevailed, with a large portion of the rural population toiling as dependent workers for large landowners. In these conditions, peasants had few freedoms.

Political reforms that gave greater voice to these workers eventually generated pressure for land reallocation. The election of Eduardo Frei to the presidency in 1964 was a game changer. Frei quickly set to reshuffling land by purchasing large estates from private landholders for reallocation among workers. A few years later, in 1967, Congress passed a new law empowering the state to acquire private land for reallocation through expropriation and to recall state-owned land for the same purpose.

Frei pressed ahead with this agenda, and his successor, Salvador Allende, doubled down on it. By 1973, when Allende was toppled in a reactionary military coup, nearly 6,000 estates covering 25 million acres of land had been reallocated among roughly 54,000 peasant households.[16] The reform enveloped the better part of all the agricultural land in the country. The government fashioned most of these former estates into worker cooperatives in a classic style of cooperative reform. Hoping to ensure continuity of production, the government retained formal ownership of the land.

The cooperative reform enveloped the Chacabuco Valley and other land concessions in the Patagonia region. The government withdrew its leasing concession in the valley from several of Bridges's business partners who had continued ranching operations after Bridges died in 1949. It put the land into the hands of interested men from the broader region who had farming experience but no land of their own. The government eventually forged a cooperative from twenty-two families and oversaw its functioning through the national land agency while retaining official ownership of the land.[17] Meanwhile, the government also designated two national reserves out of lands bordering the cooperative that would eventually be incorporated into Patagonia Park.

The land agency gave the new cooperative sheep and cattle it had purchased from Bridges's partners when it withdrew the concession, and it also built them houses. In return, families had to make regular payments to the agency in order to build capital in these investments and make them their own. One former cooperative member,

Luisa Galindo, told me that families had "hoped that the land would eventually become ours too."[18] She recounted how the cooperative had split the valley and surrounding mountains into sectors, one for each family, and everyone seasonally contributed to collective tasks such as shearing the sheep and tending portions of the herds in various pockets of the valley and its offshoots.

Cooperative families faced a steep learning curve at the start. The land agency lacked expertise in administering the ranch, as did many of the beneficiaries, and some departed to be replaced by others. But things settled in and families built a life there. They sought to care for their herds of sheep and cattle and grew them successfully following many of the standard ranching practices of the time. But those practices put more pressure on the already damaged soils and grasses. Families also drew from the southern beech forests to build fences and heat their homes, converted parts of the steppe into fields to grow vegetables for household consumption, and hired bounty hunters to cull the puma population that preyed on sheep.[19]

The challenges grew within just a few years. In 1973, General Augusto Pinochet toppled Salvador Allende in a military coup and set about reversing the land reallocation program. The government began dismantling cooperatives as it sought to forge a more capitalist economy and stoke economic growth. It returned some cooperative land to former landowners and auctioned off other lands to private parties promising to put them into production. With the land agency overseeing cooperatives operating under new military administrators, the members of the cooperative in the Chacabuco Valley lived in something of a purgatory, awaiting their fate while continuing to work the land.[20] The prospect of owning the land faded, fostering poor land stewardship. Some cooperative members abruptly withdrew, taking their investments in animals and infrastructure with them.

Eventually, in the early 1980s, the military government forced remaining cooperative workers off the land. It sold the property at auction to a Chilean entrepreneur of Belgian descent named François de Smet. The de Smet family, fleeing the ruins of Europe after World

War II, had arrived in an area north of the Chacabuco Valley in 1949 seeking the promise of frontier land from the Chilean government. Starting from scratch, the family had begun by farming and harvesting timber.[21] Just over thirty years later they were now able to purchase the Chacabuco Valley.

The environmental toll of the cooperative era and the poorly managed transition became clear as soon as the de Smets entered Chacabuco Valley. When I spoke with Charlie de Smet, who began administering the valley in 1981, he told me, "We received a very disordered and deteriorated property, in terms of the land and soils, the houses, and the machinery."[22] Cooperative members had taken, sold, or eaten most of the remaining sheep and cattle and stripped valuable parts of the ranching infrastructure that they felt they rightfully owned. The de Smets had to start over again, rebuilding infrastructure and purchasing livestock for the ranch.

The de Smets grew their new herd to nearly 30,000 sheep and cattle, and the ranch came to serve as home to several dozen families who helped to run it. It was the main employer for people living in the neighboring town of Cochrane. Some of the workers the de Smets hired had been inscribed in the former cooperative. Workers often viewed the valley as their home and saw its identity as inextricably tied to ranching. The ranch shipped wool and sheep to Chile's populated central valley and to international markets. It also sold meat locally.[23]

The de Smets managed smaller herds than in the time of Lucas Bridges and paid greater attention to sustainability. They rotated animals across different patches of land to avoid exhausting the pastureland. In the summer they pushed their herds out of the valley into the surrounding hills and mountains to graze so that the bottom valley could rest, and then they brought animals back to it during the winter months. And they tried to rehabilitate endangered deer populations and steward guanaco populations.[24]

Despite these improvements, the damaged natural landscape struggled to recuperate without a rest from endless extraction. The imperatives of running a ranch that could support the family and employ members of the local community generated tensions with the environment. The large herds of sheep continued to trample on and uproot the delicate steppe grasslands, both in the valley floor and in higher elevation basins and valley offshoots. In contrast to the native guanaco, which graze grasses and leave their roots intact, livestock tear at them and uproot portions. Cattle grazing in the beech forests at higher elevations stripped saplings from the understory, compromising forest health. Fences also interrupted habitats. Many native animals and plants remained under pressure or were crowded out of the valley, and several invasive plant species thrived.

In 2012, recalling her first visit to the valley in the mid-1990s in vivid terms, Kris Tompkins wrote, "When I drove through the Chacabuco Valley for the first time, I saw the extra-high 'guanaco fences' designed to keep these first-rate jumpers out of the best bottom grasslands, which were reserved for the cattle on the estancia. My eyes glazed over looking out on the tens of thousands of sheep grazing the bunch grasses up and down the valley. The grasses looked patchy and dead. Nothing left for wildlife. Previously one of the most biologically rich areas of Patagonia, the Chacabuco Valley was a sea of sheep and cattle."[25]

It was something she had seen in plenty of other places previously. "I come from a ranching family," she later told me, "and it's a story that's played out around the world. Generally speaking, livestock are put on the land too heavily, the management system is rudimentary, and the grasses get overgrazed. In the case of Patagonian grasslands, it only took 100 years and they were completely decimated."[26] Kris and her husband Doug would upturn the fate of the Chacabuco Valley once they began their massive conservation project.

KRIS TOMPKINS WAS the first CEO of Patagonia Inc. and helped build the company into a leading outdoor gear and clothing brand. Doug Tompkins founded the outdoor gear company North Face and cofounded the Esprit clothing company. He first traveled to Patagonia in the 1960s for climbing and mountaineering. The two married in 1993 and settled on leaving their roles in business and dedicating themselves instead to conservation efforts.

The Tompkinses' land conservation efforts began in Chile in the 1990s with what would become Pumalín Douglas Tompkins National Park. Through his nonprofit foundation, which subsequently grew and became Tompkins Conservation, Doug Tompkins purchased roughly half a million acres of land between 1991 and 1994 in central Patagonia, mostly from private absentee landowners. The punishing landscape had made the land nearly impossible to settle. The area is covered with temperate rainforest, fjords, and towering mountains, and it is home to one of the largest remaining populations of the rare alerce tree, a relative of the redwood. The Tompkinses expanded the protected territory to over 700,000 acres over the course of the next fifteen years and moved to a property next to it. Meanwhile, Tompkins Conservation made other enormous land purchases in the area, including a 200,000-acre parcel that would form the basis of the nearby Corcovado National Park.[27]

These immense private land purchases by an outsider started to turn heads in a country where conservation philanthropy was virtually unknown. Conspiracy theories arose that played into various racist tropes and national and local fears, including the notions that Doug Tompkins was trying to create a Jewish territory, a CIA base, or a nuclear waste dump in Patagonia. Politicians and the military called the land acquisitions at Pumalín—which ran from the ocean to Argentina, effectively cutting the country in half—a national security threat. They also worried that he might block important national infrastructure projects from running through the area.

While rumors swirled, Tompkins Conservation approached the government with an unusual proposal: to turn the large plot in the Corcovado area over to the Chilean government if it would form a national park from that land and adjacent federal land. Both the president and the military ultimately endorsed the idea, creating Corcovado National Park in 2005. The government also declared Pumalín a nature sanctuary, increasing its protections.

Kris Tompkins's conservation nonprofit purchased the Chacabuco Valley Estate as these negotiations with the government played out. This purchase again raised eyebrows across the country. And it met with stiff opposition from many locals, whose livelihoods and histories were deeply intertwined with ranching in the valley. Generations of locals had worked in various capacities for the ranch in the valley across the many changes in ownership. Some were even born there. They considered the land and the ranch as part of their identity and held tight the history and narrative of their forebears as pioneers. Locals also resented feeling excluded from the transformation of the land and feared the erosion of their cultural practices by an influx of outsiders. The opposition was not uniform, however. Many younger people supported the conservation goals for the area, as did people who stood to gain from ecotourism.[28]

By the time Kris Tompkins's nonprofit signed the purchase of the Chacabuco Valley, the natural landscape was severely compromised. Eighty years of grazing massive herds of sheep and cattle on the delicate grasslands had left a trail of damaged grasses, invasive species, and entirely barren patches of land suffering soil erosion. Hundreds of miles of fencing crisscrossed the valley and limited the natural range of wild animals, especially the iconic guanacos. Some animal species, such as the South American ostrich (also known as the rhea), had nearly been driven to local extinction. And hunting had dramatically thinned the number of pumas. As the ecosystem's top predator, pumas played a critical role in eliminating weak animals, keeping animal disease at bay. The remains of puma prey also provided food for other birds and animals.

The Tompkinses and their conservation organizations nonetheless saw enormous potential to restore the valley's natural ecosystem. They set about rehabilitating and "rewilding" the Chacabuco Valley after purchasing the estate and its vast sheep herds in 2004. The team wound down the ranching operation and sold off the sheep over the course of several years. With the help of volunteers, they tore out some 400 miles of fencing in order to reopen the valley to the free movement of native animals. A restoration ecologist then collected soil samples across the valley and developed a plan to reseed damaged grasslands by planting native grasses and to root out invasive species. And the group took measures to protect and enhance the populations of predators, including pumas and foxes, as well as endangered animals such as the rhea and a threatened species of deer.

Within a decade, the valley's natural environment started to thrive as it had for millennia prior to land settlement and ranching. Native grasses sprouted up in the valleys and patched up eroded areas in the delicate steppe, breathing in carbon from the air along the way. Pumas, guanacos, rheas, deer, and dozens of other species both large and small began roaming freely without the confines of fences, and their populations grew in number. There are still plenty of remnants from the former ranching era, such as fenceposts, shepherd huts in the mountains, and vehicle tracks to different sectors of the valley. Portions of the grassland and forest are still struggling to reestablish themselves and will require considerably more time to do so. But gazing across the expanse of the Chacabuco Valley from above, it is increasingly hard to detect many of the human imprints that marked it so deeply for a century.

As the Chacabuco Valley started to recover, the Tompkinses began working with the Chilean government to secure its protected status in perpetuity. They formulated a bold plan to donate more than 1 million acres of the land they had amassed for preservation if the Chilean government would agree to commit additional public land and to turn the combined areas into a network of national parks in Patagonia. In 2015, shortly before Doug Tompkins died in a tragic kayaking accident, he presented the proposal to Chile's president, Michelle Bachelet.

The complex proposal described a project that would require political leadership as well as government coordination and resources to carry out. Identifying, designating, and protecting such a vast collection of lands that had been subject to settlement and business concessions for a century was an enormous task. And it required shifting the vision of development in Patagonia from extractive and intensive land use industries, such as logging and ranching, to ecotourism and sustainability.

The Bachelet government recognized and shared this vision and worked vociferously to bring it to life. As Bachelet put it in a reflection on the creation of the new parks, "The key is to create conditions for our citizens to live in a high-quality environment and have sustainable development opportunities."[29] In the end, her government more than met the Tompkinses' proposal. It contributed over 9 million acres of land for preservation and created a series of new national parks, including Patagonia Park, while expanding several others. It drastically expanded the range of Chile's national park system while extending protections over rare plants, animals, and entire ecosystems.

The Chilean government took over control and administration of the park lands in 2018, supported by conservation foundations affiliated with the Tompkinses. Since that time, Chile's parks have become an increasing attraction for visitors both near and far who seek solace, beauty, and adventure in the natural environment, all rooted in the preservation of land and its protection from wide-scale human transformation in a world where that is becoming increasingly rare. "It represents a new future for Chile," reflected the former minister of the environment who worked to secure the parks deal. "And it has enhanced the spirit of collaboration among government bodies in the service of ecological conservation."[30] This episode shows how a turn in land power in support of sustainability can set countries on a new path to protecting the environment.

WILD SPAIN

In 1961, as Chile's Chacabuco Valley was under intensive ranching, the Netherlands' Prince Bernhard, the inaugural president of the newly formed World Wildlife Fund, sent a letter to Spanish leader General Francisco Franco as part of one of the organization's first conservation efforts. A rising Spanish naturalist named José Antonio Valverde had actually penned the letter. Valverde had fallen in love with a sprawling series of marshlands and dunes known as Doñana, a delta region on Spain's southwestern coast where the Guadalquivir River spills into the ocean. The letter's request was bold and simple: "to create a reserve for wild birds in the Guadalquivir marshes."[31]

Nearly a decade prior, in 1952, a bird enthusiast and heir to the fortune of Spain's famed González Byass winery, Mauricio González-Gordon, had invited the zoologist Francisco Bernis and Valverde, a student of Bernis at the time, to examine and track birds on his property in the heart of Doñana. Bernis and Valverde were deeply moved by what they encountered: vast wetlands and dunes teeming with bird and sea life, "true national monuments" of wildlife that inspired awe and reflected beauty.[32] Because the Doñana wetlands are located at the intersection of the European and African continents, they serve as a critical breeding ground and stopover point for millions of migratory birds. They are also home to a wide diversity of marine and terrestrial animal life, including the endangered Iberian lynx, and contain many hundreds of species of native flora.

Bernis and Valverde learned about grave threats to Doñana's landscape during their visit. The natural ecosystems of the area had suffered gradual degradation for several hundred years after the Spanish monarchy granted the land to the local nobility for settlement, and it had become a famed hunting reserve. But the fascist government that arose from the ashes of Spain's civil war in the 1930s posed an unprecedented hazard. Political and economic pressures led General Franco to embark on a campaign to convert underused land around the country into productive areas.

As part of that campaign, the Spanish government had approved an ambitious reforestation plan in the western part of Doñana. It aimed to convert sandy areas and bits of marshland into vast plantations of pine and eucalyptus to produce paper pulp and a material similar to rubber at a time when the country was isolated from the international arena and global markets. Millions of trees that tapped into Doñana's critical underground aquifer were planted at the western fringes of Doñana in 1952 and 1953.[33] At the same time, the government was building an irrigation canal in Doñana's eastern marshes to support a settler reform in the area, and it had begun draining tens of thousands of acres of ecologically sensitive marshlands. Bernis penned a letter to Franco, which González-Gordón delivered, begging him "to protect the Coto [Doñana] from its imminent industrialization."[34] The petition fell on deaf ears, and development began closing in at the edges of Doñana.

Valverde's trip with Bernis marked the start of his obsession with the Doñana area. He dreamed of turning it into a bird preserve. Valverde returned to Doñana several times in the ensuing years, most prominently as part of a "Doñana Expedition" lasting for several weeks in 1957. That trip included some of Europe's most renowned naturalists, ornithologists, and nature photographers. The team filmed a documentary titled *Wild Spain* that showed Doñana to the public at a mass scale for the first time. He also toured scientific conferences in Europe to spread awareness about the importance of the Guadalquivir marshes to bird migration routes.

In 1961, a group of the Doñana Expedition members formed the World Wildlife Fund (WWF, now the World Wide Fund for Nature) with the aim of protecting nature around the globe. One of its first objectives was to protect the Doñana by raising funds to purchase land there for conservation.[35] Valverde led the effort, crowdsourcing funds for an initial land purchase in Doñana.

When General Franco received the letter from Prince Bernhard in 1961, he was looking for opportunities to reduce the country's international isolation. He turned to Spain's main scientific body, the Higher Council of Scientific Research, to consider the request. In an ironic twist of fate, the council's head sought out the leading expert on Doñana to craft a response, someone he admired and had professionally encouraged previously—Valverde himself. Without Franco's knowledge, Valverde gleefully responded to his own letter on behalf of Spain: "From Spain we are completely in agreement with that lofty initiative."[36]

After some negotiation, in 1963 the World Wildlife Fund, with additional support from Franco's government, purchased just under 17,000 acres of the property that Mauricio González-Gordón owned along with two other families. Franco's government and the WWF put Valverde in charge of administering it as a biological reserve. Encroachment on the marshes nonetheless continued in the next several years as most of the left bank of the Guadalquivir was turned into farmland.

The WWF and Valverde continued their efforts to expand and protect the Doñana reserve. They raised funds to purchase additional properties over the next several years and beat back a government attempt to exploit the heart of Doñana by building a mammoth dam at the southern end of the marshes. And in 1969 they achieved what few had thought possible: the declaration of Doñana as a national park covering 86,000 acres of land. Subsequent legislation in 1978, just after Spain's transition to democracy, expanded the national park to nearly 126,000 acres. And in 1989 the government of Andalusia designated an additional buffer area, larger than the park itself, as a reserved natural area intended to protect the national park from neighboring local settlements.

Today Doñana National Park and associated nature reserve areas form the largest biological reserve in all of Europe. Doñana is also Europe's largest marshland. Many portions of the marshes in the broader Doñana area that existed seventy-five years ago were swallowed up by land settlement and industrial projects, and what remains is under threat as a result of climate change and the water demands and pollution of nearby farms, tourist resorts, and mines. But environmental protections and restoration have also advanced in recent decades. The remaining portions of the original Doñana landscape stand as one of Europe's last great natural gems. And the fight to preserve Doñana's land helped to spark an environmental movement that has achieved protections on lands across the country and beyond, and that has forestalled dozens of initiatives that would have resulted in major damage to the land and the natural and human life it sustains.

THE DOÑANA AREA formed at the end of the last glacial period as glaciers melted and sea levels rose, creating a series of marshes, lagoons, estuaries, and ponds on the southwest coast of Spain where the Guadalquivir River runs into the Atlantic Ocean and forms a delta. The area progressively filled with sand and silt from the tides and currents of the Atlantic Ocean and the Guadalquivir River. Shifting dunes and tidal bars along the coast protect the inland wetlands and hem them in.

Humans have inhabited and traversed the Doñana region for thousands of years. Phoenicians, Greeks, Romans, and other civilizations left traces in the area. But fundamental alterations to the landscape and the natural resources it hosted did not occur until the Spanish Crown recaptured the territory from the Moors and began granting it out in an exclusive type of settler reform to local nobility. In the late 1400s, the third Duke of Medina Sidonia introduced deer to the area for hunting, drove out wolves, began grazing cattle in parts of the marshes, and started to harvest forested areas around the wetlands. This lineage of dukes largely held the land into the 1800s and slowly transformed it through hunting, ranching, and the introduction of pine trees for forestry purposes.[37] Eventually other nobles and wealthy elites came to buy up or lease parts of the area, and in the early 1900s Spain's king hunted frequently in Doñana, accompanied by royal guests.

Hunting, forestry, and limited ranching degraded parts of the marshland habitats and altered marine and terrestrial ecosystems. An experiment in draining and diking a northern section of the marshes in the 1920s and 1930s directly destroyed marshland but was initially rather limited. An existential threat to Doñana's natural environment only emerged when a fascist government came to power in Spain in 1939 and sought to convert the area into land suitable for agriculture and logging through large-scale irrigation works and forest plantations.

Spain in the 1930s was a preindustrial society of haves and have-nots. Half the workforce labored in agriculture, and a large portion of it as wage laborers without their own farms. In southern Spain, where landlessness was most acute, the top 1 percent of large landowners together held more than half the land.[38] This stark inequality fueled strikes and land invasions in the countryside and generated enormous pressure for the reallocation of private land to the poor. A highly controversial, predominantly tiller-style reform began in 1936 following an electoral win by the left, but it quickly crumbled as a coup threw the country into civil war.[39] Three years of bitter partisan warfare and atrocities followed until General Francisco Franco and his nationalist forces crushed the left and secured their hold on power.

Firmly allied to large landowners, Franco sought to alleviate land pressure on their estates and avoid a rerun of the civil war. He also sought to increase food production in a country reeling from the twin forces of civil war and the Great Depression, and now marginalized on the European stage just as World War II was breaking out. The plan was simple: put more land into agricultural production. Inspired by programs such as Mussolini's efforts to drain Italy's swamps and recover agricultural land, Franco's government aimed to irrigate arid lands and to drain marshes and swamps in order to make them suitable for farming. It would then build new farming villages in these areas and relocate agricultural workers to them.

The government purchased portions of private farms for settlement and repurposed some national lands and farmlands owned by municipalities, paving the way for a blend of settler- and tiller-style reforms. From the 1940s to the 1970s, the government created almost 300 new villages and built more than 30,000 houses. It built dams and channels, dug irrigation ditches, and constructed infrastructure such as roads and power lines. The program came to encompass nearly 2.5 million acres of land.[40]

The Doñana region became one of the government's targets for land conversion through this program. Engineers, agronomists, and military men envisioned transforming the area into farmland by draining the swamps and installing infrastructure. They were encouraged by an experiment by a private company in the northern fringes of the Doñana region that had built dikes and dug drainage channels in the 1920s and 1930s and had eventually begun cultivating rice.

Construction on the Lower Guadalquivir Canal began in 1940 with the intent of eventually draining the swamps on the left bank of the river and bringing fresh water to the area in order to wash the salts from the land and make it more suitable for farming. It was a massive and labor-intensive effort that took more than twenty years to complete. The project eventually became known as the Prisoner's Canal, because it relied heavily on the labor of thousands of political prisoners from Spain's civil war and its aftermath.[41]

Bernis and Valverde embarked on their fateful trip to Doñana as the canal progressed and the government began draining portions of Doñana's marshes. The government declared the transformation of marsh areas into cropland a major national interest shortly after their visit in 1955. At the same time, it began constructing the first new town in the area. It built ten towns from scratch on the left bank in the swamp and on its outskirts over the course of the next decade and constructed over 1,000 homes for new settlers.[42] These towns and their agricultural fields eventually swallowed the entirety of the marshes on the left bank of the Guadalquivir, which made up roughly one-third of the marshland in the Doñana area. In place of the marshes arose neatly arrayed fields of rice, cereals, legumes, and vegetables.

The result was severe loss of the natural ecosystems in the Doñana area. Nearly 185,000 acres of marshland were converted into agricultural land.[43] This was roughly the same size as the Chacabuco Valley that Tompkins Conservation donated to Chile for Patagonia National Park. It was an immediate blow to bird nesting grounds along with fish, reptile, amphibian, and insect populations. Damage to the remaining natural ecosystems was also severe. Farmers began dumping pesticides on their crops, including DDT, that trickled into the broader water system and compromised bird populations and health.

Soil erosion associated with intensive agricultural use increased sedimentation in the marshes, disturbing habitats and the natural flooding cycles.

Meanwhile, the threat from reforestation was brewing on the other side of the Doñana. Millions of pine and eucalyptus trees were planted in sandy areas and on portions of marshland at the western edges of the area in 1952 and 1953. The plantations, especially of eucalyptus, sucked up vast quantities of water from underground aquifers, desiccating the neighboring marshland habitats. Human activity was destroying the Doñana from both sides.

Focused instead on development, Franco visited the area in 1953 to supervise the reforestation progress. He also visited Mauricio González-Gordón's property in Doñana, where he had hunted years earlier. In contrast to Bernis and Valverde's visit the previous year to examine and inquire about bird life and the natural ecosystems, Franco had a more self-interested query that stemmed from one of his few hobbies: "Are the plantations good for hunting?" Not long after the visit, González-Gordón paid a visit to Franco to answer that question with a letter written by Bernis but signed by González-Gordón. It described the threats that the reforestation project posed to Doñana's natural environment—and to its use as a hunting ground.[44] A decade later, following the birth of the World Wildlife Fund and the activism of Valverde, Bernis, and other naturalists, a piece of González-Gordón's property formed the kernel of what would become Doñana National Park.

PROTECTIONS OF THE natural landscape and its ecosystems at Doñana sought to dial back the damage wrought by the prior settler reforms in and around the park. The government bought out the private landowners within the national park's boundaries. It banned hunting and agriculture within the park, placed strict limitations on grazing for the remaining cattle, and uprooted invasive species such as eucalyptus trees. These conservation steps enabled damaged habitats and threatened species to regenerate. Tight regulations were imposed on hunting, fishing, and agriculture in the buffer areas of the park.

With José Antonio Valverde's guidance and political finesse, the government also built a landmark biological station at Doñana that Valverde stepped in to run. It came to manage two reserve areas within the park that are solely devoted to wildlife conservation and scientific research on ecology, biological diversity, and the impacts of development and climate change on the environment. The station started monitoring water quality in Doñana for heavy metals, pesticides, and other contaminants.

Environmental protections in Doñana increased further after its declaration as a UNESCO World Heritage Site in 1994 and in the wake of a 1998 mining disaster that unleashed millions of tons of toxic waste in rivers and marshes upstream from Doñana, destroying bird habitats and killing an enormous number of fish. Environmental groups, including the WWF, along with the Spanish government, the European Union, and even corporate donors, stepped up conservation and restoration efforts.[45] In 2005, the government began a marsh restoration project. It reverted several thousand acres of converted agricultural land back into marshland in the northern part of Doñana and annexed them to the national park in 2006. It also reconnected parts of the marshes to the river that had been blocked off from them by walls built in the 1980s and that had reduced the flow of sediments into the marsh, enabling the return of amphibians, reptiles, and fish.[46] The government more recently started making major investments to limit water extraction from the aquifers on which the wetlands, as well major agricultural interests, depend. And the provincial government of Andalusia expanded the natural buffer area around the park in 2016. Today some 30 percent of the Doñana region's wetlands have status as protected natural areas.[47]

One of the greatest legacies of land conservation in Doñana for the environment actually extends beyond its boundaries. The fight to save Doñana's natural landscape birthed one of the world's premier organizations for wilderness preservation and sparked environmental activism across Spain and internationally. Groups like the Spanish Ornithological Society (SEO Birdlife), which Valverde helped to found, Spain's branch of the WWF, Spain's branch of Greenpeace, Ecologists in Action (Ecologístas en Acción), and other groups all organize to protect environmentally sensitive Spanish territory threatened by development initiatives. While they have various roots, all have been propelled by the fight against ongoing environmental damage wrought by a myopic focus on development and industrialization that Franco crystallized in areas such as Doñana but that carried on well past his rule. These groups have time and again halted extensions of Franco's vision to manipulate the natural environment in the service of economic development. One recent example is the shuttering of the Ebro River Transfer, a herculean plan to build a network of dams and pipes to transfer water out of the Ebro river system in the north of Spain into four other river systems hundreds of miles away.

Today a sea of greenhouses under white plastic sheets extend as far as the eye can see to the northwest of Doñana. The sheets cover the area's billion-dollar strawberry, raspberry, and blueberry industry that feeds Europe's insatiable berry appetite. These berries are the new eucalyptus trees for Doñana: their growers draw vast quantities of water from the aquifer that feeds Doñana, a considerable portion of it illegally.[48] That puts water resources for the marshes at risk. Local water authorities troll the area in search of illegal wells that are overdrawing water resources, but so far they have been no match for the powerful industry.

The fact that Doñana has become progressively encircled by agricultural and industrial activity over the past seventy-five years puts it in peril. In addition to episodic threats such as the 1998 mining disaster, and the water-hungry berry industry, other intensive agricultural use at the edges of the park and the neighboring Matalascañas beach resort are placing major stresses on the water supplies on which local ecosystems rely. The settlements on the left bank of the Guadalquivir that the Franco government created in the 1950s and 1960s, for instance, are now hot spots for environmental violations in the area.[49]

Water inputs to the Doñana are now half of what they were in the 1960s, and one-fifth of what occurred naturally before modifications to the river systems that feed it.[50] Climate change further exacerbates this problem. In the summer of 2022, the last permanent freshwater lagoon in the park temporarily dried up as temperatures soared and a multiyear drought continued.

Precarious as it is, the heart of Doñana nonetheless remains an unrivaled natural area and critical wildlife sanctuary. And it serves as a monument to the idea that humans can repurpose land to reclaim and protect the natural environment. Other natural areas of Spain suffered more than the Doñana area under the Franco government as it transformed the landscape through land settlement. For instance, while it was building the Lower Guadalquivir Canal and new farming settlements in the marshes of the Doñana, it was also building a series of dams and new towns in the Upper Ebro Valley at the foot of the Pyrenees Mountains. While the projects opened up more land for agriculture, they also severely compromised the environment. Agriculture on the new farmlands increased the salinity of local soils and introduced a wave of chemicals and pesticides that poisoned watersheds. The dams and reservoirs also drastically reduced the sediment flowing out to the ecologically rich but sensitive Ebro Delta, weakening it against rising seas and storms and putting bird and sea-life habitats at even graver risk than in Doñana. The government now spends millions of euros annually to truck sediment from the Upper Ebro River to the coast to try to stabilize it and prevent the Mediterranean Sea from running far upstream and washing over the delta.

* * *

HUMANS AND THE natural environment coevolved for millennia before people started to destroy it. Indigenous peoples in particular are well versed in stewarding natural areas across the globe in ways that preserve biodiversity and natural resources and that respect the environment. Humans can also develop more environmentally friendly practices on private land. Those practices can range from homeowners sowing native plants in their yards in support of pollinators to farmers adopting organic and regenerative agriculture that restores soils and watersheds rather than depleting them.

Governments and their land policies play a critical role in encouraging sustainable practices through regulations, subsidies and other incentives, and protections. The Conservation Reserve Program in the United States, for example, a program under the US Department of Agriculture, provides funding for agricultural producers to take environmentally sensitive lands out of production and undertake active restoration and conservation measures. Government agencies can also contract with private landowners for conservation easements that provide environmental protections for land. Minnesota's Department of Natural Resources runs a program along these lines as it seeks to restore native prairies.

Land use regulations and sustainable management practices will have increasing importance as growing populations continue to place pressure on natural resources and landscapes. They are weaker and messier tools than the creation of parklands, are more subject to reversals, and often have a greater effect on slowing the degradation of the natural environment than on restoring it to its more robust and complete prior state. Humans have yet to harness the willpower and to master the art and science of reconstructing whole ecosystems at a large scale. But if climate change and the extinction crisis are to be slowed or reversed, land has to be put to work for conservation across the globe, and fast.

CHAPTER 10

THE RETURN OF THE DISPOSSESSED

THE TYPICALLY QUIET TENBOSCH SUGARCANE FARM ACROSS THE Crocodile River from Kruger National Park in South Africa was abuzz. On June 19, 2007, Black residents from nearby communities, white businesspeople, and government functionaries gathered under the expansive, mostly cloudy sky. South Africa's minister for agriculture and land affairs, Lulama Xingwana, stepped to the front of the crowd to do something seismic in a country undergoing rapid change: return an enormous swath of prime agricultural land to four Black indigenous communities that had been forced off of it during the country's racially discriminatory apartheid era. The date marked the anniversary of the fateful 1913 Natives Land Act, which had enabled the white-run government to forcibly remove millions of Black South Africans from their land and relocate them into cramped and far-flung "homelands." "The dispossession of land rights," Minister Xingwana noted, "stripped the communities of their dignity and rendered them landless and second class citizens in the country of their birth." She made a solemn vow: "I want to say to the four communities, the African National Congress (ANC) led government is committed to ensure that the wrongs of the past are corrected, and that there is redress for the victims of racially motivated land dispossessions."[1]

The joyous ceremony marked one of the largest land transfers in South Africa's land restitution program until that point. Several other communities extended the restitution claim shortly after the ceremony. By 2008, the government had settled claims transferring over 150,000 acres of land to seven Black communities in South Africa's northeastern Nkomazi region with more than 20,000 beneficiaries.[2] It paid white farmers nearly half a billion dollars to hand over their land.

When I spoke with the chairperson of the trust representing one of the communities, Petros Silinda of the Ngomane Siboshwa, he vividly recalled signing the agreement with the government to return the land: "That was an experience that I will take to the grave. It was so emotional."[3] Another member of the same community whose parents, like Silinda's, had suffered forced removal from their land—in their case in 1954, only to be dumped far away with nothing but the clothes on their backs—reported that "after they got the beneficiary number, especially my mother she was so excited, even today she is still excited."[4]

The minister also gave a nod to the land's former white owners, saying, "I am pleased with the commitment shown by TSB . . . and the others to offer settlement support to the new land owners." TSB was one of South Africa's major sugar producers and plantation owners. All of its sugarcane came from fields in and around the Nkomazi area. The company began cooperatively working with the government and communities on restitution in 1998 and eventually sold the government over 90 percent of its land for reallocation to Black communities. It also helped to bring along other white commercial sugarcane farmers.

The land restitution shifted sugarcane production in the region away from white commercial growers and toward Black communities.[5] But after decades of marginalization away from their ancestral land, most beneficiaries of the land claim were poor and had little knowledge of commercial farming. As Silinda, who eventually came to work with TSB and the company that later acquired it, RCL Foods, on his community's behalf, told a reporter, "It was challenging for us as a community because we didn't have the expertise. . . . We had to look for a partner with experience."[6]

TSB wanted to remain in the lucrative sugar industry and stepped up to work with the Nkomazi communities. As the company's director of agricultural operations, Dawie van Rooy, put it, the company made the judgment that "if we want a stable community, we don't have an option. We have to sell this land. And we have to implement a . . . [community] partnership . . . that ensures sustainable cane supply."[7]

TSB spent years planning a smooth handover to communities and ways to form an enduring partnership. It forged fifty-fifty joint venture agreements with several communities and began leasing sugarcane farmland from the community trusts and associations, which in turn also pay a share of profits to communities. It gave the joint ventures technical and operational support and provided training and skills development to members as well as jobs. That included a scholarship program to train and educate community members for operational and strategic management, in effect grooming them for leadership positions. The company began hiring more community members at its sugar mills, and the joint ventures started to hire community members for contract work such as farm maintenance. And TSB invested in Black small-scale sugarcane growers who farmed lands they had been forcibly removed to decades prior, helping to establish and capitalize their enterprises and similarly forging a joint venture agreement with them as a group to foster sustainable production.

Within several years, the partnership that TSB forged with these communities became a model for land restitution and reallocation elsewhere in the country. Reflecting on this legacy, van Rooy said that "it really felt great to make a difference. It was not an easy go. Everything was much more difficult than normal and there were a lot of emotions involved, but the fact that a balanced model was negotiated and implemented with all parties as winners [meant that] there was a lot to be celebrated considering the sustainability and success of this process."[8]

This episode of land restitution is one of thousands being used to dismantle South Africa's racial hierarchy that began with white colonial settlement and reached its apex during apartheid with mass forced removal of Black indigenous communities from their land. It is a fraught, expensive, and exceptionally complex project, given the monumental scale of racially motivated land dispossession and rights violations. It has encountered controversy, opposition, and plenty of failures. But it has also restored dignity, a sense of justice, and even economic opportunity to many Black South Africans. The project is an evolving model of how land can be put to the service of racial justice and reconciliation.

Land is a potent tool in the construction of racial hierarchy. Racial and ethnic groups can rise to dominate others by stealing their land and livelihoods, carving deep ruts across civilizations that endure generations. Those ruts cut straight through economies, politics, and communities.

Yet land reallocation can also be used to deconstruct that hierarchy. The recognition and restitution of land among disadvantaged groups, or reparations to remedy the deep scars of indignity, abuse, and neglect through land takings, can be put to the service of reconciliation and the creation of more just, inclusive, and equitable societies. It is not possible to erase the past through restitution and reparations or to reconstruct it. Histories of dispossession live on through marginalization and inequality that can endure generations or even centuries. Falling behind makes it even harder to catch up when opportunities have passed over several generations of people, descendants have dispersed, and economies have changed. Because of this, land returns cannot easily "undo" what has been done.

But progress can be made. Power has shifted before and it can be shifted again. Land restitution and reallocation are not as new and impossible as we might think. It is a mistake to think that some types of land reallocation are set in stone or irreversible and others are pie in the sky.

Distant though an unwinding of these hierarchies and disparities may seem, the stories of South Africa and Australia reveal the work that is already being done to remedy racial injustice through land restitution, reparations, and reallocation. South Africa is deploying all of these policies to grapple with a brutal and racist British colonial legacy that removed indigenous Blacks from their land and cordoned them off into "black homelands." Putting land back into the hands of Blacks is a critical step in reconciling with and remedying this past. The process has been rocky, but the change is undeniable. Australia is recognizing Aboriginal rights to ancestral land across the country after long-standing policies that sought to push Aboriginals aside, exploit them, and finally to assimilate them into mainstream Australian culture. Aboriginal communities are safeguarding and reclaiming land by demonstrating ties to it through traditional songs, stories, and artwork. These communities now have rights or ownership to more than half of Australia's land, and they are increasingly being treated as partners in resource and land management.

To understand how to right the wrongs of land power, we have to understand how the Great Reshuffle has been steered in the wrong directions over the centuries. What we learn from these stories informs the corrections that are being fought over today.

JUSTICE IN SOUTH AFRICA

Land appropriation was central to the colonial projects in what is now South Africa. Over the course of several centuries, European settlers progressively pushed indigenous groups off their ancestral lands and claimed the land as their own. Europeans linked to the Dutch East India Company first started settling around the Cape of Good Hope in the 1650s. They began competing with local indigenous groups for resources and land as their numbers grew and they moved inland. When the British gained control of the Cape in the early 1800s, many Dutch settlers moved north and east to escape their control. Both the British and the Dutch pushed aside more indigenous groups as settlement expanded and diamonds and gold were discovered.

Land dispossession and racial segregation advanced shortly after the country became independent from Great Britain in 1910.[9] The 1913

Natives Land Act was one of the most consequential policies that the white-minority South African government adopted. The act set up a series of "reserves" for the Black population that covered less than 10 percent of the country's land area. These areas mostly contained marginal, poor-quality land, and they were located in peripheral areas far from centers of power. The act also banned the purchase or lease of land by Blacks outside of those areas. And it outlawed tenant farming and sharecropping on white-owned land, driving Black farmers in those areas into more subservient wage-labor roles. The government separated Blacks from whites in urban residential areas a decade later.

Racial hierarchy and segregation deepened still further several decades later. Apartheid began with the election of the National Party in 1948. The government classified everyone into one of four racial categories: white, Black, coloured, or Indian. Blacks made up over three-quarters of the population and whites about 10 percent. A little less than 10 percent of the population was considered coloured; they lived mainly in western South Africa and had mixed ancestry. Indians made up just a few percent of the population and mostly lived in urban areas.

Each racial category had its own rights and rules under apartheid. A series of removal policies then enabled the government to forcibly displace non-whites from their homes and land in areas of South Africa designated for whites. It relegated most to rural "homelands" (also known as *bantustans*) that largely corresponded to the 1913 reserves. In urban areas, the government instituted rigid racial segregation of residential and business areas and moved non-whites into designated "townships," typically shantytowns at the outskirts of cities.[10] Some 3.5 million people suffered forced relocation.[11]

This process severely disrupted the various communities that ended up in Nkomazi. In the late nineteenth and early twentieth centuries they were dispersed across a wider area and their populations shifted somewhat across territory owing to changing economic opportunities, relations with neighboring communities, and pressure from the government over the creation of a game reserve in what is now Kruger National Park. Eventually the communities became more settled within the Tenbosch area, and many families came to have their own lands that they passed down within their clan-based lineages. These settlements, too, then came under threat as the South African government first sold the area to a land speculation company and then repossessed it in order to dole it out in pieces to white settlers, including some veterans of World War II. Local communities, faced with rising pressure to work in white mining operations or on white-owned farms, resisted being forced into unwanted labor arrangements. The apartheid state considered their residence outside of a "homeland" and among increasing numbers of white farmers as a "black spot" to be removed.

The main episode of removal occurred in late 1954. Government trucks arrived to quickly haul off 7,000 Ngomane people and dump them into a cramped and fractured smaller "homeland" in the south of Nkomazi that later became known as KaNgwane.[12] Petros Silinda of the Ngomane Siboshwa, a current farm manager for his community trust's joint venture with RCL at Tenbosch, told me what his parents and elders had told him about the experience of removal. First, the government "called [the Tenbosch communities] in Komatipoort. Some of the chiefs did not go there. The only chief among the Ngomane that went there was Chief Mpoti, who was with the Lugedlane clan. . . . When Chief Mpoti was with his people he was going there . . . to tell the delegation that we are not going anywhere." When government agents invited Chief Mpoti into a room as the representative of the Ngomane, however, "they closed the door" and "escorted him to the other side where there was a van," to detain him and send him into exile. "By the time it was around 5 p.m., [his] people were hungry, they were waiting for their chief. . . . Then one guy came and said, 'Your chief has agreed that you are going to be removed.' People were angry, and they started throwing stones." Silinda started loudly and repeatedly snapping his fingers to mimic the sound of throwing stones as he continued. "They asked, 'Where is the chief now?' The chief is gone. And they had to go back home. By the time they went home, already the trucks . . . [had] started to remove these people. And it's not like the chief agreed. That's why it was a forced removal. . . . My grandfather was one of the indunas [headmen], and he did not agree. [The Ngomane] Siboshwa did not actually agree, and even the Hoyi group did not actually agree. But they were all removed."

People lost nearly everything they owned during the removal. It occurred just before the maize harvest and happened so quickly that people could not take their animals or possessions with them. There was no infrastructure, housing, or on-site water access where the government trucks dumped them. "We were thrown into the bush where there was nothing," the current chief of the Ngomane Lugedlane explained.[13]

Evictions of neighbouring communities accompanied this removal. And the Black populations that already lived in the south of Nkomazi had to cede territory and move to accommodate the displaced communities.[14] Under apartheid, the government defined and delimited these communities as distinct "tribes." It forced them into areas with limited land access, depriving them of traditional livelihoods and consigning them to poverty. Many community members still live in these areas. TSB had already begun buying up land in the Tenbosch area at this point, and it continued to do so in the ensuing years as it established sugarcane farming in the region.

In tandem with removing non-whites from their land and cordoning them off from the rest of society, the National Party stripped them of their South African citizenship and voting rights, assigning them citizenship within the Black "homelands." The ostensible aim was tribal self-government in these homelands, though in practice the National Party curated cooperative partners in homelands. Every aspect of South African society became infused with racial discrimination propped up by rigid segregation.

The apartheid system began cracking under the weight of its own brutality in the 1980s. Black activists and social movements put increasing pressure on the National Party and cast harsh light on its repressive and anti-democratic core. Foreign governments and investors began to boycott the country and levy sanctions on it. Eventually the National Party came to the negotiating table. In 1990, it released the country's most famous political activist, Nelson Mandela, from prison and legalized opposition movements and parties such as the African National Congress.

IN A WATERSHED moment, South Africa held open democratic elections in 1994. The Black-majority ANC party won in a landslide. The landscape it inherited was deeply scarred by the racialized policies of apartheid and European settlement. Nearly half of the population still lived in rural areas, yet racial inequity rooted in land was stark. The white minority, 11 percent of the population, held 86 percent of all farmland in the country. Most of this land was concentrated in the hands of about 60,000 white farmers.[15] Meanwhile, 13 million Blacks, many of whose forebears had been dispossessed through racially discriminatory practices, were packed into former homelands on largely poor-quality land.

Blacks across the country demanded the restitution of their land rights. The new South African government vowed to reallocate some 60 million acres of agricultural land, about 30 percent of the country's total, by 1999 to redress historical racially based land dispossession. South Africa was poised to embark on one of the most ambitious attempts ever to use land as a tool for deconstructing racial hierarchy.

Land reallocation became a stand-in for the many meanings of reconciliation and justice. A nationally representative survey taken in 2004 showed that 85 percent of Black South Africans felt that "most land in South Africa was taken unfairly by white settlers, and they therefore have no right to the land today."[16] As a valuable asset and a basis for livelihoods that white settlers disrupted, land was a fundamental material demand. Land also held deep symbolic meaning as the embodiment of social and economic loss, the evocation of memory, and the restoration of individual and collective hope.

South Africa's transition to democracy both responded to and placed limits on the demand for land reallocation. There was consensus that the past had to be addressed and remedied. Victims of dispossession won rights of redress. The constitution laid the legal foundation for land reallocation. As Nelson Mandela put it in 1995, "With freedom and democracy last year, came restoration of the right to land. And with it, the opportunity to address the effects of centuries of dispossession and denial. . . . At last we can, as a people, look our ancestors in the face and say: Your sacrifices were not in vain."[17]

But the handover from the apartheid-era National Party to the ANC was painstakingly negotiated and carefully choreographed in ways that restricted this promise. The white minority won major concessions to protect their property and power in exchange for opening up the political system. They secured constitutional protections for property rights, a government of national unity for the first five years of democracy that included the National Party, limits to policies of transitional justice, and a devolution of selected federal powers.

Land reallocation under democracy advanced under two distinct tracks.[18] Both tracks blend tiller-, collective-, and settler-style reforms in that they allocate both private and state-owned land to individuals and community groups as a whole. The first track aims at restitution. The government promised to restore land rights to people who were forcibly removed from their land under racially discriminatory laws and practices after the 1913 Natives Land Act. Victims of land dispossession had to file a restitution claim with the state by the end of 1998 to be eligible to have their land returned or to have access to an alternative remedy, either a grant of a different area of land or financial compensation. The displaced Nkomazi communities pursued getting their land back through the restitution track.

Individuals and communities made nearly 80,000 restitution claims on the part of over 1.5 million people covering both rural and urban land. Most of these cases had been resolved by the mid-2000s through financial compensation, restoration of state-owned land, or grants of private land to claimants that the government had purchased through voluntary sales from owners. But approximately 6,700 claims remained unresolved in 2022, mostly in rural areas.[19] Many of these are complicated and especially consequential claims. Notwithstanding these remaining claims, some 10 million acres of land has been restituted to victims so far. Much of this land has come from the state rather than private farmers.[20] Victims have opted for financial compensation in their removal from another 6 million acres of land.[21]

The second track entails the distribution of land to non-whites as part of reconciliation and reparations that go beyond strictly restitution. It was widely recognized that the extremely high rates of poverty and landlessness among Black indigenous South Africans and those of mixed ancestry at the end of apartheid were due to systematic racial discrimination. This situation cried out for a remedy even for populations that could not concretely trace their family histories to forced removal policies after 1913 or that did not file restitution claims. The goal essentially was to transfer land held overwhelmingly by wealthy white landowners to Black farmers.

The main thrust of a more general policy of land distribution and land reallocation is a market-based "willing seller, willing buyer" reform in line with the World Bank's recommendations. Through this program, the government purchases voluntarily offered private farmland at market value rates.[22] It then gives grants to individual or group applicants to enable them to purchase land in a blended tiller/collective-style reform. Applicants have to be non-white and live on or near the land they aim to acquire.[23]

This policy has also affected the Nkomazi region and the sugar industry there. A number of Black farmers separate from the Nkomazi restitution claimants have applied for and been granted land from previously white-owned farms. Some of these Black farmers began to grow sugarcane and have forged partnerships and contracts with TSB (and later RCL Foods) like those of the land restitution communities.[24]

The market-based land reallocation program has guided the transfer of approximately 18 million acres of land to Black farmers.[25] Research demonstrates that land transfers through the program generate higher consumption and household living standards for most land beneficiaries within several years. These farmers receive clear title deeds to their property, though in some cases the deeds have been delayed by restitution claims over the same land.[26]

Other state programs of land reallocation support and run in parallel to the market-based reform. Most notable is a program that subsidizes beneficiaries to start commercial farms on state-owned property with leases that can be converted to ownership if a farm proves successful and productive. This is essentially a settler-type reform, because it involves state land rather than private land. Although the government has doled out 6 million acres of land in this way, the program has been riddled with corruption and mismanagement and the vast majority of farms have failed.[27]

ONE OF SOUTH Africa's powerful national mythologies in its transition from apartheid to democracy is that the country transcended a rigid racial hierarchy that pitted ruling whites against marginalized Blacks and came to embrace its multicultural diversity as a "rainbow nation." This diversity is reflected in the many indigenous cultures that preceded South Africa's formation as well as in the waves of white settlers, Indians, and others that arrived to its shores. These ideas are wired into the heroization of Nelson Mandela's ascendance, and politicians, social commentators, and church leaders spread them widely in the years after apartheid crumbled.

Critics ranging from populist firebrands to social activists argue that the term is used as empty rhetorical cover for the real racial reconciliation and transformation required for authentic multiculturalism. They point to legacies of racism, inequality, and crime that live on from the apartheid era in brutal ways. The country remains one of the most unequal places on earth. Blacks earn on average a sixth of what whites earn.[28] Unemployment has been stuck above 20 percent for years. And murder rates are among the highest in the world. Other critics who are dissatisfied with the new role of Blacks in society point to these same figures as evidence that emphasizing diversity and multiculturalism has failed and that the country is mismanaged and on the wrong path.

But the abundant challenges that continue to face the country do not negate significant advances in restitution and reconciliation. These are unambiguously complicated and messy processes. Yet to South Africa's credit, it has seriously grappled with them. It has restituted and restored millions of acres of land to rural Black South Africans, transferred many thousands of housing plots to urban Blacks, and provided reparations to a large set of victims of apartheid-era human rights abuses. Many people who have received land are better off now than in the past even if it has not made them wealthy. And many of those who have opted for compensation over land have invested their awards in durable benefits such as improvements in their homes.[29]

The symbolic value of these national efforts has also helped construct and sustain a shared narrative, replicated in national discourse, memorials, and museums, of past racial transgressions and the necessity to reconcile with them. And for individual claimants, restitution invokes memory and is used to create meaning. As one study of restitution beneficiaries put it, "While the bulldozing of their homes symbolized the demolition of their dignity, the commission's provision of land and homes became a symbol of dignity resurrected."[30] Even cash payments have been imbued with meaning through creative uses that are often linked to home and belonging and in various ways to symbolizing history.[31]

The settlement between TSB, now RCL, and the Nkomazi communities reflects this historic shift. The communities that received land and formed joint ventures with RCL have sustained high levels of productivity. Community members now serve as farm managers and officers, work in large numbers at the sugar mills, and engage in contract labor with the joint ventures.[32] Small-scale sugar farmers in the former homeland regions have seen rising incomes, and many have been able to afford improved housing, vehicles, and better education for their children.[33] There has also been growth in midsize Black farms and the development of a Black professional and managerial class within the sugar industry.[34] All of this has transpired over the course of years amid turnover at RCL, within the communities and their trusts, and within the joint ventures.

Some beneficiaries of the restituted communities are now members of the Black professional class working with RCL as joint venture managers, straddling what was previously a stark and impenetrable divide. One of them is Edward Ndlovu, whom I interviewed. "You have to have two characters, one as a [joint venture] employee with RCL and another as a beneficiary. . . . It's so challenging, but it's so exciting, to work in that place knowing that you are giving something back to the community that raised you. . . . We call it the spirit of ubuntu in South Africa: A person is a person by another people," he said. "We are so happy to work for this wonderful company and also make money for them so that they can get to the end of the year. When [beneficiaries] get the money [annual trust payouts], they don't even know you, you see them in town, you meet them at the bus station, they will be talking, they will say they have received the certificate [payment]. They are so happy, and you played a big role in making them benefit."[35]

Land conflict between the Nkomazi communities and whites in the area has also subsided, even if it has not entirely resolved. The secretary of one of the community trusts, recalling the period before restitution, said, "We would at times fight with the white people because they did not want to let go of the land. We are all happy now that it is over."[36] When I spoke with Dave Thomson, the RCL executive of the partnership with small-scale growers and a director of the community joint ventures, he echoed that sentiment. Amid a climate of contestation over ownership and labor in farming communities around the country, he noted that "not one of the farms have been invaded, damaged, burnt, vandalized, or protested around and shut down. . . . The community feels they are RCL/TSB, and TSB feels they are the community."[37]

There are plenty of other similar cases. The Makuleke community reclaimed ownership of part of the renowned Kruger National Park and now leases it to the park while jointly managing its conservation and profiting from its commercial use for tourism. The Giba community reclaimed its ancestral land from white farmers in Mpumalanga

Province and turned to growing high-value crops while employing women and starting a program to train young people in farming. The Cremin community, which had been forcibly removed from land in KwaZulu-Natal in the 1970s, regained it and reconstituted itself. And while urban land restitution is complicated by population pressure and high real estate prices, there are some successes there, too, such as in Gqeberha (formerly Port Elizabeth).

These episodes have deeply marked the people in these communities and have contributed to restoration and reconciliation. The Giba community trust leader reported that "the farm will restore hope and create more job opportunities. The Giba community is already benefitting."[38] In Cremin, one community member, reflecting on how whites returned their land, said that "it means the wounds were really healed." Another said of the community, "We are consoled."[39] In Port Elizabeth, the land restitution authority chief executive reflected that "it was important for people to acknowledge there was an injustice and that, in some way, there was compensation for it."[40]

Of course, with a past so brutal and the path out of it so complex and charged, there are also many failures and disappointments. Some high-profile restitution projects have collapsed, such as Elandskloof in the Western Cape, and the initially successful Zebediela citrus farm in Limpopo. Others have underdelivered and faced long delays, such as the resettlement of the District Six area of Cape Town, which the apartheid government bulldozed to the ground.

These flops are only a small sample of a heap of discouraging failures.[41] And many smaller projects have failed to live up to the expectations of beneficiaries. Those failures understandably cast a shadow on successes.

There is even ample discontent among some members of land restitution communities from the Nkomazi area. Some people criticize the deal with TSB even while recognizing its importance for skills transfer and farming continuity, arguing that TSB and other white-dominated commercial sugar enterprises received handsome payments for land that was previously stolen from indigenous Blacks, retained control of sugar operations through their joint ventures, and should pay more in leasing fees and dividends to communities. The chairperson of one community trust in the region that has suffered management problems feels that land restitution "was a bitter pill to swallow." In an interview, he told me, "We can say the land did come back to us as the dispossessed. But in reality, if . . . I give you something back but you must partner with so and so, that means that the land didn't really come back to me. It's only a business transaction."[42] Furthermore, joint ventures with several communities of the broader Tenbosch restitution claim not linked to TSB failed and communities had to forge a different path. And there are continuing struggles over governance within some of the community trusts and associations that have held up community distributions and hampered community involvement, souring beneficiaries on the broader arrangements.

PROGRESS ON LAND restitution and racial reconciliation has been both rocky and real. That is in keeping with South Africa's broader struggles. Black South Africans now dominate politics and the government, and the civil service, police, and military are far more representative of the population than they were in the apartheid era. But it remains a land of inequality and unfulfilled dreams.

Restitution and reparations in South Africa remain incomplete. While the government has transferred about 34 million acres to Black farmers since the end of apartheid, this is still only half of what it promised to complete by 1999. The government has pushed back the deadline to finish land transfers several times and is now aiming for 2030. Even that date remains a pipe dream. Meanwhile, urban restitution has been truncated. Restoring whole urban landscapes is politically infeasible and practically impossible given both the cost and the intervening changes in the population and economy.

Part of the reason that restitution and reparations have been so difficult, slow, and messy is that Black South Africans are not a simple, undifferentiated group. The creation of Blacks as a racial category was a long-term and incomplete project of domination that sought to erase differences among indigenous communities and regions and replace those differences with a single, monolithic underclass. Under that socially constructed facade of commonality lay different communities with different relations to the land and property and unique histories of dispossession. The reality is that these different communities, and the people within them, require tailored treatment in restitution and reparations.

There is also a litany of more prosaic reasons why restitution has proceeded slowly and fitfully. Some of these derive from the fact that society has radically changed since the time of the Natives Land Act and early policies of forced removal under apartheid. Applying restitution at the local level requires distinguishing specific legitimate beneficiaries from others. It entails grappling with what are often poorly documented histories and addressing inevitable conflicts between landowners and claimants, between claimants and the state, and even between different claimants to the same land.[43] These issues are complicated by others, including advancing urbanization, as well as generational change, which shifts interests, memories, and opportunities. Such factors are commonplace in restitution and not unique to South Africa.

In addition to a slower than anticipated restitution process, many new farmers struggle on the rural land they receive. The land restitution commission originally viewed its role as simply transferring plots of land, and its job as complete once it handed over a farm to a claimant. That narrow focus led to failure among many early land recipients. Beneficiaries need comprehensive and sustained support from both national and local-level governments in order to begin down the path to a more holistic restoration and then thrive in the longer term as they build a new life in the modern economy. Those receiving commercial farms also need partnerships with existing commercial farmers to more quickly gain access to capital, markets, and expertise. The government has learned this lesson and has turned some floundering projects around and set other recent ones off on better footing. But it still faces limited budgets and turnover in policies and personnel within the institutions charged with restoring material losses and a sense of justice to the majority of the population.

Individual land struggles are aggravated by changing population dynamics. South Africa's population has multiplied rapidly since the time of land displacement. There are far more descendants of victims than victims themselves. Descendants often have very different views of what to do with the land and struggle to reach common ground among themselves. This situation fuels infighting, underinvestment, corruption, and an inability to effectively work with critical government, private-sector, and nonprofit partners.

The government is responding to growing popular discontent with the slow pace and spotty record of land restitution and reparations by trying to do more, and to do it faster. It is formulating a path to hasten land reallocation by dropping the "willing seller, willing buyer" principle in favor of a "just and equitable" principle that opens the door to government-led expropriation of land at submarket rates. This approach is especially popular among those who believe that the very notion of paying white landowners at market rates for land that had been stolen from indigenous Blacks is rotten at its core. It simultaneously faces stiff resistance from critics who view it as a form of populist pandering, or even reverse racism, sacrificing white commercial farmers to Blacks who may have little experience farming.

The government is also trying to expand the land restitution track by reopening the claims process that initially ended in 1998. President Jacob Zuma supported this idea in a 2014 speech to traditional leaders around the country, saying, "The critical problem that we found was that the process of taking the land from indigenous people took centuries, it took different forms and finally ended with the huge majority of the indigenous people with no land. It took wars, it took laws, many things. But when we were supposed to address this matter, we were only given a few years to deal with it. We felt it was unfair and indeed it excluded many other people."[44] The government reopened the claims process that year, but it was subsequently halted because of a conflict between the Constitutional Court and the legislature.[45] This tense holdup promises another attempt at expanding land restitution in the future.

It is easy to focus on the growing pains and shortfalls of this process and to miss the progress. South Africa has forged a path toward correcting the mistakes of previous land reshuffles in the country. But it is only one of many. There are rumblings of other projects to give the land back elsewhere.

THE AUSTRALIAN PATH TO RECONCILIATION

In mid-May 2023, Aboriginal communities in Australia's northeast Arnhem Land celebrated the life of the former longtime Gumatj clan leader of the Yolngu people, Galarrwuy Yunupingu. Yunupingu had been a lifelong champion of Aboriginal land rights across the country. Australian prime minister Anthony Albanese attended his public memorial and celebrated his "unbending belief in the need for Aboriginal people to hold their future in their own hands."[46]

Four days later, on May 22, that belief became closer to reality. In a landmark decision with wide-ranging repercussions, the Federal Court ruled that the Gumatj clan was potentially eligible for compensation over a government land grab of a chunk of Yolngu territory that the government held in their interest.[47]

The main episode occurred in early 1963. While apartheid was at its height in South Africa and the government was forcibly removing Blacks from their land, the Australian government intervened in the Yirrkala area with the aim of handing a piece of the Yolngu reserve over to a company to mine bauxite. When the government created the "exclusively Aboriginal" Arnhem Land Aboriginal Reserve in 1931, the Yolngu thought their land was safe from outside incursions. But they were wrong. The government caved two decades later to mining interests and opened their region up to prospecting.

The Yolngu were not consulted in the land seizure and they resisted it. They sent a petition to the House of Representatives demanding their land back. Although he was only a teenager at the time, Yunupingu attended the drafting of the petition. The argument in the petition was simple: "The land in question has been hunting and food gathering land for the Yirrkala tribes from time immemorial: we were all born here." Furthermore, the Yolngu argued, "the procedures of the excision of this land and the fate of the people on it were never explained to them beforehand, and were kept secret from them."[48] The government denied the Yolngu petition, and a court case the Yolngu launched in 1969 also failed. Mining went ahead. The Yolngu began receiving mining royalties under statutory land rights in the region that came several years later, but they still wanted a more direct say in the control and use of their land.

Decades later, after a transformation in the treatment of Aboriginal and Torres Strait Islander people's land and communities, including the recognition of Aboriginal "native title" to ancestral land, Yunupingu tried again. In 2019, on behalf of his Gumatj clan, Yunupingu filed a claim for native land title in Arnhem Land and also lodged an application for compensation for the government's actions in the area that adversely affected the community and its land. The government argued in court that it had the authority to overrun native title and that it did not have to provide just compensation for property it repurposed in that region of Australia. The Federal Court rejected all of the government's arguments and allowed the case to proceed.

The new leader of the Gumatj clan, Yunupingu's brother Djawa Yunupingu, hailed the decision. "Although my brother did not live to hear today's judgment, he would have been pleased that the Federal Court's decision recognised the fundamental right of First Nations People to be treated equally by Australian law," he said. The case, he noted, is "a continuation of his [Galarrwuy Yunupingu's] life's work . . . to have Native Title properly recognised as the heart of the identity of all First Nations People."[49]

The Yolngu case is part of a momentous transformation in the treatment of Aboriginal and Torres Strait Islander people, also known as First Nations people, in Australia. As Djawa Yunupingu indicated, land is at the core of that transformation. The recognition of indigenous authority over their land serves as a bedrock for autonomy, self-determination, and symbolic parity in social status with other Australians. It also confers control of valuable resources that can be used to enhance the welfare of Aboriginal communities and chip away at Australia's racial hierarchy, in which whites fare far better than Aboriginals on nearly every social and economic indicator. Paired with a growing share of government support aimed at remedying centuries of abuse and maltreatment, Australia for the first time in its history has the chance to flatten its racial hierarchy. "To live comfortably with the rest of Australia," Djawa told me, "is what we have always been trying to do."[50]

The recognition and return of land to First Nations people in Australia has been long overdue and it has been contested in every way for decades. But it has also advanced considerably in ways that cannot easily be undone, putting Australia on a new trajectory in its relations with Aboriginal communities. First Nations people now have native title over about 40 percent of Australia, and that figure is growing.[51] Along with First Nations ownership in other areas and shared land access, First Nations communities now have rights or ownership in slightly over 50 percent of Australia's land.

The nature of these rights and ownership differ considerably across Australia's states and territories in accordance with differences in statutory and common law. First Nations people own more land and have stronger land rights in the western half of Australia than in the east. The Northern Territory where the Yolngu live stands out as the high point of Aboriginal land rights, notwithstanding remaining contestation over claims and rights. But land rights are slowly expanding in prized eastern and coastal areas as well.

GREAT BRITAIN STARTED settling Australia in the late 1700s, just a few decades prior to gaining a beachhead at the tip of South Africa. Captain James Cook first mapped the east coast and claimed it for Great Britain in 1770. The British then set up a penal colony there in 1788, and a mix of free white settlers and convicts began trickling over to the continent that is known today as Australia.

The new settlers encountered some of the oldest human cultures on the planet when they arrived. Aboriginal Australians descended from an early wave of human migration out of Africa a little over 70,000 years ago.[52] At the time of British contact, they were divided into hundreds of groups across the continent and spoke several hundred different languages. Most were hunter-gatherers, and their ties to the land were intimate and complex. Tribal members traditionally inherited land access and use rights to clan or sub-clan territories through the male line, but could also hunt and gather in other selected areas and had additional access rights from the mother's side. These arrangements were infused with spiritual and religious elements. The land, animals, and people have their origins in "Dreamtime," a reference to a creation story that continues to operate, manifest, and be revealed in the present. For the Yolngu, ties to the land since time immemorial and the meanings, "dreams," and songlines associated with it form a constitution of sorts.[53]

This rich history was unknown to the British at the time of their settlement. And it did not prevent them from making one of the largest land grabs in their imperial history. Over the course of the next century and then some, Britain plowed ahead with an expansive settler reform in Australia similar to the one in South Africa. It settled Australia with a mix of racism and willful ignorance. As top British government advisers put it in 1887, Australia was a "land practically unoccupied without settled inhabitants or settled law" and without settled farming.[54]

By that time, however, it was well known that Aboriginals had inhabited most of the continent. The British nonetheless justified taking their land based on the fact that Aboriginal cultures did not have a centralized sovereign state that could speak on their behalf or anything like British conceptions of individual and excludable property rights. As a House of Commons report put it in an 1837 report, Aboriginals were "barbarous" and "entirely destitute of the rudest forms of civil polity."[55] In essence, and without formally invoking it at the time, the British operated in accordance with an international legal doctrine known as *terra nullius,* which enables sovereign powers to occupy, claim, and administer land that "belongs to no one." For the British, who judged Aboriginal civilizations as barbaric and without government, Aboriginals were not equals and their land could simply be taken.

On Australia's Eastern Seaboard, colonial state governments doled out tract after tract of land to white settlers and gave them legal ownership, expelling Aboriginals. Other white settlers squatted on eastern Aboriginal lands and eventually came to own them, too. White pastoralists that ranched cattle or sheep claimed sections of the vast arid areas of interior central and western Australia, setting up what became known as "stations." The stock destroyed the local ecosystems on which Aboriginals relied for food. With no good alternatives, many Aboriginals formed encampments at the headquarters of stations and worked for settlers, often under exploitative or even slave-like conditions, in exchange for food staples. Others migrated to towns or missions. Yet another set of Aboriginals lived in more lightly managed "reserves" separate from whites.

As the British and Australian colonial governments displaced Aboriginals en masse from their land and European diseases ravaged their populations, a second strain of British policy arose: "protection." The British government appointed "chief protectors" of Aboriginals in each colony to safeguard them from violence and the vices of white settlement, especially alcohol. Protection policy amounted to segregation in practice. It quickly devolved into an ugly form of control and included restrictions on movement and the forced removal of mixed children from their parents.

Segregation policy endured well into the 1950s and 1960s when a new policy of assimilation replaced it. The Australian government pivoted to treating Aboriginals like other Australians before the law, focusing on individual rights and liberties and ignoring their unique ties to the land and any desires to live autonomously. For the first time since Australia had become independent, it extended voting rights to Aboriginals and included them in the census. But it continued to ignore the core issue for Aboriginals that had driven them to the bottom of Australia's racial hierarchy on nearly every social, economic, and symbolic dimension: their dispossession from the land.

The Yolngu people helped force land into the foreground of public consciousness in the 1960s. Their petition to the government to drop its appropriation of their land to a mining company, crafted on tree bark, touched off a national stir. The House of Representatives organized a committee to determine how to proceed. The committee held several hearings, including one in Yirrkala where the Yolngu lived. When the committee chair asked the Yolngu elder Milirrpum about whether mining should come to their land, and could perhaps benefit them, Milirrpum replied, in language invoking the rich array of cultural ties and responsibilities to land associated with the term "country": "This [is] aboriginal people's place. We want to hold this country. We do not want to lose this country."[56] The government ignored their pleas and went ahead with the mining project. In 1968, it signed its approval for a Swiss and Australian mining conglomerate called Nabalco to exploit the bauxite reserves. In the coming years, Djawa Yunupingu recounted to me, "they came and they destroyed the land and they put a mine in the middle of my ancestors' country."[57]

The Yolngu did not give up. Against a backdrop of growing Aboriginal activism, most notably the Gurindji people's walk-off at the Wave Hill cattle station to demand their land back, several Yolngu clan leaders, including Milirrpum and Galarrwuy Yunupingu's father, launched a legal case against the company, arguing that they had held land rights to the area since time immemorial and that the government should recognize those rights. The judge in the case instead ruled that "the doctrine of native title" had no legal basis in Australian law.

Although the Yolngu lost the case, it marked a turning point for Aboriginals. A 1972 election brought the Labor Party into power. Under party leader Gough Whitlam, Labor leaders incorporated Aboriginal land rights into their campaign. Whitlam appointed one of the lawyers who worked on the case for the Yolngu, Edward Woodward, to head an Aboriginal Land Rights Commission, charging it with making recommendations for introducing land rights legislation. Woodward's report advocated for "the provision of some basic compensation in the form of land for those Aborigines who have been irrevocably deprived of the rights and interests which would otherwise have been inherited from their ancestors."

This call was met through landmark legislation in 1976 known as the Aboriginal Land Rights (Northern Territory) Act. For the first time, Aboriginals could claim ownership over their land or over state-owned land in the Northern Territory, where a disproportionately large share of Aboriginals live, if they could prove traditional association to it through songs, stories, or rituals. The land could not be bought, sold, or mortgaged, and therefore could not be taken or given away. Ownership also came with some control of key resources and royalty streams, making Aboriginal land rights in the territory superior to those elsewhere, both at the time and up to the present. In practice, the government vested ownership in Aboriginal land trusts and set up land councils to mediate between trusts and outside parties.

The legislation marked a radical repositioning of the Australian government toward Aboriginals. It came with broader social change. Discourse on Aboriginal policy shifted from assimilation to self-determination. And in the 1980s, in the Northern Territory and elsewhere, many Aboriginals began to move out of larger Aboriginal towns into smaller homeland communities where they had traditional ties to the land.

The act and claims eventually came to transfer half of the Northern Territory to Aboriginal ownership, more than initially envisioned. Subsequent litigation extended land claims into the productive intertidal coastal fisheries. But the act had limitations. The biggest was that it only applied to the Northern Territory, which was administered by the federal government. Most of the Aboriginal population living in other Australian states, with a few exceptions, still lacked recourse to traditional land claims.[58] That would change in the 1990s with a bombshell court decision that finally opened the door to broader Aboriginal land recognition.

AUSTRALIA'S HIGH COURT issued a historic decision in 1992 that upended policy dating back to the time it was a British colony: they ruled that Aboriginal and Torres Strait Islander people could hold "native title" to land based on traditional laws and customs that would be recognized under Australian common law. The case revolved around a claim brought by Eddie Mabo of the Meriam people against the state of Queensland. Mabo, who was from the Murray Islands in the Torres Strait, argued that because the Meriam people had occupied the Murray Islands since time immemorial and farmed there for centuries, they effectively had ownership over the land, and that Queensland had no claim over it even if the Crown still held the root title.

The court largely agreed. While it held that the British Crown and subsequently the Australian government could extinguish native title, it ruled that native title could survive in places where the state did not dispose of it. The court also roundly rejected the more than two-century-old doctrine of *terra nullius* as applied to Aboriginal land. As Justice Gerard Brennan wrote for the majority, "The common law of Australia does not embrace the enlarged notion of *terra nullius* or persist in characterizing the indigenous inhabitants as people too low in the scale of social organization to be acknowledged as possessing rights and interests in land."

The historic court case and the Native Title Act, passed in parliament the following year, gave greater protection to Aboriginal and Torres Strait Islander lands and established a legal basis for lodging claims to recuperate land wrested from them. Several years later the court strengthened native title further by enabling it to operate concurrently with pastoral or mining leases. In other words, those leases did not extinguish native title in remote areas.

Some of the wins for land protections for First Nations peoples of the early and mid-1990s subsequently came under fire. Their scope of rights and ability to claim land through native title diminished under legislation and court decisions in the late 1990s and 2000s. In some circumstances, especially in parts of Australia settled by whites, rights crept toward ensuring protection of heritage and access to sacred sites rather than full control over land. Such rights fall far short of statutory Aboriginal land rights in the Northern Territory, which today remain the "high-water mark" within Australia.[59]

But the process of reconciliation with First Nations peoples has marched on, with land recognition and restitution at the core. Indigenous communities have notched a host of high-profile wins that signify the power that new land policies hold in deconstructing Australia's racial hierarchy by returning dignity, autonomy, and economic resources to indigenous groups. These wins have extended beyond the arid lands of the interior to coastal areas, to valuable resources such as national parks, and to the country's more populous east coast.

In 2021, for instance, the Queensland government returned four national parks, including the iconic Daintree National Park, to the Eastern Kuku Yalanji people. The parks included in the agreement span about 400,000 acres. Dozens of other parks in the area had also been transferred to Aboriginal ownership. The community will regain management over the land after a temporary period of joint stewardship with the Queensland government. Marking the land handover, the Queensland minister for the environment, Meaghan Scanlon, said, "The Eastern Kuku Yalanji people's culture is one of the world's oldest living cultures and this agreement recognises their right to own and manage their Country, to protect their culture and to share it with visitors."[60] The land return "rights the wrongs of the past," the minister noted, and marks "a step forward in that path to reconciliation."[61] A Yalanji leader, reflecting on the deep meaning of getting the land back, also commented on the signing of the agreement, saying, "This is where we belong. . . . All our ancestors called us back to home. I broke down—to get it all back in a battle that we've lost so many, young and old, that fought for country and now it's all back."

A year later, the Queensland government returned an even larger tract, spanning two national parks, two reserves, and other lands, to three indigenous groups that had long campaigned for it. Upon the return of the land, Scanlon emphasized that "this program is fundamentally about land justice." The Aboriginal communities, she said, "were the traditional custodians of this land for thousands and thousands of years—they've cared for country and they rightfully are the best people to work with Queensland Parks and Wildlife Service to manage these really important ecosystems."[62] The communities were thrilled to finally receive their land back. As one community member reported, "There's definitely going to be a brighter future for our kids, our grandkids, our great-great-grandkids. It's such a wonderful feeling—I'm feeling on top of the world."

Land returns like these are taking place around the country. In 2023, the state of Victoria recognized the Eastern Maar people as owners of a considerable tract of coastal land, including part of a national park. Victoria's treaty and First Peoples minister Gabrielle Williams made clear at a land transfer ceremony that the handover was "geared towards one outcome and that is achieving better outcomes for our First Nations people."[63] An Eastern Maar woman who was at the ceremony agreed, saying, "It's a recognition of rights that provides a platform for all things; from economic development to meaningful recognition, so we can ensure that we have the self-determination to secure our rightful place in the future."[64] An Eastern Maar man, filled with pride, said, "The seeds of justice are finally starting to blossom."[65]

DESPITE THE FACT that First Nations people now have rights or ownership of over half of Australia's land, the processes of recognition, restitution, and reconciliation remain incomplete. There remain hard and controversial limits to land returns in Australia. "Settled Australia," and particularly urban areas and lands the British and Australian governments doled out to whites in the process of the colonization of Australia, are off-limits to claims of native title. Most of the land recognized as belonging to Aboriginals is located in remote areas of the country that are peripheral to centers of power, population hubs, and areas of economic dynamism. And the Australian government retains the power to extinguish native title for reasons of state.

Aboriginal communities also have to jump through many bureaucratic hoops in order to claim native title. The claims process is complicated by the fact that demonstrating continuous spiritual and ancestral ties to the land is in many cases difficult, given their histories of displacement and land dispossession and the government movement of people. Reclaiming access to or compensation for lost land faces even steeper hurdles. The result is that the generations that initially suffered land losses have often passed by the time justice is served. Galarrwuy Yunupingu's death prior to the Yolngu receiving native title or compensation for their seized land is a case in point. At a minimum, Aboriginal communities must spend years navigating a purgatory of requirements, gathering proof of their ties to the land or engaging in drawn-out lawsuits to recuperate what is rightfully theirs while missing out on opportunities to enjoy the rights that are due to them.

As for the Yolngu, notwithstanding the recent win for the Gumatj clan in Federal Court, their six-decade-long battle for land continues. Yunupingu's win on behalf of the Gumatj was appealed and therefore faces further tests before a final resolution. Even if the win holds, the Gumatj will only receive compensation for their land that has been lost, rather than the land itself. And other Yolngu clans from the Yirrkala area will need to go through their own processes. Djawa told me that the ongoing struggles and litigation give a sense of powerlessness, even as he holds hope and believes the community is going in the right direction.[66]

History has a long shadow, and for Aboriginal Australians, that shadow is dark. Two centuries of dispossession, cultural erasure, segregation, and assimilation cannot be remedied in a generation or two, even with the best of policies. Discrimination against Aboriginal and Torres Strait Islander people in the media, the workplace, health settings, and elsewhere remains prevalent. Aboriginals earn less income, have poorer health, and suffer higher incarceration rates than non-indigenous Australians.[67]

The growing but still incomplete recognition of Aboriginal land rights in recent decades can serve as a foundation for closing the gap with whites on social and economic well-being. Some Aboriginal communities have already made concrete gains. The process to restitute and recognize Aboriginal land is slow, messy, and fraught, but Australia is making progress in the right direction. If it stays the course for several more generations, its long-standing racial hierarchy rooted in the colonial project of land-taking will notably diminish.

* * *

THE DEMANDS TO return land to dispossessed populations and decolonize society are gaining more and more traction, especially among young people and activists. These demands are radical and profound. But they are not unprecedented. The whole history of the Great Reshuffle shows us that societies have done the unthinkable over and over again: they have reallocated their lands in response to radical demands before. It's not impossible to imagine them doing the same again—and doing it right this time.

The few societies that have engaged in land returns to help undo the racial hierarchies that land appropriation wrought have inevitably grappled with a mountain of quandaries. Why should one generation pay for the past and not another? In many cases, the original transgressors and victims have passed away, and their descendants are left to sort things out, often in a radically different social and political environment. But if a remedy is to be applied, some group has to be the one to take action. How should restitution be weighed against the prospect of disrupting an entire society? Many major cities sit atop stolen lands and serve as home to millions. In some cases, the vast majority of entire countries could be subject to restitution. And where does restitution end? The past cannot be reconstructed. Ways of living have been altered irreversibly. And well-being and opportunity can take generations to repair even under the best of circumstances.

Navigating the mountain of moral and practical questions that come with a new reshuffling of land can be difficult. It can be challenging to get beyond the knee-jerk assumption that reallocating land means choosing a new group of winners and losers. But the reality is that land power has an outsized ability to accelerate prosperity for all. No doubt, the considerations that must go into these decisions are nuanced and context-specific. What is owed to dispossessed Aboriginal Australians, Black South Africans, Native Americans, indigenous Canadians, or Palestinians can differ wildly. But only the societies that open these debates can get to the heart of racial reconciliation using the symbolic and material tool that has deepened division from the time of their founding—land.

CONCLUSION

THE GREAT RESHUFFLE IS NOT OVER. THE TWO BIG MOMENTS that forever shifted land's power in human society correspond to moments when the curve of human population meaningfully shifted. Land first began to acquire power as humans found ways to flourish, harnessing surplus and developing agriculture to build complex early societies. Reshuffling then spread like wildfire as technological and social change began multiplying human populations to an extent that strained and then broke old landholding patterns. This second, more intense phase of reshuffling was further fueled by political drives to create and consolidate nation-states and to commandeer them for reasons of personal gain, ideological fulfillment, and social control. We are still living in this second phase of reshuffling.

It can sometimes feel as if land reshuffles are something very distant, particularly in countries with stable and even calcified political systems. A similar feeling probably prevailed in the years before the French and American Revolutions, before the Great Reshuffle began in earnest. But the same dynamics that subsequently forced land to be reallocated are still present today. Population pressure on the land, strong states with a deep reach into society, and political battles over the control of land and resources are still fueling land competition. As those factors shift and grind like tectonic plates across societies, they spark demands and efforts to reallocate land. More reshuffles are coming.

Current population models suggest that the global human population will peak at 10 billion people before the year 2100. Land pressure will be at its peak in the coming decades. It will also be distributed unevenly. Sub-Saharan Africa, for instance, is anticipating a population boom that will dramatically increase human density on agricultural land in a dynamic reminiscent of what occurred in Europe several hundred years ago and in Latin America a century ago. Popular demands to reshuffle land and political desires to do so will be overwhelming.

The world's population crunch is also occurring at a time when the climate is changing in unprecedented ways, rendering some long-inhabited land unusable and converting previously undesirable land into prime areas for settlement and agriculture. This will generate a rush to extract value from land where it is rapidly disappearing and efforts to appropriate and exploit promising territories. The writing is already on the wall for places that will be submerged with rising sea levels, such as lowland Bangladesh and the Maldives. Northeastern Brazil, the American Southwest, and the African Sahel are also in the danger zone, with long droughts and land degradation already rendering land less usable than in the past, and in some areas even causing it to be barren. By contrast, Canada, Finland and Norway, and even Siberia are becoming more attractive as future destinations. Globalization will supercharge these trends as multinational firms with global supply chains compete with locals to snap up prime lands around the world.

We can already see the surge of competition over land in battles over territory and resources playing out today. Conflicts over cobalt mines in the Congo, the strategic and fertile grain-producing plains of eastern Ukraine, palm oil plantations in Colombia, and agricultural land in the Nuba Mountains of Sudan offer grim harbingers of what may lie ahead when desperate efforts to accumulate land and its resources spill over into violence. But violence and war are not the only possible outcomes. Competition for land could remain fierce but mostly peaceful. For instance, as global ice shields and permafrost melt, remote, far-flung territories could become desirable, touching off a new wave of land grabs in an increasingly cramped and changing world.

Land power has defined the era of recorded human history and the Great Reshuffle has framed modern life—but it could take a radical new turn in the coming centuries. Human population growth triggered land scarcity, but the process could just as easily reverse itself. If some long-range demographic predictions hold true, the next century and the following one could be characterized by an implosion in the global population.[1] The main driving factor is the low birth rates that are spreading around the globe in tandem with wealth and development. A majority of people already live in places with below-replacement fertility, which averages to roughly two children for every two people. Most societies in Europe and in East and Southeast Asia are near or beyond peak population. The population of the United States is being propped up only by immigration, and the populations of Japan, China, and Germany are declining. Humanity could rapidly retrace its steps back below 1 billion. The disappearance of hundreds of millions of landowners could lead to a lot of different outcomes, but among them is a completely altered relationship to land and land scarcity, and with it a wholly new round of reshuffling.

A new reshuffling in a shrinking world could finally provide breathing space for major projects of land restitution to communities dispossessed in the population run-up. But there may still be a fight to make restitution to these communities a priority. Although no one can know precisely how it will unfold, political power in a shrinking, heating world is going to be volatile, and societies will almost certainly struggle with authoritarianism. There will be global competition to secure access to shrinking stocks of temperate land and water and remaining resources. Major projects of geoengineering may envelop economies and huge swaths of land alike. Meanwhile, wealthy and privileged countries may harden their borders, heightening inequality between nations and people in their climate suffering. These dynamics could both transform and elongate the enduring relevance of land power and land reshuffling even as population pressures on the land wane.

In the meantime, living generations are charging ahead with using land power to remedy some of the problems of land power in the past. A number of societies are showing how land, when in the right hands, can play a role in dismantling racial hierarchies, righting gender inequities, healing the environment, and advancing development. These efforts are both top down and bottom up. Governments are experimenting with it, social movements and philanthropists are advocating it, and slogans and ideas are increasingly being translated into practical policy prescriptions.

Governments, communities, and individuals around the globe are turning to innovative new arrangements on the land to craft a better future. Increasingly, this means turning away from traditional, narrow conceptions of exclusive and individual ownership in favor of shared land use, partial common ownership, land stewardship layered over private property, conservation and other easements, community land trusts, and the like. These arrangements seek to balance the benefits of ownership and economic growth with environmental management, equality, land and housing access, and a voice for broader communities. In doing so, they aim to curtail some of the undesirable consequences of land power as it was exercised in the past.

Success depends on an alignment of timing, leverage, and ideas. It requires reformers to recognize and seize upon the unique moments when power shifts and an opportunity arises to address the past. In some places on earth this is already happening. But too many societies miss these moments. That is a core reason why I wrote this book, after years of moving back and forth between compiling and crunching datasets; reading and publishing studies on development, democracy, and inclusion; interviewing people; and getting out on the land the world over. I came to realize that people have been underestimating how important land is to the way societies work, how much a poorly done reallocation of land can lock in future problems, and how powerful a surgical reallocation can be to improve our most pernicious problems. I also came to realize that people marching on the streets for lofty and seemingly distant, idealistic goals—such as reparations and land returns that mainstream politicians and observers claim will never happen—and the legions of policymakers, bureaucrats, and lawyers sweating over land use policy changes are working toward a common goal more often than they recognize.

To change our world for the better now, and to seed the consciousness that we will need to make a better future fifty or a hundred years from now when another unique moment of humanity on the land arrives, requires us to see land power for what it is and to learn how to use it for good. That is the mission of this book.

LAND'S LINK TO power is ironclad—for now. How societies use their land and who owns that land determines how people live, who flourishes, who falters, and who has a say in what happens next.

Land has changed hands before, and when it did, the decisions that were made set the stage for the most pressing social problems that define our world to this day. If human civilization is to have a more just and equitable future, we must take land power seriously. The stakes are high: we are closer to the next reshuffle than we realize, and we must be ready to choose the right path when it arrives.

ACKNOWLEDGMENTS

Ever since some early formative research trips up and down Latin America, I have made sure to get out onto the land wherever I go. The land is the home and in many cases the caretaker of the world's many diverse cultures, the source of its food, and the host of its natural beauty. Most of the people who live on the land hold it as a part of their identity and treat it as a wellspring of life and livelihood. It is irreversibly etched into them, and so it has become to me.

In years of research around the world, I have come to realize that even for people who have left the land for cities and urban life, and for those born into cities, the land is just a few steps behind them. Take Peru. On March 16, 2020, I took a cab to the Lima airport in the wee, gray hours of the morning. Peru's president had announced that the country was closing its borders that evening in response to fears over the spreading global pandemic. As I scrambled to catch one of the final flights out of the country, another exodus was brewing. In the days and weeks that followed, a tidal wave of people flooded out of Lima and other Peruvian cities and back to the land where family and friends awaited. Many of them stayed for months.

The knee-jerk turn back to the land in the face of crisis was a natural one in a country where urbanity is only a couple generations old. As I have come to learn in trips back and forth to the country, nearly everyone in the cities has fairly shallow roots there. Many families still span the rural-urban divide, and the young shift seamlessly between education and jobs in the cities and family gatherings in the countryside. But Peru is not alone. The same is true in societies across Latin

America, South and East Asia, Eastern Europe, and Africa. The roots are deeper in more advanced industrial economies, but only by a few generations. We all come from the land. The shadows of that past might still be stark, as in Peru, or more faded, but they are all around us, whether a pandemic conjures them up or not.

In equal parts, this book explores the land in today's light as well as its flickering shadows. Writing it gave me a greater understanding of the shadows of land in my own life. My father had been working for a decade to piece together the story of his separated Polish grandparents and just recently cracked the code. Like many first- and second-generation Americans, we had a gap in our understanding of what life had been like for our European ancestors and why they had come to America when they did. And in my father's case, that story was about being both rooted in and uprooted from the land. As I was writing this book, he was contacting family members and archivists in Poland about land records. Before long, all signs pointed back to serfdom in southern and eastern Poland. Although it is difficult to uncover the precise arrangements for reasons rooted in poverty, an utter lack of self-determination, and the land power that enabled large landowners to rebuff government, those facts of life persisted beyond the end of serfdom until the building pressures of World War I finally led some family members to flee to America while others got caught behind. But this story is just one among many I collected in the process of writing this book.

It is hard to know where exactly most of my debts lay for this project, because it contains insights and understandings that first began to incubate over fifteen years ago, as well as a few stories that predate this book. Fieldwork in the fields, streets, and buses of Mexico, Peru, Bolivia, Colombia, China, Spain, Portugal, Italy, Ireland, Venezuela, and elsewhere taught me lessons I never could have gained from a distance. Gladly, I have already thanked many of the people who assisted me along the way in previous publications, which gives me cover to shine the brightest spotlight on the people who most recently supported this particular book.

I am especially grateful for the people who shared their stories and their lives with me, because it is through them that I came to understand the centrality and complexities of life tied to land. The group is large and growing, but it expanded in new ways in the writing of this book. From Southern California, I would like to particularly thank Sean Milanovich and Moraino Patencio, Tribal members of the Agua Caliente Band of Cahuilla Indians, for sharing their experiences and perspectives with me; Julie Hause at the Agua Caliente Cultural Museum, for digging up fascinating historical material from the museum's archival collections; and community members at the inauguration of the new Agua Caliente Cultural Museum in late 2023 who spoke to and welcomed me.

I am humbled and thankful for my conversations with a group of hardworking and determined women activists and land restitution beneficiaries in Colombia. Elena Antonio Parodis and María Eugenia Ríos shared their difficult and long stories with me about violent displacement from the land and efforts to win it back. Luz Margarita, a land restitution attorney, spoke with me about the legal issues and practical complications around restitution to Elena's family and in her region, and Blanca Irene from the legal foundation Corporación Jurídica Yira Castro provided insights into grassroots advocacy for land restitution mechanisms and the foundation's work to help Elena and her community get their land.

In South Africa, Stella Mthembu and RCL Foods graciously hosted sugarcane farm tours in the Nkomazi region and interviews with farm managers. Many community members of the Ngomane Siboshwa, Ngomane Lugedlane, Ngomane Hoyi, and Mhlaba generously shared their time and stories with me, including Stella, Nontobeko Zulu, Petros Silinda, Edward Ndlovu, Patrick Vilakazi, and Sizwe Mkhulu, as did former TSB executive Dawie van Rooy and trust administrator Jacob van Garderer. Their willingness to grapple with the legacies of apartheid and dedication to making an inclusive vision of restitution work is deeply inspiring.

My research in Chile was likewise rewarding. I thank Carolyn McCarthy of Tompkins Conservation for facilitating connections into many sides of the Patagonia National Park story. Kris Tompkins generously shared her story and motivations for land preservation and the creation of the park. Ingrid Espinoza and Cristián Saucedo from Rewilding Chile reflected with me on the making of the park, as did Marcelo Mena, the former minister of the environment who worked to convert the land deal into law. François de Smet, who owned the Chacabuco Valley before its conversion into parkland, and his brother Charlie de Smet, who administered the estate, generously spoke to me about their family and their ranching operations. Luisa Galindo, a former cooperative member who made a life in the valley in the 1970s, welcomed me into her home to share her family's experiences. I also thank Elvis Valdés, who shared information about the cooperative era based on the experiences of his father, whom the cooperative called in periodically to hunt and kill mountain lions to protect the sheep and cattle.

I am immensely appreciative of Paola Villa Paro's work to connect me with a new set of land and property title beneficiaries in Peru, as well as officers of several land titling and legal agencies. Wilber Vivanco, William Paño, Juan de Dios Condori, Pablo Villa Incattito, and Wilbert Huamani graciously shared their stories and those of their families and communities with me. They spoke with fortitude, courage, and optimism about family histories of servitude and work on the land, cultural preservation, and rural development. Countless other Peruvians have done the same over the years, inspiring my work. One of them, whose voice appears in this book, is Justina López, an incredibly strong woman I met years ago who, in the early 1970s, was freed from the hacienda where she was born.

I thank Liam Flanagan for working to connect me with Djawa Yunupingu in Australia's northeast Arnhem Land. Djawa, the current Gumatj clan leader of the Yolngu people and a champion of their land rights, generously shared with me how he thought about the Yolngu's connection to their land, the community's relationship with the rest of Australia, and his dreams and goals for future Yolngu generations.

I also give thanks to the research assistants who worked with me to make this book a reality. Philippe Becker, Ellie Grimm, Michael

Rendon, Andrea Marino Varela, and Yinghui Zhou helped to conduct plausibility probes of several cases of land reallocation that I chose to highlight in this book and provide an academic backdrop for them. Siobhan Finnerty helped to reach out to and track down interview subjects. Without this help, it would have been far harder to fulfill the ambitions of this book.

The book benefited greatly from the insights and feedback of colleagues and experts who read and commented on drafts of most of the chapters. That group included brilliant colleagues at the University of Chicago and an international network of connections. Especially helpful were conversations with and reflections from several Australia experts and interlocutors, including Frances and Howard Morphy, Clare Wright, Fred Myers, Kendall Trudgen, Diane Bell, and Tom Keely; interactions with Federico Valverde regarding Doñana National Park in Spain; and feedback from Alex Dyzenhaus, At Fischer, and Kathy Hurly on land issues in South Africa.

I had the good fortune of having the developmental editors Thomas LeBien and Amanda Moon to help shape my initial ideas into a workable outline and book proposal. From there, I could not have imagined a more attentive and effective editor than Brandon Proia at Basic Books. His discerning eye and elegant edits turned the manuscript into something far more readable and engaging and at every turn helped me to convey its most important points.

The project was supported by the Center for International Social Science Research at the University of Chicago. Fieldwork was conducted following review by the University of Chicago Social and Behavioral Sciences Institutional Review Board (IRB23-1388).

Meanwhile, on the home front I had the lucky support and inspiration of a growing family that provides a foundation to life and that encourages me to reflect on what we are creating for future generations. From my mother double-checking my metaphors to my youngest daughter, who is obsessed with bears, they all bring me new energy, joy, and hope every day.

NOTES

INTRODUCTION

1. The value of land in advanced economies alone reached approximately $130 trillion by 2022. See Rudiger Ahrend and Matteo Schleicher, "Land-Value Capture: Money Doesn't Grow on Trees, It Grows Below Them," Organisation for Economic Co-operation and Development (OECD), *OECD Cogito* (blog), October 7, 2022, https://oecdcogito.blog/2022/10/07/land-value-capture-money-doesnt-grow-on-trees-it-grows-below-them. The real estate company Savills estimates that property values globally, including land, housing, offices, factories, and machinery, had reached nearly $400 trillion by 2022. Global economic output and equities were each estimated at around $100 trillion, and global debt at $130 trillion. Paul Tostevin and Charlotte Rushton, "Total Global Value of Real Estate Estimated at $379.7 Trillion—Almost Four Times the Value of Global GDP," Savills, September 25, 2023, www.savills.com/insight-and-opinion/savills-news/352068/total-global-value-of-real-estate-estimated-at-$379.7-trillion---almost-four-times-the-value-of-global-gdp.

2. "Rural Population," from United Nations Population Division, World Urbanization Prospects, 2018, at World Bank, https://data.worldbank.org/indicator/SP.RUR.TOTL.

CHAPTER 1: LAND AND POWER IN HUMAN HISTORY

1. James C. Scott, *Against the Grain: A Deep History of the Earliest States* (New Haven, CT: Yale University Press, 2017), 10.

2. Roger Kain and Elizabeth Baigent, *The Cadastral Map in the Service of the State: A History of Property Mapping* (Chicago: University of Chicago Press, 1992), 1.

3. Notwithstanding this increase, archaeological evidence indicates that the slow shift from hunting and gathering to agriculture in most societies was associated with initial declines in dietary and overall health, lifespans, and leisure. See Scott, *Against the Grain*, 10.

4. See, for instance, Arthur A. Joyce, "The Founding of Monte Albán: Sacred Propositions and Social Practices," in *Agency in Archaeology*, ed. Marcia-Anne Dobres and John Robb, 71–91 (London: Routledge, 2000).

5. Benjamin Isaac, *Empire and Ideology in the Graeco-Roman World* (Cambridge: Cambridge University Press, 2017), chap. 8.

6. This shift occurred earlier and more decisively in agricultural societies that centered on cereal crops than in those focusing on root crops. There is also anthropological and archaeological evidence of gender roles in many societies absent established agriculture and the plow, but those changes still deepened them. Alberto Alesina, Paola Giuliano, and Nathan Nunn, "On the Origins of Gender Roles: Women and the Plough," *Quarterly Journal of Economics* 128, no. 2 (2013): 469–530; Casper Worm Hansen, Peter Sandholt Jensen, and Christian Volmar Skovsgaard, "Modern Gender Roles and Agricultural History: The Neolithic Inheritance," *Journal of Economic Growth* 20, no. 4 (2015): 365–404.

7. Fernand Braudel, *The Mediterranean in the Ancient World* (London: Allen Lane, 1998), 71.

8. Usage of the term "indigenous" did not become widespread until the period of global decolonization following World War II and is most commonly understood as people whose origins predate colonial contact.

9. Life among these groups was not always egalitarian and peaceful. Some of them developed inequality and hierarchy. However, this stratification was typically due to earned rather than inherited social rank, and there were sharp limits to it. Accumulation was quite limited, and inequality was frequently tempered by norms of reciprocity and gift-giving. See Kent Flannery and Joyce Marcus, *The Creation of Inequality: How Our Prehistoric Ancestors Set the Stage for Monarchy, Slavery, and Empire* (Cambridge, MA: Harvard University Press, 2012).

10. For one account of indigenous land and property in early North America, see Allan Greer, *Property and Dispossession: Natives, Empires and Land in Early Modern North America* (Cambridge: Cambridge University Press, 2018). Even many whole communities rarely had exclusive and well-delineated territories. Among many Aboriginal groups in Australia, for instance, there was overlapping land use across groups based on descent.

11. See Greer, *Property and Dispossession*, 43–55.

12. Colin Scott, "Property, Practice and Aboriginal Rights Among Quebec Cree Hunters," in *Hunters and Gatherers*, vol. 2, *Property, Power and Ideology*, ed. Tim Ingold, David Riches, and James Woodburn (London: Routledge, 1988), 35–51.

13. Kathleen Bragdon, *Native People of Southern New England, 1650–1775* (Norman: University of Oklahoma Press, 2009).

14. A couple of the many thousands of examples include the Yolngu of northeast Arnhem Land in Australia and the Tsimané of Bolivia's Yungas region. Clans among the Yolngu have territorial land claims, but these claims have reciprocal implications with other matrilineally affiliated clans and individuals in terms of land access, use, and decision-making. The Tsimané practice subsistence slash-and-burn agriculture supplemented with hunting and gathering. Land is considered joint territory of the community and is not parceled into anything like individual or family ownership.

15. Count Hermann zu Dohna-Kotzenau, quoted in Shearer Davis Bowman, *Masters and Lords: Mid-19th Century U.S. Planters and Prussian Junkers* (New York: Oxford University Press, 1993), 176.

16. Baron Theodor von der Goltz, writing in 1896, quoted in Bowman, *Masters and Lords*, 168. Some *Junkers* instead spoke of serfdom more along the lines of benevolent patriarchy.

17. Bowman, *Masters and Lords*, 172.

18. Bowman, *Masters and Lords*, 33.

19. The figure was 6,500 landlords in the 1870s. See Terence Dooley, *Sources for the History of Landed Estates in Ireland* (Dublin: Irish Academic Press, 2000), 3–16.

20. Quoted in Anne Kane, "Finding Emotion in Social Movement Processes: Irish Land Movement Metaphors and Narratives," in *Passionate Politics: Emotions and Social Movements*, ed. Jeff Goodwin, James M. Jasper, and Francesca Polletta, 251–266 (Chicago: University of Chicago Press, 2001).

21. William Hinton and Fred Magdoff. *Fanshen: A Documentary of Revolution in a Chinese Village* (New York: NYU Press, 2008), 22. The book is based on Hinton's exceptional work in northern China from 1945 to 1948; it was originally published in 1966.

22. Hinton and Magdoff, *Fanshen*, 33, 39.

23. This statement was filed on January 15, 1970, to the Ministry of Agriculture's regional director of Zone XI of the agrarian reform. Accessed by the author at the Centro Bartolomé de las Casas, Cusco, Peru. The landowner was department prefect of Cusco.

24. This statement was filed on January 15, 1970, to the Ministry of Agriculture's regional director of Zone XI of the agrarian reform. Accessed by the author at the Centro Bartolomé de las Casas, Cusco, Peru.

25. Market forces and government regulations in many places have nonetheless encouraged agglomeration over time.

CHAPTER 2: THE GREAT RESHUFFLE

1. Theresa Finley, Raphaël Franck, and Noel D. Johnson, "The Effects of Land Redistribution: Evidence from the French Revolution," *Journal of Law and Economics* 64, no. 2 (2021): 233–267, 242.

2. This shift nonetheless took time. Amid political instability and resistance, it took several years for feudal rights to be abolished in practice and to sell off church and noble lands. And it took still more time for some pieces of this land to end up in the hands of peasants, because land speculators and ascendant entrepreneurs became involved in some of the initial auctions.

3. Michael Albertus, *Autocracy and Redistribution: The Politics of Land Reform* (Cambridge: Cambridge University Press, 2015).

4. Paul Frymer, "'A Rush and a Push and the Land Is Ours': Territorial Expansion, Land Policy, and US State Formation," *Perspectives on Politics* 12, no. 1 (2014): 129–131. The "Five Civilized Tribes" were the Cherokees, Chickasaws, Choctaws, Muscogees (Creek), and Seminoles.

5. The groups constituting these divisions shifted over time. However, early European settlers were consistently categorized as white and Indians as non-white. See, for instance, Jennifer Hochschild and Brenna Marea Powell, "Racial Reorganization and the United States Census 1850–1930: Mulattoes, Half-Breeds, Mixed Parentage, Hindoos, and the Mexican Race," *Studies in American Political Development* 22, no. 1 (2008): 59–96. See also Matthew Frye Jacobson, *Whiteness of a Different Color: European Immigrants and the Alchemy of Race* (Cambridge, MA: Harvard University Press, 2009).

6. See Lachlan McNamee, *Settling for Less: Why States Colonize and Why They Stop* (Princeton, NJ: Princeton University Press, 2023).

7. Sheila Fitzpatrick, *Stalin's Peasants: Resistance and Survival in the Russian Village After Collectivization* (New York: Oxford University Press, 1994), 3–4.

8. Elisabeth Croll, "Women in Rural Production and Reproduction in the Soviet Union, China, Cuba, and Tanzania: Socialist Development Experiences," *Signs: Journal of Women in Culture and Society* 7, no. 2 (1981): 361–374.

9. Ronald Dore, *Land Reform in Japan* (London: Oxford University Press, 1959), 30–35.

10. Ronald Dore, *Shinohata: A Portrait of a Japanese Village* (New York: Pantheon, 1978), 65.

11. For instance, see Joe Studwell, *How Asia Works: Success and Failure in the World's Most Dynamic Region* (New York: Grove/Atlantic, 2013).

12. Enrique Mayer, *Ugly Stories from the Peruvian Agrarian Reform* (Durham, NC: Duke University Press, 2009), 90, 125.

13. There were two types of reform cooperatives. One type was formed of permanent workers managing a single estate, and a second brought together workers from neighboring estates and nearby indigenous communities.

14. Mayer, *Ugly Stories*, 3.

CHAPTER 3: LANDS DIVIDED BY RACE

1. Author interview with Dr. Sean Milanovich, enrolled member of the Agua Caliente Band of Cahuilla Indians, November 13, 2023. Dr. Milanovich comes from a long family line of caring for the land, plants, animals, and the water. He is an advocate for the traditional lands of his people.

2. I follow Agua Caliente conventions in referring to themselves as a band, community, people, or Tribe.

3. Mona De Crinis, "Cahuilla Territory," *Me Yah Whae*, Fall/Winter 2021–2022, https://aguacaliente.org/documents/Cahuilla_Territory.pdf, 58–69, 66.

4. Author interview with Sean Milanovich, November 13, 2023.

5. *Grants of Land in California Made by Spanish or Mexican Authorities*, California State Lands Commission, 1982, available at https://slcprdwordpressstorage.blob.core.windows.net/wordpressdata/2019/09/1982-GrantsSpanishMexican.pdf.

6. The relationship between the two groups was, however, fractious over time. See, for instance, John Booss, "Survival of the Pilgrims: A Reevaluation of the Lethal Epidemic," *Historical Journal of Massachusetts* 47, no. 1 (2019): 108.

7. Russell Thornton, *American Indian Holocaust and Survival: A Population History Since 1492* (Norman: University of Oklahoma Press, 1987).

8. Carly Severn, "'How Do We Heal?' Toppling the Myth of Junípero Serra," KQED, July 7, 2020, www.kqed.org/news/11826151/how-do-we-heal-toppling-the-myth-of-junipero-serra.

9. Quoted in Paul Frymer, "'A Rush and a Push and the Land Is Ours': Territorial Expansion, Land Policy, and US State Formation," *Perspectives on Politics* 12, no. 1 (2014): 119–144, 124.

10. Quoted in Frymer, "A Rush and a Push," 124.

11. Sean Milanovich, "The Treaty of Temecula: A Story of Invasion, Deceit, Stolen Land, and the Persistence of Power, 1846–1905" (PhD diss., University of California Riverside, 2021).

12. US National Archives and Records Administration (NARA), NARA Record Series 75, Microfilm M-234, Letters received by the Office of Indian Affairs, 1824–1881, California Superintendency, 1849–1880, Roll 35 (1856–1857).

13. The US government also directly loaned them credit in the form of bonds. Richard White, "Information, Markets, and Corruption: Transcontinental Railroads in the Gilded Age," *Journal of American History* 90, no. 1 (2003): 19–43, 22.

14. Frymer, "A Rush and a Push." Note that "whiteness" at the time was not always a straightforward or consistent category but an ongoing category of social and political construction.

15. Ross Mattheis and Itzchak Tzachi Raz, "There's No Such Thing as Free Land: The Homestead Act and Economic Development," December 31, 2019, available at Scholars at Harvard, https://scholar.harvard.edu/sites/scholar.harvard.edu/files/iraz/files/Raz_JMP_2019.pdf, 9.

16. The barriers were especially steep for Black Americans, who were still reeling from the legacies of slavery and faced rigid Jim Crow laws in the South.

17. Timothy J. Hatton and Jeffrey G. Williamson, "What Drove the Mass Migrations from Europe in the Late Nineteenth Century?," NBER Historical Paper No. 43, 1992, National Bureau of Economic Research, www.nber.org/papers/h0043.

18. White, "Information, Markets, and Corruption."

19. D. M. Ellis, "The Forfeiture of Railroad Land Grants, 1867–1894," *Mississippi Valley Historical Review* 33, no. 1 (1946): 27–60.

20. P. W. Gates, "The Homestead Law in an Incongruous Land System," *American Historical Review* 41, no. 4 (1936): 652–681; P. W. Gates, "Land Policy and Tenancy in the Prairie States," *Journal of Economic History* 1, no. 1 (1941): 60–82.

21. Some Agua Caliente took advantage of the stagecoach and early railroad to help transport goods and find employment, but with increasing land competition others were forced into low-wage labor working to construct the railroads.

22. The government terminated one of these reservations (Mission Creek) in 1970.

23. Lowell Bean and Harry Lawton, *The Cahuilla Indians of Southern California: Their History and Culture* (Banning, CA: Malki Museum Press, 1965), 3–4.

24. "How Desert Became a Checkerboard," *Palm Springs Desert Sun* 43, no. 124 (1969), available at University of California, Riverside, Center for Bibliographical Studies and Research, California Digital Newspaper Collection, https://cdnc.ucr.edu/?a=d&d=DS19691229.2.120.

25. Rachel Dayton Shaw, "Evolving Ecoscape: An Environmental and Cultural History of Palm Springs, California, and the Agua Caliente Indian Reservation, 1877–1939" (PhD diss., University of California, San Diego, 1999), 115, 117.

26. Shaw, "Evolving Ecoscape," 119.

27. Shaw, "Evolving Ecoscape," 122.

28. Land access was nonetheless governed by clans with distinct territorial claims.

29. Letter to the secretary of the interior from Pedro Chino and signatories, Agua Caliente Indian Reservation, Palm Springs, California, May 1, 1923, available at US

National Archives and Records Administration (NARA), National Archives Catalog, Record Group 75, Records of the Bureau of Indian Affairs, Series: Individual Indian Probate Case Files, Probate File Numbers 92347-20-103168-20 (part), 1920 (1 of 2), https://catalog.archives.gov/id/197708891?objectPage=806.

30. In its abortive effort to strip the Tribe of its culturally important palm canyons by turning Indian Canyons into a national park, the all-white Palm Springs Indian Committee argued that because the community practiced periodic burns in the area (which served to regenerate soils and control fire risk), they should not be trusted to steward the area, and it should be turned over to the parks system without compensation. The Tribal community successfully fought that attempted land grab.

31. Letter to the Agua Caliente from Charles Burke, commissioner of the Bureau of Indian Affairs, stamped May 4, 1923, available at US National Archives and Records Administration (NARA), National Archives Catalog, Record Group 75, Records of the Bureau of Indian Affairs, Series: Individual Indian Probate Case Files, Probate File Numbers 92347-20-103168-20 (part), 1920 (1 of 2), https://catalog.archives.gov/id/197708891?objectPage=788.

32. Author correspondence with Moraino Patencio, enrolled member of the Agua Caliente Band of Cahuilla Indians, January 4, 2024. The Patencio family has long been involved in Tribal governance.

33. Holders of individual trust lands initially had very restricted property rights and could not sell or transfer their land. Land held in trust could in theory be converted to fee simple ownership with full property rights after twenty-five years had elapsed. Later, after the passage of the Burke Act in 1906, a local Bureau of Indian Affairs officer could convert trust land to fee simple if the officer deemed an individual "competent" to manage the property.

34. Author interview with Moraino Patencio, November 8, 2023.

35. Bureau of Indian Affairs (BIA), press release, June 19, 1957, available at BIA, www.bia.gov/as-ia/opa/online-press-release/department-proposes-equalization-legislation-palm-springs-indians.

36. *Arenas v. United States*, 322 U.S. 419 (1944).

37. Renee Brown, "History of Equalization of Property Rights by Members of Agua Caliente Band of the Cahuilla Indians," *Palm Springs Desert Sun*, April 30, 2023, www.desertsun.com/story/life/history/2023/04/30/history-property-rights-struggle-by-members-of-agua-caliente-band-of-the-cahuilla-indians-has-been-d/70165045007. Additional details from author correspondence with Moraino Patencio, January 5, 2024.

38. Because the land allotments in downtown Palm Springs had become very valuable by this time, this implied assigning large tracts of less valuable land outside the downtown area to members, covering and therefore maintaining the Tribal land base. Author correspondence with Moraino Patencio, January 4, 2024.

39. Shaw, "Evolving Ecoscape," 122.

40. Author interview with Dr. Sean Milanovich, November 13, 2023.

41. Miranda Caudell, "A People's Journey," *Me Yah Whae*, Fall/Winter 2016–2017: 50–54, www.aguacaliente.org/documents/OurStory-10.pdf.

42. Author communication with Moraino Patencio, November 8, 2023.

43. *Journal of the Senate, Legislature of the State of California* (Sacramento: California State Print Office, 1961).

44. Arewen Nuttall, "Section 14: The Agua Caliente Tribe's Struggle for Sovereignty in Palm Springs, California," *American Indian Magazine* 20, no. 2 (2019), www.american indianmagazine.org/story/section-14.

45. The evictions largely affected tenants and less so members of the Agua Caliente. A number of the Agua Caliente had established business arrangements around the hot springs and elsewhere and in a few cases had white employees.

46. "Frank Bogert: Palm Springs' Civic Leadership, Institutionalized Segregation, and Racial Bias, 1958–1966," Palm Springs City Hall Monument Report, April 28, 2021, available at minutes of the City of Palm Springs, Human Rights Commission, meeting of May 5, 2021, www.palmspringsca.gov/home/showpublisheddocument/78757/6375537 44496070000.

47. Quoted in the exhibit "Section 14: The Other Palm Springs, California," National Museum of the American Indian, Washington, DC.

48. Author interview with Moraino Patencio, November 8, 2023.

49. J. David Hacker and Michael R. Haines, "American Indian Mortality in the Late Nineteenth Century: The Impact of Federal Assimilation Policies on a Vulnerable Population," NBER Working Paper No. 12572, 2006, National Bureau of Economic Research, published version in *Annales de démographie historique* 110, no. 2 (2005): 17–29, 20.

50. Andrew Mollica and Dominic Parker, "What Makes Economic Growth Inclusive? Evidence on the Role of Ethnicity from Native Americans," April 24, 2017, available at Projects at Harvard, https://projects.iq.harvard.edu/files/canada/files/mollica_and_parker _4-24-2017_a.pdf.

51. Ronald Trosper, "American Indian Poverty on Reservations, 1969–1989," in *Changing Numbers, Changing Needs: American Indian Demography and Public Health*, ed. Gary D. Sandefur, Ronald R. Rindfuss, and Barney Cohen (Washington, DC: National Academies Press, 1996).

52. Donna Feir, "The Landscape of Opportunity in Indian Country: A Discussion of Data from the Opportunity Atlas," Center for Indian Country Development, Research Brief No. 2019-03, April 19, 2019, available at Federal Reserve Bank of Minneapolis, www.minneapolisfed.org/-/media/files/community/indiancountry/the-landscape -of-opportunity-in-indian-country-04-19-19.pdf.

53. Alexia Fernández Campbell, "How America's Past Shapes Native Americans' Present," *The Atlantic*, October 12, 2016.

54. Dedrick Asante-Muhammad, Esha Kamra, Connor Sanchez, Kathy Ramirez, and Rogelio Tec, "Racial Wealth Snapshot: Native Americans," National Community Reinvestment Coalition, 2022, https://ncrc.org/racial-wealth-snapshot-native-americans.

55. Kelli Mosteller, "For Native Americans, Land Is More Than Just the Ground Beneath Their Feet," *The Atlantic*, September 17, 2016.

56. "Native Land Law: Can Native American People Find Justice in the US Legal System?," Indian Land Tenure Foundation, 2016, https://iltf.org/wp-content/up loads/2016/11/native_land_law_2010_MR6.pdf. In this vein, the 2012 HEARTH Act

provides tribes an opt-in mechanism for greater autonomy in managing land use decisions. Though the program has been successful, only sixty-nine tribal nations had been enrolled as of late 2021.

57. Wil Del Pilar, "Degree Attainment for Native American Adults," Education Trust, November 15, 2018, https://edtrust.org/resource/degree-attainment-for-native-american-adults.

58. "Disparities," Indian Health Services, www.ihs.gov/newsroom/factsheets/disparities, accessed May 15, 2024.

59. Rebecca Carron, "Health Disparities in American Indians / Alaska Natives: Implications for Nurse Practitioners," *Nurse Practitioner* 45, no. 6 (2020): 26–32.

60. "Leading Causes of Death—Females—Non-Hispanic American Indian or Alaska Native—United States, 2016," Centers for Disease Control and Prevention, 2016, www.cdc.gov/women/lcod/2016/nonhispanic-native/index.htm.

61. Mary Findling, Logan Casey, Stephanie Fryberg, Steven Hafner, Robert Blendon, John Benson, Justin Sayde, and Carolyn Miller, "Discrimination in the United States: Experiences of Native Americans," *Health Services Research* 54 (2019): 1431–1441.

62. Author interview with Moraino Patencio, November 8, 2023.

63. Moraino Patencio's father, a former Tribal chairman, first leased out his childhood home when it became too expensive to live in Section 14 and later witnessed it being knocked down to build the Hilton Hotel, which currently stands in its place across from the mineral springs. Author interview with Moraino Patencio, November 8, 2023.

64. "2013–2017 ACS 5-Year Estimates," US Bureau of the Census, American Community Survey, 2017, www.census.gov/programs-surveys/acs/technical-documentation/table-and-geography-changes/2017/5-year.html.

CHAPTER 4: THIS LAND IS MEN'S LAND

1. In a controversial omission that remains contested today, the Canadian government never compensated First Nations for the land.

2. Another loophole for women obtaining homestead land opened in 1908 with the Volunteer Bounty Act. Canadian veterans of the Boer War could claim up to 320 acres of homesteading land through the act or name a substitute. Because there were no gender restrictions on substitutes, a small number of women claimed land through the act.

3. Constance Backhouse, "Pure Patriarchy: Nineteenth-Century Canadian Marriage," *McGill Law Journal* 31, no. 2 (September 1985): 272–273.

4. Sarah Carter, *The Importance of Being Monogamous: Marriage and Nation Building in Western Canada to 1915* (Edmonton: University of Alberta Press, 2008), 59.

5. Women did win homesteading rights in Alberta in 1930 when the Alberta Lands Act replaced the Dominion Lands Act in the province. But by this point, the best land had been taken, and then the Great Depression complicated homesteading.

6. Seymour Martin Lipset, *Continental Divide: The Values and Institutions of the United States and Canada* (New York: Routledge, 1991), 10–11.

7. Lipset, *Continental Divide*, 43. Both British liberal and selected Canadian continental political forces were against many elements of confederation but could not successfully oppose them.

8. The property requirement for the Senate remains in place today, though its impact is close to negligible. However, it periodically resurfaces. One example is the 1997 appointment of Peggy Butts, a Catholic nun who had taken a vow of poverty. She had to have a small parcel of land transferred to her name in order to be sworn into office.

9. Sarah Carter, "'Daughters of British Blood' or 'Hordes of Men of Alien Race': The Homesteads-for-Women Campaign in Western Canada," *Great Plains Quarterly* 29, no. 4 (2009): 270.

10. Carter, "Daughters of British Blood," 71.

11. These dower rights sought to protect spouses who were not on the title of a homestead property from dispossession without their consent and to enable them to stay on the land in the case of the death of their spouse.

12. "Spinsters Want Homesteads," *Edmonton Bulletin*, May 21, 1893, quoted in Carter, "Daughters of British Blood," 273.

13. Bill Waiser, "History Matters: No Female Homesteaders Need Apply," *Saskatoon (Saskatchewan) StarPhoenix*, February 14, 2017, https://thestarphoenix.com/opinion/columnists/history-matters-no-female-homesteaders-need-apply.

14. Binnie-Clark also advocated for the exclusion of foreigners from access to homestead land as the tide of immigration in Canada was rising.

15. Letter to the editor by Reverend R. W. Beveridge, January 15, 1910, published in Winnipeg, read by Roche to Oliver in the House of Commons session, April 30, 1910, in *House of Commons Debates*, vol. 97, *Second Session, Eleventh Parliament, 1909–1910* (Ottawa: Canada Parliament, 1910), 8488.

16. *House of Commons Debates*, April 30, 1910, 97:8489–8490.

17. Carter, "Daughters of British Blood," 281.

18. A series of resolutions passed at the United Farmers of Alberta convention sought homesteading rights for women in 1929. See Carter, "Daughters of British Blood," 283.

19. The act continued to operate in the Northwest Territories, but even that ended in 1950.

20. "Uneven Progress, 1867–1919," in *A History of the Vote in Canada*, 3rd ed. (Quebec: Public Enquiries Unit, Elections Canada, 2020), www.elections.ca/res/his/WEB_EC%2091135%20History%20of%20the%20Vote_Third%20edition_EN.pdf.

21. Catherine Cavanaugh, "The Limitations of the Pioneering Partnership: The Alberta Campaign for Homestead Dower, 1905–25," *Canadian Historical Review* 74, no 2 (June 1993): 198–225.

22. Cristine Georgina Bye, "'I Like to Hoe My Own Row': A Saskatchewan Farm Woman's Notions About Work and Womanhood During the Great Depression," *Frontiers: A Journal of Women Studies* 26, no. 3 (2004): 135–167, 136. Rural women on the American side of Canada's western frontier border received considerably more state resources than women on the Canadian side.

23. See, for instance, Veronica Strong-Boag, "Pulling in Double Harness or Hauling a Double Load: Women, Work and Feminism on the Canadian Prairie," in *The Prairie West: Historical Readings*, ed. R. Douglas Francis and Howard Palmer, 2nd ed. (Edmonton:

Pica Pica Press, 1992), 401–423; Christa Scowby, "'I Am a Worker, Not a Drone': Farm Women, Reproductive Work and the Western Producer, 1930–1939," *Saskatchewan History* 48, no. 2 (Fall 1996): 3–15.

24. Bye, "I Like to Hoe My Own Row."

25. Mary Kinnear, *Female Economy: Women's Work in a Prairie Province, 1870–1970* (Montreal: McGill-Queen's University Press, 1998).

26. Marjorie Griffin Cohen, *Women's Work, Markets and Economic Development in Nineteenth-Century Ontario* (Toronto: University of Toronto Press, 1988).

27. Clarence Lochhead and Katherine Scott, *The Dynamics of Women's Poverty in Canada* (Ottawa: Status of Women Canada, 2000), 19.

28. Norah Keating and Maryanne Doherty, *A Study of Alberta Farmers* (Edmonton: Agricultural Research Council of Alberta, 1985).

29. Statistics are from the 2011 agricultural census. See "Highlights and Analysis," Statistics Canada, www.statcan.gc.ca/en/ca2011/ha.

30. Ratan Ghosh, "Effect of Agricultural Legislations on Land Distribution in West Bengal," *Indian Journal of Agricultural Economics* 31, no. 3 (1976): 40–46.

31. B. K. Chowhury, "Land Reform Legislation and Implementation in West Bengal," *Indian Journal of Agricultural Economics* 17, no. 2 (1962): 141–151.

32. The limit of five hectares was for irrigated land and the seven-hectare limit applied to unirrigated land. These limits applied to households of five members. Additional family members qualified the household for an additional half hectare each, up to a maximum of seven irrigated hectares.

33. See P. S. Appu, *Land Reforms in India: A Survey of Policy, Legislation and Implementation* (New Delhi: Vikas, 1996), Appendix IV.3.

34. Timothy Besley and Robin Burgess, "Land Reform, Poverty Reduction, and Growth: Evidence from India," *Quarterly Journal of Economics* 115, no. 2 (2000): 389–430, 401.

35. The maximum was up to 50 percent if the landlord provided all material inputs.

36. Pranab Bardhan and Dilip Mookherjee, "Subsidized Farm Input Programs and Agricultural Performance: A Farm-Level Analysis of West Bengal's Green Revolution, 1982–1995," *American Economic Journal: Applied Economics* 3, no. 4 (2011): 186–214; Abhijit V. Banerjee, Paul J. Gertler, and Maitreesh Ghatak, "Empowerment and Efficiency: Tenancy Reform in West Bengal," *Journal of Political Economy* 110, no. 2 (2002): 239–280.

37. Klaus Deininger, Songqing Jin, and Vandana Yadav, "Long-Term Effects of Land Reform on Human Capital Accumulation: Evidence from West Bengal," WIDER Working Paper No. 2011/82, 2011, United Nations University World Institute for Development Economics Research (UNU-WIDER), www.econstor.eu/bitstream/10419/53978/1/678366586.pdf.

38. Pranab Bardhan, Michael Luca, Dilip Mookherjee, and Francisco Pino, "Evolution of Land Distribution in West Bengal, 1967–2004: Role of Land Reform and Demographic Changes," *Journal of Development Economics* 110 (2014): 171–190, 174.

39. Sonia Bhalotra, Abhishek Chakravarty, Dilip Mookherjee, and Francisco J. Pino, "Property Rights and Gender Bias: Evidence from Land Reform in West Bengal," *American Economic Journal: Applied Economics* 11, no. 2 (2019): 205–237.

40. Prashant K. Trivedi, "Reinforcing Exclusions: Caste, Patriarchy and Land Reforms in India," *Journal of Land and Rural Studies* 10, no. 2 (2022): 262–277.

41. Furthermore, inheritance of agricultural land occurred under prevailing state-level land reform laws, which were highly gender unequal.

42. Sanchari Roy, "Empowering Women? Inheritance Rights, Female Education and Dowry Payments in India," *Journal of Development Economics* 114 (2015): 233–251.

43. On female child mortality rates, see Daniel Rosenblum, "Unintended Consequences of Women's Inheritance Rights on Female Mortality in India," *Economic Development and Cultural Change* 63, no. 2 (2015): 223–248. On female suicides (and a rise in male suicides as well) and wife beating, see Siwan Anderson and Garance Genicot, "Suicide and Property Rights in India," *Journal of Development Economics* 114 (2015): 64–78.

44. Until recently, agricultural censuses and household surveys have not collected gender-disaggregated data on ownership holdings. Nonetheless, studies such as Bhalotra et al., "Property Rights and Gender Bias"; Trivedi, "Reinforcing Exclusions"; and others suggest that land reforms, if anything, have perpetuated or even deepened gender biases in landholding and inheritance.

45. Bina Agarwal, Pervesh Anthwal, and Malvika Mahesh, "How Many and Which Women Own Land in India? Inter-Gender and Intra-Gender Gaps," *Journal of Development Studies* 57, no. 11 (2021): 1807–1829. These data are from a 2009–2014 survey across nine of India's states.

46. Yuvaraj Krishnamoorthy, Karthika Ganesh, and Karthiga Vijayakumar, "Physical, Emotional and Sexual Violence Faced by Spouses in India: Evidence on Determinants and Help-Seeking Behaviour from a Nationally Representative Survey," *Journal of Epidemiology and Community Health* 74, no. 9 (2020): 732–740.

47. Dana Smith, "More Than a Third of Female Suicides Are Committed by Indian Women," *Scientific American*, December 1, 2018. The official numbers are likely a considerable undercount, perhaps by a factor of six to nine. See Anderson and Genicot, "Suicide and Property Rights in India," 64.

48. Sharangee Dutta, "In 2021, Over 45K Women Died by Suicide in India, 23,000 of Them Are Housewives: NCRB Data," *Hindustan Times*, August 30, 2022, www.hindustantimes.com/india-news/in-2021-over-45k-women-died-by-suicide-in-india-23-000-of-them-are-housewives-101661855990564.html.

49. Yunping Tong, "India's Sex Ratio at Birth Begins to Normalize," Pew Research Center, August 23, 2022, www.pewresearch.org/wp-content/uploads/sites/20/2022/08/PR_2022.08.26_India-sex-ratio_REPORT.pdf.

50. This episode is reported in detail in Rolando Antonio Velis Polío, "La Reforma Agraria de 1980 en El Salvador: Lucha política, diseño y ejecución," *Revista de humanidades y ciencias sociales* 3 (2012): 95–120, retold in Eduardo Montero, "Cooperative Property Rights and Development: Evidence from Land Reform in El Salvador," *Journal of Political Economy* 130, no. 1 (2022): 48–93.

51. Michael Albertus, *Autocracy and Redistribution: The Politics of Land Reform* (Cambridge: Cambridge University Press, 2015), 31.

52. Paul Almeida, *Waves of Protest: Popular Struggle in El Salvador, 1925–2005* (Minneapolis: University of Minnesota Press, 2008), 114.

53. Almeida, *Waves of Protest*, 37.

54. Karen Musalo, "El Salvador—A Peace Worse Than War: Violence, Gender and a Failed Legal Response," *Yale Journal of Law and Feminism* 30, no. 3 (2018): 32–35.

55. Vincent McElhinny, "Inequality and Empowerment: The Political Foundations of Post-War Decentralization and Development in El Salvador, 1992–2000" (PhD diss., University of Pittsburgh, 2006), 283.

56. Montero, "Cooperative Property Rights and Development," 56–57.

57. Carmen Diana Deere, "Rural Women and State Policy: The Latin American Agrarian Reform Experience," *World Development* 13, no. 9 (1985): 1037–1053, 1041; Cristóbal Kay, "Latin America's Agrarian Reform: Lights and Shadows," Land Reform / Réforme agraire / Reforma agraria, 1998/2, https://openknowledge.fao.org/server/api/core/bitstreams/323dde22-f6e6-44cd-8244-da9d69c7d51a/content, 23.

58. Carmen Diana Deere and Magdalena León, *Empowering Women: Land and Property Rights in Latin America* (Pittsburgh: University of Pittsburgh Press, 2001), 98.

59. Deere and León, *Empowering Women*, 98.

60. Deere, "Rural Women and State Policy," 1046–1050.

61. Fabrice Lehoucq and Harold Sims, "Reform with Repression: The Land Reform in El Salvador," ISHI Occasional Papers in Social Change No. 6, 1982, Institute for the Study of Human Issues, https://libres.uncg.edu/ir/uncg/f/F_Lehoucq_Reform_1982.pdf.

62. Deere and León, *Empowering Women*, 98.

63. The group's name in Spanish is the Frente Farabundo Martí para la Liberación Nacional.

64. Morena Soledad Herrera, *Movimiento de mujeres en El Salvador, 1995–2006: Estrategias y miradas desde el feminismo* (San Salvador: Fundación Nacional para el Desarrollo [FUNDE], 2008), 89.

65. Albertus, *Autocracy and Redistribution*, 314.

66. Deere and León, *Empowering Women*, 212.

CHAPTER 5: THE DISAPPEARING WILDERNESS

1. Robert Wilson, "Authoritarian Environmental Governance: Insights from the Past Century," *Annals of the American Association of Geographers* 109, no. 2 (2019): 314–323, 317.

2. Robert Marks, *China: An Environmental History*, 2nd ed. (London: Rowman and Littlefield, 2017), 327.

3. Zhang Xiaofang, "The Early Exploration of the Road to Socialist Industrialization in China," *Journal of Peking University (Philosophy and Social Science Edition)* 56, no. 4 (2019): 11–20, 17.

4. Marks, *China*, 327.

5. See, for instance, Robert Marks, *Tigers, Rice, Silk, and Silt: Environment and Economy in Late Imperial South China* (New York: Cambridge University Press, 1998).

6. Marks, *China*.

7. Tenancy overall was roughly 20 percent in the late 1930s. The largest 3–4 percent of landowners held 20–30 percent of the arable land in northern China and 30–50 percent of

the arable land in southern China. These rates were not as severe as in nearby Taiwan and South Korea. See Michael Albertus, *Property Without Rights: Origins and Consequences of the Property Rights Gap* (Cambridge: Cambridge University Press, 2021), 295.

8. John Wong, *Land Reform in the People's Republic of China: Institutional Transformation in Agriculture* (New York: Praeger, 1973), 129–130.

9. Marks, *China*, 322.

10. Liu Dachang, "Tenure and Management of Non-State Forests in China Since 1950: A Historical Review," *Environmental History* 6, no. 2 (2001): 239–263.

11. Marks, *China*, 1.

12. "Sichuan People's Surprise Siege of Sparrows," *People's Daily*, March 25, 1958, 7, http://data.people.com.cn.

13. Ruigang Bi, Hanyi Chen, Qinyun Wang, and Xuebin Wang, "Sparrow Slaughter and Grain Yield Reduction During the Great Famine of China," April 22, 2021, 3, available at SSRN, https://ssrn.com/abstract=3832057.

14. Ruigang Bi et al., "Sparrow Slaughter."

15. Basil Ashton, Kenneth Hill, Alan Piazza, and Robin Zeitz, "Famine in China, 1958–61," in *The Population of Modern China*, ed. Dudley L. Poston and David Yaukey, 225–271 (Boston: Springer, 1992). Land collectivization compounded the mismanagement of agriculture and associated environmental causes of the famine. By divorcing income from work input and eliminating private property, collectivization eroded work incentives and cauterized private investment in agriculture. It was a perfect storm for the human and natural environment. Career incentives and the political radicalism of officials pursuing political advancement also exacerbated decision-making problems. See James Kai-Sing Kung and Shuo Chen, "The Tragedy of the *Nomenklatura*: Career Incentives and Political Radicalism During China's Great Leap Famine," *American Political Science Review* 105, no. 1 (2011): 27–45.

16. Peter Ho, "Mao's War Against Nature? The Environmental Impact of the Grain-First Campaign in China," *China Journal* 50 (July 2003): 37–59, 41.

17. Marks, *China*, 327.

18. Marks, *China*, 328.

19. Naiping Song and Zhang Fengrong, "Re-evaluation of the 'Grain as the Key Link' Policy and Its Impact on the Ecological Environment," *Economic Geography* 26, no. 4 (2006): 628–631, 629.

20. Jintao Xu, Runsheng Yin, Zhou Li, and Can Liu, "China's Ecological Rehabilitation: Unprecedented Efforts, Dramatic Impacts, and Requisite Policies," *Ecological Economics* 57, no. 4 (2006): 595–607, 597.

21. Liu Dachang, "Reforestation After Deforestation in China," in *Good Earths: Regional and Historical Insights into China's Environment*, ed. Ken-ichi Abe and James E. Nickum, 90–105 (Kyoto: Kyoto University Press, 2009), 91.

22. Marks, *China*, 329.

23. Sandra Postel and Lori Heise, "Reforesting the Earth," Worldwatch Paper 83, 1988, Worldwatch Institute, 51–52, https://files.eric.ed.gov/fulltext/ED293701.pdf.

24. Marks, *China*, 316.

25. Yuxuan Li, Weifeng Zhang, Lin Ma, Gaoqiang Huang, Oene Oenema, Fusuo Zhang, and Zhengxia Dou, "An Analysis of China's Fertilizer Policies: Impacts on the

Industry, Food Security, and the Environment," *Journal of Environmental Quality* 42, no. 4 (2013): 972–981.

26. See, for instance, W. L. Zhang, Z. X. Tian, N. Zhang, and X. Q. Li, "Nitrate Pollution of Groundwater in Northern China," *Agriculture, Ecosystems and Environment* 59, no. 3 (1996): 223–231. Also see Marks, *China*, 367–370.

27. "Why Protect the Amazon," Amazon Conservation Association, www.amazonconservation.org/the-challenge/why-the-amazon, accessed May 16, 2024.

28. "Why Protect the Amazon," Amazon Conservation Association.

29. Jake Spring, "Amazon Biome Hurtles Toward Death Spiral as Deforestation Jumps," Reuters, January 27, 2021, www.reuters.com/business/environment/amazon-hurtles-toward-death-spiral-deforestation-jumps-2020-2021-01-27.

30. Kiley Price, "Study: How Years of Wildfires Have Devastated the Amazon," Conservation International, September 1, 2021, www.conservation.org/blog/study-how-years-of-wildfires-have-devastated-the-amazon. See also Zoe Sullivan, "The Real Reason the Amazon Is on Fire," *Time*, August 26, 2019, https://time.com/5661162/why-the-amazon-is-on-fire.

31. "Threats to the Amazon," Amazon Conservation Association, www.amazonconservation.org/the-challenge/threats, accessed May 16, 2024.

32. Matt Sandy, "The Amazon Rainforest Is Nearly Gone. We Went to the Front Lines to See If It Could Be Saved," *Time*, September 12, 2019, https://time.com/amazon-rainforest-disappearing.

33. One particularly important law was the 1850 Land Law, which legally prohibited land squatting but in practice enabled powerful large landowners to systematically incorporate frontier lands. It also legalized existing de facto landholdings and legitimized pre-independence imperial land grants. See Michael Albertus, Thomas Brambor, and Ricardo Ceneviva, "Land Inequality and Rural Unrest: Theory and Evidence from Brazil," *Journal of Conflict Resolution* 62, no. 3 (2018): 557–596.

34. Martin T. Katzman, "The Brazilian Frontier in Comparative Perspective," *Comparative Studies in Society and History* 17, no. 3 (1975): 266–285, 276.

35. Gabriel Ondetti, *Land, Protest, and Politics: The Landless Movement and the Struggle for Agrarian Reform in Brazil* (University Park: Pennsylvania State University Press, 2008).

36. Brazil's landholding Gini was 0.83. See International Fund for Agricultural Development (IFAD), *Rural Poverty Report 2001: The Challenge of Ending Rural Poverty* (Oxford: Oxford University Press for IFAD, 2001), chap. 3.

37. Michael Albertus, "Landowners and Democracy: The Social Origins of Democracy Reconsidered," *World Politics* 69, no. 2 (2017): 233–276. Data from the United Nations Food and Agriculture Organization, World Census of Agriculture.

38. Jessica Intrator, "From Squatter to Settler: Applying the Lessons of Nineteenth Century U.S. Public Land Policy to Twenty-First Century Land Struggles in Brazil," *Ecology Law Quarterly* 38, no. 1 (2011): 179–232, 187.

39. Lee Alston, Gary Libecap, and Bernardo Mueller, *Titles, Conflict, and Land Use: The Development of Property Rights and Land Reform on the Brazilian Amazon Frontier* (Ann Arbor: University of Michigan Press, 1999), 37.

40. Luiz Carlos Kopes Brandão, "A colonização brasileira, do descobrimento ao estatuto da terra," unpublished manuscript, 2009, 7.

41. The settlements were Goiás (1941), Amazonas (1941), Maranhão (1942), Pará (1943), "General Osório" in Paraná (1943), Dourados (1943), Piauí (1944), and Jaíba (1948). Lucas Felicio Costa and Ricardo Trevisan, "Colônias Agrícolas Nacionais: Laboratórios experimentais de exploração e ocupação do território brasileiro, um arranjo possíve," *Eixo: A construção da cidade sul-americana contemporânea. História e historiografias* (Belo Horizonte, Brazil: Asociación de Escuelas y Facultades Públicas de Arquitectura de América del Sur, 2019); Wagner Abadio Freitas and Marcelo de Mello, "A Colônia Agrícola Nacional de Goiás e a redefinição nos usos do território," *Sociedade e natureza* 26, no. 3 (2014): 471–482.

42. Martin Katzman, "Colonization as an Approach to Regional Development: Northern Paraná, Brazil," *Economic Development and Cultural Change* 26, no. 4 (1978): 709–724, 712.

43. Ondetti, *Land, Protest, and Politics*, 11.

44. The 1964 land statute law required the country's land reform agency to issue certificates to beneficiaries in order for them to be able to sell, partition, lease, or mortgage their land. But in many cases it did not issue titles and it did not link them to a land cadaster, leaving beneficiaries in legal limbo.

45. Charles Wood and Marianne Schmink, "The Military and the Environment in the Brazilian Amazon," *Journal of Political and Military Sociology* 21, no. 1 (1993): 81–105, 88.

46. See Nigel Smith, *Rainforest Corridors: The Transamazon Colonization Scheme* (Berkeley: University of California Press, 1982), 17. Also see Robert Walker, Stephen Perz, Eugenio Arima, and Cynthia Simmons, "The Transamazon Highway: Past, Present, Future," in *Engineering Earth: The Impacts of Megaengineering Projects*, vol. 1, ed. Stanley Brunn, 569–599 (Dordrecht: Springer, 2011), 580.

47. Wood and Schmink. "The Military and the Environment," 89.

48. Georgia Carvalho, Daniel Nepstad, David McGrath, Maria del Carmen Vera Diaz, Márcio Santilli, and Ana Cristina Barros, "Frontier Expansion in the Amazon: Balancing Development and Sustainability," *Environment: Science and Policy for Sustainable Development* 44, no. 3 (2002): 34–44, 37.

49. Aurora Miho Yanai, Paulo Maurício Lima de Alencastro Graça, Leonardo Guimarães Ziccardi, Maria Isabel Sobral Escada, and Philip Martin Fearnside, "Brazil's Amazonian Deforestation: The Role of Landholdings in Undesignated Public Lands," *Regional Environmental Change* 22, no. 1 (2002): 1–14.

50. Jesse Hyde, "The Lawless Frontier at the Heart of the Burning Amazon," *Rolling Stone*, September 17, 2019, www.rollingstone.com/politics/politics-features/amazon-burning-bolsonaro-novo-progresso-deforestation-885114.

51. The group's name in Portuguese is Movimento dos Trabalhadores Rurais Sem Terra.

52. On limiting urbanization and crime through agrarian reform, see Belén Fernández, *Agrarian Elites and Democracy in Latin America* (Cambridge: Cambridge University Press, 2024).

53. On property rights and organization within settlements on privately owned land, see Aldiva Sales Diniz and Bruce Gilbert, "Socialist Values and Cooperation in Brazil's Landless Rural Workers' Movement," *Latin American Perspectives* 40, no. 4 (2013): 19–34.

54. Michael Albertus, Thomas Brambor, and Ricardo Ceneviva, "Land Inequality and Rural Unrest: Theory and Evidence from Brazil," *Journal of Conflict Resolution* 62, no. 3 (2018): 557–596. Based on data from the Instituto Nacional de Colonização e Reforma Agrária.

55. For instance, in 2019 President Jair Bolsonaro passed a provisional measure (MP-910) that allowed individuals to legalize "self-declared" ownership of up to 1,500 hectares (3,700 acres) in Amazonia. Ownership is often demonstrated by putting land to use, first by clear-cutting the forest. See Lucas Ferrante, Maryane Andrade, and Philip Fearnside, "Land Grabbing on Brazil's Highway BR-319 as a Spearhead for Amazonian Deforestation," *Land Use Policy* 108 (2021): 2.

56. Karin-Marijke Vis, "The Road Transforming the Amazon," BBC, November 4, 2014, www.bbc.com/travel/article/20141028-the-road-transforming-the-amazon.

57. Albertus et al., "Land Inequality and Rural Unrest."

58. Albertus et al., "Land Inequality and Rural Unrest."

59. Veronica Orellano, Paulo Furquim Azevedo, Maria Sylvia Saes, and Viviam Ester Nascimento, "Land Invasions, Insecure Property Rights and Production Decisions," *Journal of Agricultural Economics* 66, no. 3 (2015): 660–671.

60. Stephen Aldrich, Robert Walker, Cynthia Simmons, Marcellus Caldas, and Stephen Perz, "Contentious Land Change in the Amazon's Arc of Deforestation," *Annals of the Association of American Geographers* 102, no. 1 (2012): 103–128; Claudio Araujo, Catherine Araujo Bonjean, Jean-Louis Combes, Pascale Combes Motel, and Eustaquio Reis, "Property Rights and Deforestation in the Brazilian Amazon," *Ecological Economics* 68, no. 8 (2009): 2461–2468.

61. Philip Fearnside, "Desmatamento na Amazônia brasileira: História, índices e consequências," *Megadiversidade* 1, no. 1 (2005): 113–123; Amintas Brandão Jr. and Carlos Souza Jr., "Deforestation in Land Reform Settlements in the Amazon," Imazon, no. 7 (June 2006): 1–4, https://imazon.org.br/PDFimazon/Ingles/the_state_of_amazon/deforastantion_land.pdf.

62. Brandão and Souza, "Deforestation in Land Reform Settlements in the Amazon."

63. Gabriel Cardoso Carrero, Philip Martin Fearnside, Denis Ribeiro do Valle, and Cristiano de Souza Alves, "Deforestation Trajectories on a Development Frontier in the Brazilian Amazon: 35 Years of Settlement Colonization, Policy and Economic Shifts, and Land Accumulation," *Environmental Management* 66, no. 6 (2020): 966–984.

64. Yiyun Wu, Xican Xi, Xin Tang, Deming Luo, Baojing Gu, Shu Kee Lam, Peter M. Vitousek, and Deli Chen, "Policy Distortions, Farm Size, and the Overuse of Agricultural Chemicals in China," *Proceedings of the National Academy of Sciences* 115, no. 27 (2018): 7010–7015, 7010.

65. Laura Mallonee, "The Lush Billion-Tree Spectacle of China's Great Green Wall," *Wired*, October 10, 2017, www.wired.com/story/ian-teh-chinas-great-green-wall.

66. Jintao Xu et al., "China's Ecological Rehabilitation."

CHAPTER 6: THE UNDERDEVELOPMENT PLAYBOOK

1. Alonso Domínguez Rascón, *La política de reforma agraria en Chihuahua, 1920–1924* (Mexico City: Instituto Nacional de Antropología e Historia, Plaza y Valdés, 2003), 74.

2. Domínguez Rascón, *La política de reforma agraria en Chihuahua*, 74.

3. Quoted in Hans Werner Tobler, "Los campesinos y la formación del estado revolucionario, 1910–1940," in *Revuelta, rebelión, y revolución*, ed. Friedrich Katz (Mexico City: Ediciones Era, 1990), 439.

4. The party's name in Spanish is the Partido Revolucionario Institucional.

5. Quoted in Domínguez Rascón, *La política de reforma agraria en Chihuahua*, 75.

6. Susan Walsh Sanderson, *Land Reform in Mexico, 1910–1980* (Orlando, FL: Academic Press, 1984), 16.

7. There were 11.7 million rural inhabitants and 3.5 million urban ones according to the 1910 census.

8. Sanderson, *Land Reform in Mexico*, 18, 19.

9. Article 27 followed from a 1915 decree in response to intense pressure from Zapata, Pancho Villa, and other revolutionaries. See Sanderson, *Land Reform in Mexico*.

10. Emilio Kourí, "La invención del ejido," *Nexos*, January 2015, www.nexos.com.mx/?p=23778.

11. A considerable faction of PRI leaders in the 1930s had communist ideological leanings and viewed the ejido as a step toward collectivized agriculture. A set of pragmatists viewed group-based land redistribution as more efficient, rapid, and manageable than individual redistribution. And a group of nationalists viewed the ejido as a unique and venerable link to Mexico's great indigenous civilizations. See Kourí, "La invención del ejido."

12. Gerardo Otero, "Agrarian Reform in Mexico: Capitalism and the State," in *Searching for Agrarian Reform in Latin America*, ed. William Thiesenhusen, 276–304 (Boston: Unwin Hyman, 1989).

13. Over the course of its rule and including postrevolutionary land redistribution in the lead-up to the PRI's formation, Mexico redistributed 126 million acres of land. Redistribution is closer to 210 million acres when including the recognition or confirmation of communities that already had de facto, relatively autonomous control of their property (*reconocimiento* or *confirmación y titulación de bienes comunales*).

14. The Gini index of landholding inequality (which ranges from 0 to 1, with 0 representing perfect equality) dropped from 0.96 in 1930 to 0.62 by the 1960s. For the 1930 figure, see Susan Eckstein, "The Impact of Revolution on Social Welfare in Latin America," *Theory and Society* 11, no. 1 (1982): 43–94. For the 1960s figure, see International Fund for Agricultural Development (IFAD), *Rural Poverty Report 2001: The Challenge of Ending Rural Poverty* (Oxford: Oxford University Press for IFAD, 2001), 118.

15. Jesus Silva Herzog, *El agrarismo mexicano y la reforma agraria* (Mexico City: Fondo de Cultura Económica, 1959); Eyler Simpson, *The Ejido: Mexico's Way Out* (Chapel Hill: University of North Carolina Press, 1937); Michael Albertus, Beatriz Magaloni, Barry Weingast, and Alberto Diaz-Cayeros, "Authoritarian Survival and Poverty Traps: Land Reform in Mexico," *World Development* 77 (2016): 154–170.

16. Albertus et al., "Authoritarian Survival and Poverty Traps."

17. Alain de Janvry, Marco Gonzalez-Navarro, and Elisabeth Sadoulet, "Are Land Reforms Granting Complete Property Rights Politically Risky? Electoral Outcomes of Mexico's Certification Program," *Journal of Development Economics* 110 (2014): 216–225.

18. The leveling of wealth through the revolution and radical policy shifts from the 1910s through the 1930s also drove down economic inequality for several subsequent decades. See David Felix, "Income Inequality in Mexico," *Current History* 72, no. 425 (1977): 111–116.

19. William Thiesenhusen, *Broken Promises: Agrarian Reform and the Latin American Campesino* (Boulder: Westview Press, 1995), chap. 2.

20. Albertus et al., "Authoritarian Survival and Poverty Traps," 156.

21. Gustavo Gordillo, Alain de Janvry, and Elisabeth Sadoulet, "Between Political Control and Efficiency Gains: The Evolution of Agrarian Property Rights in Mexico," *CEPAL Review* 66 (1998): 151–169, 158.

22. Gustavo Perez-Verdin, Yeon-Su Kim, Denver Hospodarsky, and Aregai Tecle, "Factors Driving Deforestation in Common-Pool Resources in Northern Mexico," *Journal of Environmental Management* 90, no. 1 (2009): 331–340; Marcela Vásquez-León and Diana Liverman, "The Political Ecology of Land-Use Change: Affluent Ranchers and Destitute Farmers in the Mexican Municipio of Alamos," *Human Organization* 63, no. 1 (2004): 21–33.

23. Angus Wright, "Downslope and North: How Soil Degradation and Synthetic Pesticides Drove the Trajectory of Mexican Agriculture Through the Twentieth Century," in *A Land Between Waters: Environmental Histories of Modern Mexico*, ed. Christopher R. Boyer, 22–49 (Tucson: University of Arizona Press, 2012).

24. Gordillo et al., "Between Political Control and Efficiency Gains," 159.

25. Alejandro Encinas and Fernando Rascón, *Reporte y cronología del movimiento campesino e indígena*, vol. 5 (Mexico City: Universidad Autónoma de Chapingo, 1983), 130.

26. One example was the Comité Coordinador Empresarial. See Carlos Arriola, "Los grupos empresariales frente al Estado (1973–1975)," *Foro internacional* 16, no. 4 (1976): 449–495, 475.

27. Julio Calderón Cockburn, "Luchas por la tierra, contradicciones sociales y sistema político: El caso de las zonas ejidales y comunales en la ciudad de México (1980–1984)," *Estudios demográficos y urbanos* 2, no. 2 (1987): 301–324; Gordillo et al., "Between Political Control and Efficiency Gains."

28. Gordillo et al., "Between Political Control and Efficiency Gains," 158; Albertus et al., "Authoritarian Survival and Poverty Traps," 158.

29. Eckstein, "The Impact of Revolution on Social Welfare in Latin America," 71.

30. Gordillo et al., "Between Political Control and Efficiency Gains."

31. Because of the implications of an entire family losing land access, migrants were frequently members of a larger household, though not heads of household who held agrarian rights within the ejido.

32. Felix, "Income Inequality in Mexico," 112.

33. Albertus et al., "Authoritarian Survival and Poverty Traps."

34. Data from the Food and Agriculture Organization indicate that average yields per agricultural worker from 2015 to 2017 for corn, beans, wheat, sugarcane, and cereal grains—the bulk of Mexico's top agricultural products by planted area—were higher than

the 1989–1991 averages on the eve of the Program for Certification of Rights to Ejido Lands (PROCEDE). The vast majority of this production came from small and medium producers. Furthermore, just over 14 percent of the rural population lived below the World Bank's international poverty line of $1.90 per day in 2014, down from around 28 percent at the equivalent marker in the early 1990s. See Paloma Villagómez Ornelas, "Rural Poverty in Mexico: Prevalence and Challenges," National Council for the Evaluation of Social Development Policy, Mexico City, 2019, 2, available at United Nations, www.un.org/development/desa/dspd/wp-content/uploads/sites/22/2019/03/RURAL-POVERTY-IN-MEXICO.-CONEVAL.-Expert-Meeting.-15022019.pdf.

35. Speech by President Hugo Chávez at Santa Inés de Barinas, December 10, 2001, transcript at Todo Chávez, www.todochavezenlaweb.gob.ve/todochavez/2943-intervencion-del-comandante-presidente-hugo-chavez-en-la-promulgacion-de-la-ley-de-tierras-y-desarrollo-agrario.

36. Margarita López Maya, "Venezuela: El paro cívico del 10 de diciembre," *Nueva Sociedad* 177 (2002): 8–12.

37. Michael Albertus, *Autocracy and Redistribution: The Politics of Land Reform* (Cambridge: Cambridge University Press, 2015), 237.

38. It vacillated between about 40 percent and 70 percent of revenue depending on the oil price. See Osmel Manzano and Jose Sebastian Scrofina, "Resource Revenue Management in Venezuela: A Consumption-Based Poverty Reduction Strategy," 2013, available at Natural Resource Governance Institute, www.resourcegovernance.org/sites/default/files/Venezuela_Final.pdf.

39. Gregory Wilpert, "Land for People Not for Profit in Venezuela," Venezuelanalysis.com, August 23, 2005, https://venezuelanalysis.com/analysis/1310.

40. Michael Albertus, "The Role of Subnational Politicians in Distributive Politics: Political Bias in Venezuela's Land Reform Under Chávez," *Comparative Political Studies* 48, no. 13 (2015): 1667–1710.

41. The properties targeted included those larger than the regional average and with productivity less than 80 percent of what was possible.

42. Meanwhile, the government asked all landowners to register their property. But because the vast majority could not trace their land title back to 1848, few landowners did so.

43. These examples draw from Michael Albertus, "This Land Was Your Land," *Foreign Policy*, November 13, 2015.

44. Albertus, *Autocracy and Redistribution*, 240.

45. Michael Albertus, "The Role of Subnational Politicians."

46. Land reallocation was not solely responsible for the collapse. A decline in the price of oil, other economic policies, and increasing authoritarianism also caused economic fallout. But land reallocation was part and parcel of the problems.

47. "Will Venezuela's Dictatorship Survive?," *The Economist*, March 9, 2017; Amelia Cheatham, Diana Roy, and Rocio Cara Labrador, "Venezuela: The Rise and Fall of a Petrostate," Council on Foreign Relations, March 10, 2023, www.cfr.org/backgrounder/venezuela-crisis.

48. Marco Arena, Emilio Fernandez Corugedo, Jaime Guajardo, and Juan Francisco Yepez, "Venezuela's Migrants Bring Economic Opportunity to Latin America,"

IMF Country Focus, December 7, 2022, www.imf.org/en/News/Articles/2022/12/06/cf-venezuelas-migrants-bring-economic-opportunity-to-latin-america.

49. This account is drawn from Paul Ginsborg, *A History of Contemporary Italy, 1943–1988* (London: Penguin, 1990), 124–125; Paolo Cinanni, *Lotte per la terra e comunisti in Calabria (1943–1953): Terre pubbliche e Mezzogiorno* (Milan: Feltrinelli, 1977), 84–87. Ginsborg draws from both other scholars and firsthand accounts.

50. Giovanni Mottura and Umberto Ursetta, *Il diritto alla terra* (Milan: Feltrinelli Economica, 1981), 201–202.

51. Ethan Kapstein, *Seeds of Stability: Land Reform and US Foreign Policy* (New York: Cambridge University Press, 2017), chap. 4.

52. These included the upland region of Calabria in southern Italy, parts of Campania in the center south, the Delta Podano region in northern Italy, Maremma in western central Italy, the Fucino Basin in the center of the country, a broad swath of Lucania, Molise, and Puglia in the southeast, the entirety of the island of Sardinia, and all of Sicily.

53. In practice, relatively little land was exempted from expropriation in this way.

54. The Ministry of Agriculture calculated the cost of land reform over its operative period from 1950 to 1964 at 709 billion lire—a large sum that computed to over 5 million lire per land reform beneficiary family. I converted these figures to contemporary US dollars using an inflation calculator.

55. Kapstein, *Seeds of Stability*, 119–122.

56. Giovanni Marciani, *L'esperienza di riforma agraria in Italia* (Rome: Giuffrè Editore, 1966).

57. The size of "self-sufficient" farms varied across region even beyond this range. And given imperfect knowledge of soils and growing conditions, as well as the high demand for land, many of these farms were far from sufficient to support a family.

58. In some regions it was substantially quicker: in the Maremma, for instance, expropriation was largely complete within approximately one year of the land reform law's passage.

59. Russell King, "Italian Land Reform: Critique, Effects and Evaluation," *Tijdschrift voor economische en sociale geografie* 62, no. 6 (1971): 368–382, 377, 372.

60. Bruno Caprettini, Lorenzo Casaburi, and Miriam Venturini, "Redistribution, Voting and Clientelism: Evidence from the Italian Land Reform," CEPR Discussion Paper No. DP15679, September 2021, https://papers.ssrn.com/sol3/papers.cfm?abstract_id=3783894; King, "Italian Land Reform," 372.

61. Ginsborg, *History of Contemporary Italy*, 135.

62. Ginsborg, *History of Contemporary Italy*, 135.

63. Calabria and Maremma are not unique in their outcomes. A number of observers anticipated some of the same eventual consequences that transpired in Maremma in other parts of Italy as well. See, for instance, Alessandro Bonanno, "Theories of the State: The Case of Land Reform in Italy, 1944–1961," *Sociological Quarterly* 29, no. 1 (1988): 131–147; Guido Fabiani, *L'agricoltura italiana tra sviluppo e crisis* (Bologna: Il Mulino, 1979); King, "Italian Land Reform."

64. Social and material vulnerability are higher in reform areas. These areas also rank lower on a countrywide index of well-being. See Michael Albertus, "The Persistence of

Rural Underdevelopment: Evidence from Land Reform in Italy," *Comparative Political Studies* 56, no. 1 (2023): 65–100.

65. The average land beneficiary in the Maremma received about twenty-two acres of land compared with the local average of thirty-two acres. The smaller farms struggled to compete with larger ones, and many of the smaller ones failed to support the large, multigenerational families living on them. Furthermore, many new farm owners took years to learn critical skills relating to crop rotation and fertilizer use.

66. For instance, twenty years after the reform, 90 percent of the original beneficiaries in Calabria and over 80 percent of the beneficiaries in Sicily still held their land. See Ginsborg, *History of Contemporary Italy*, 131–137.

67. The old-age ratio is about 5 percent higher in the Maremma zone compared with municipalities just outside the zone. See Albertus, "The Persistence of Rural Underdevelopment."

68. Bonanno, "Theories of the State."

69. Lorenzo Belotti, "An Analysis of the Italian Agrarian Reform," *Land Economics* 36, no. 2 (1960): 118–128.

CHAPTER 7: THE ARC OF HISTORY IS LONG, BUT IT BENDS TOWARD DEVELOPMENT

1. Eric Hobsbawm, "A Case of Neo-Feudalism: La Convención, Perú," *Journal of Latin American Studies* 1, no. 1 (1969): 31–50, 35.

2. Author interview with Wilber Vivanco, January 22, 2024.

3. Author interview with Wilber Vivanco, January 18, 2024.

4. Data are from the 1961 agricultural census and the 1961 population census.

5. Author interview with Justina López at a former hacienda in Huarán, June 20, 2014.

6. This hacienda was in Huarán in the department of Cusco.

7. Michael Albertus, *Property Without Rights: Origins and Consequences of the Property Rights Gap* (Cambridge: Cambridge University Press, 2021), 213–215.

8. Michael Albertus, "Land Reform and Civil Conflict: Theory and Evidence from Peru," *American Journal of Political Science* 64, no. 2 (2020): 256–274.

9. William Long, "Peru's Big Debate. Novelist Takes on Charismatic Leader: Garcia's Plan to Nationalize Banks Has Polarized His Nation," *Los Angeles Times*, September 14, 1987.

10. Susan Stokes, "Democratic Accountability and Policy Change: Economic Policy in Fujimori's Peru," *Comparative Politics* 29, no. 2 (1997): 209–226, 214–215.

11. Stokes, "Democratic Accountability and Policy Change," 217.

12. Grigore Pop-Eleches, *From Economic Crisis to Reform: IMF Programs in Latin America and Eastern Europe* (Princeton, NJ: Princeton University Press, 2008), 274.

13. Timothy Mitchell, "The Work of Economics: How a Discipline Makes Its World," *European Journal of Sociology* 46, no. 2 (2005): 297–320.

14. The program's name in Spanish was the Proyecto Especial de Titulación de Tierras y Catastro Rural.

15. Author interview with William Paño, January 20, 2024.

16. The program's name in Spanish is the Comisión de Formalización de la Propiedad Informal.

17. Pablo Bandeira, José María Sumpsi, and Cesar Falconi, "Evaluating Land Administration Systems: A Comparative Method with an Application to Peru and Honduras," *Land Use Policy* 27, no. 2 (2010): 351–363.

18. Author interview with Juan de Dios Condori, January 16, 2024.

19. Marlene Castillo, Laureano del Castillo, Carlos Monge, and Minda Bustamante, *Las comunidades campesinas en el siglo XXI* (Lima: Grupo ALLPA, 2004), 27.

20. Román Robles Mendoza, "Tradición y modernidad en las comunidades campesinas," *Investigaciones sociales* 8, no. 12 (2004): 25–54, 28.

21. Instituto del Bien Común and Centro Peruano de Estudios Sociales, *Directorio de Comunidades Campesinas del Perú* (Lima: Tarea Asociación Gráfica Educativa, 2016), 6–7. More than half of these communities have been recognized and titled since the 1980s.

22. *Multi-Dimensional Review of Peru*, vol. 3, *From Analysis to Action*, OECD Development Pathways (Paris: Organisation for Economic Co-operation and Development, 2019), www.oecd-ilibrary.org/sites/d9afdddd-en/index.html?itemId=/content/component/d9afdddd-en.

23. Owen Dyer, "Covid-19: Peru's Official Death Toll Triples to Become World's Highest," *BMJ* 373 (2021): n1442.

24. Albertus, *Property Without Rights*, 255–256.

25. Guro Glavin, Kristian Stokke, and Henrik Wiig, "The Impact of Women's Mobilisation: Civil Society Organisations and the Implementation of Land Titling in Peru," *Forum for Development Studies* 40, no. 1 (2013): 129–152, 129–130.

26. John Crabtree, "The Impact of Neo-liberal Economics on Peruvian Peasant Agriculture in the 1990s," *Journal of Peasant Studies* 29, no. 3 (2002): 131–161, 140–141.

27. Author interview with Wilber Vivanco, January 18, 2024. Vivanco's career trajectory as a lawyer working on land titling is a testament to government shifts in titling. He began his career in 1997 with the Special Land Titling and Cadaster Project (PETT), then worked under the Commission for the Formalization of Informal Property (COFOPRI) starting in 2006 as titling competencies shifted there, and again moved to the regional government of the Cusco region in 2011 as competencies again shifted and became decentralized.

28. "Estos son los 68 congresistas que tienen procesos en investigación en el Ministerio Público," *Caretas*, November 9, 2020.

CHAPTER 8: ONE SMALL STEP FOR WOMEN

1. Author interview with Elena Antonia Parodis Medina, October 4, 2023.

2. The displaced group, including Elena's family, won a favorable ruling for restitution in 2011 as there was a new push to restitute land to people displaced during Colombia's conflict. But it took another eight years before the land was finally granted to Elena's family and they could go back.

3. Author correspondence with Elena Antonia Parodis Medina, December 13, 2023.

4. Author interview with Elena Antonia Parodis Medina, October 4, 2023.

5. Michael Albertus and Oliver Kaplan, "Land Reform as a Counterinsurgency Policy: Evidence from Colombia," *Journal of Conflict Resolution* 57, no. 2 (2013): 198–231, 203.

6. Michael Albertus, *Autocracy and Redistribution: The Politics of Land Reform* (New York: Cambridge University Press, 2015), 30.

7. Carmen Diana Deere and Magdalena León, *Empowering Women: Land and Property Rights in Latin America* (Pittsburgh: University of Pittsburgh Press, 2001), 43.

8. The group's Spanish name is Fuerzas Armadas Revolucionarias de Colombia.

9. Instituto Colombiano de Desarrollo Rural (INCODER), "Resoluciones Históricas de Baldíos," 2015.

10. Carmen Diana Deere and Magdalena León, "The Gender Asset Gap: Land in Latin America," *World Development* 31, no. 6 (2003): 925–947, 937.

11. Deere and León, *Empowering Women*, 87.

12. Deere and León, *Empowering Women*, 87.

13. Another law in 1990 went a further step still in stipulating that the work product in a partnership belonged to both partners equally.

14. Deere and León, *Empowering Women*, 87.

15. Deere and León, "The Gender Asset Gap," 937. The figure is 45 percent.

16. João Márcio Mendes Pereira, "The World Bank and Market-Assisted Land Reform in Colombia, Brazil, and Guatemala," *Land Use Policy* 100 (2021): 7.

17. Deere and León, "The Gender Asset Gap," 939.

18. Marcelo M. Giugale, Olivier Lafourcade, and Connie Luff, *Colombia: The Economic Foundation of Peace* (Washington, DC: World Bank, 2003), 581.

19. This mechanism was available for those victimized between 1991 and the closing of the law.

20. Estimates are that about 90 percent of violent conflict deaths were men. See Donny Meertens and Richard Stoller, "Facing Destruction, Rebuilding Life: Gender and the Internally Displaced in Colombia," *Latin American Perspectives* 28, no. 1 (2001): 132–148, 133.

21. *Octavo informe de seguimienteo al Congreso de la República* (Bogotá: Comisión de Seguimiento y Monitoreo a la Implementación de la Ley 1448 de 2011, 2021), 411.

22. This is of the nearly 150,000 people registered as victims of land dispossession or forced abandonment. This figure is considerably lower than the government's initial estimation that roughly 350,000 families would be eligible to reclaim roughly 5 million acres of land. The figures are likely lower because some victims do not feel safe in petitioning for their land back and because informal possession makes it difficult for some to imagine reclaiming claim or to provide sufficient documentation.

23. "Mujeres lideran la restitución de tierras en Colombia," *Semana*, July 25, 2019, www.semana.com/las-mujeres-se-han-convertido-en-lideres-en-los-procesos-de-restitucion-de-tierras/1047.

24. *Octavo informe de seguimienteo al Congreso de la República*, 182, 160.

25. Vanesa Botero Blandón and Ana María Serrano Ávila, "Reforma rural integral y construcción de paz para las mujeres en Colombia," *Estudios políticos* 62 (2021): 152–182.

26. María Juliana Gómez Mendoza and Luisa Paola Sanabria Torres, "Las mujeres rurales y su derecho a la tierra: Retos de la política pública en Colombia," *Trabajo social* (Universidad Nacional de Colombia) 22 (2020): 85–104, 89.

27. That figure hovered from about 80 percent to 95 percent in the 1970s to the 1990s. Giugale et al., *Colombia*, 569.

28. "Left Undefended: Killings of Rights Defenders in Colombia's Remote Communities," Human Rights Watch, www.hrw.org/report/2021/02/10/left-undefended/killings-rights-defenders-colombias-remote-communities.

29. For instance, as of late 2020, the Land Fund was providing 10 percent more land to households run by men than by women. The land formalization program benefited households run by men relative to women by a 1.4 to 1 ratio (in acreage). Adam Isacson, *A Long Way to Go: Implementing Colombia's Peace Accord After Five Years* (Washington, DC: Washington Office on Latin America, 2021), 55.

30. See, for instance, Zapata Serna, Gloria Estella, Antonio Iáñez-Domínguez, José Roberto Álvarez, and Múnera Antonio J. Pareja Amador, "Mujeres víctimas del conflicto armado: Análisis de su reparación en el marco de la ley 1448 de 2011," *Investigación y desarrollo* 28, no. 1 (2020): 157–184.

31. Isacson, *A Long Way to Go*, 56–57.

32. "Silvia Lazarte, mujer del año en Bolivia," *CIMAC Noticias*, December 28, 2007.

33. The full name is the Confederación Nacional de Mujeres Campesinas Indígenas Originarias de Bolivia, or National Confederation of Campesino, Indigenous, and Native Women of Bolivia.

34. Albertus, *Autocracy and Redistribution*, 29.

35. Sandra Ramos, *Transformaciones en la participación política de las mujeres* (La Paz: Instituto de Investigaciones Sociológicas, 2013), 45.

36. In practice, many groups partitioned their grants into family units for farming but did not have title to their plots.

37. Albertus, *Autocracy and Redistribution*, 132.

38. Deere and León, *Empowering Women*, 43.

39. Deere and León, *Empowering Women*, 74.

40. The Spanish name is the Confederación Sindical Única de Trabajadores Campesinos de Bolivia, or CSUTCB.

41. Lucila Mejía, with Irma García, Marcela Valdivia, Celinda Sosa, Lidia Anti, Florentina Alegre, Jacinta Mamani, and Bernardina Laura, *Las hijas de Bartolina Sisa* (La Paz: HISBOL, 1984).

42. Stéphanie Rousseau, "Indigenous and Feminist Movements at the Constituent Assembly in Bolivia: Locating the Representation of Indigenous Women," *Latin American Research Review* 46, no. 2 (2011): 5–28, 18.

43. Rousseau, "Indigenous and Feminist Movements," 17.

44. Deere and León, *Empowering Women*, 75.

45. The 1996 law did include gender equity criteria in the distribution and administration of land, as promoted by urban women's movements and NGOs, but these components of the law were minor relative to land titling.

46. The agency's Spanish name is the Instituto Nacional de Reforma Agraria.

47. Susana Lastarria-Cornhiel, "Land Tenure, Titling, and Gender in Bolivia," *St. Louis University Public Law Review* 29 (2009): 193–242, 224.

48. At the same time, in 2002 the Bartolinas charted a more autonomous path from the Confederation of Peasant Workers of Bolivia.

49. Carmen Diana Deere, "Women's Land Rights, Rural Social Movements, and the State in the 21st-Century Latin American Agrarian Reforms," *Journal of Agrarian Change* 17, no. 2 (2017): 258–278, 262–263.

50. Morales was a family friend of the Lazartes. See Ramos, *Transformaciones*, 46.

51. Deere, "Women's Land Rights," 268. Morales also started doling out state-owned land to peasants in a settler-type reform, as well as reallocating a small amount of privately held land.

52. Deere, "Women's Land Rights," 269.

53. Stéphanie Rousseau and Anahi Morales Hudon, *Indigenous Women's Movements in Latin America: Gender and Ethnicity in Peru, Mexico, and Bolivia* (New York: Palgrave Macmillan, 2016), 61.

54. Lastarria-Cornhiel, "Land Tenure, Titling, and Gender in Bolivia," 237.

55. See Deborah Carvalho, "Patriarchy, Culture and Land: Challenges in Securing Women's Ownership and Titling Rights in La Paz, Bolivia" (master's thesis, Simon Fraser University, Canada, 2012), 47.

56. Quoted in Melissa Camille Buice, "Indigenous Women, the State, and Policy Change: Evidence from Bolivia, 1994–2012" (PhD diss., University of Tennessee, 2013), 77.

57. Deere, "Women's Land Rights," 270.

58. Buice, "Indigenous Women, the State, and Policy Change," 187.

59. Deere, "Women's Land Rights," 270.

CHAPTER 9: RECLAIMING NATURE

1. Author interview with Kris Tompkins, December 18, 2023.

2. Kristine Mcdivitt Tompkins, "Protecting Wilderness as an Act of Democracy," *New York Times*, February 1, 2018.

3. Author correspondence with Marcelo Mena, December 20, 2023.

4. Michelle Bachelet, "Foreword," in *Pumalín Douglas Tompkins National Park*, Tompkins Conservation, 2021, 27, www.rewildingchile.org/web/wp-content/uploads/2021/08/Pumalin-Douglas-Tompkins-National-Park.pdf.

5. Ingrid Espinoza and Lorena Valenzuela, "Carbon Capture and Sequestration in the Route of Parks," Tompkins Conservation Chile, 2020. Carbon concentration in the area, particularly in the soils but also in biomass, rivals and in some aspects surpasses parts of the Amazon basin and the Pacific coast of Colombia.

6. Martín Martinic, *La trapanada al Aysén* (Chile: Pehuen Editores, 2005).

7. William Norris, *Triumph and Tragedy*, 1939, Biblioteca Patagónica (Patagonia Bookshelf), Memoirs, 5–6, https://patlibros.org/wn/memoirs.php?lan=esp.

8. Lucas Bridges, *Memorias del Baker*, n.d., Biblioteca Patagónica (Patagonia Bookshelf), Memoirs, https://patlibros.org/elb/memorias.php.

9. Claudia Sepúlveda Luque and Montserrat Lara Sutulovp, *Comunidades y áreas protegidas de la Patagonia Chilena* (Santiago: Andros, 2001), 66, available at Educación Ambiental y Participación Ciudadana (Environmental Education and Citizen Participation), Ministry for the Environment, Chile, https://educacion.mma.gob.cl/wp-content/uploads/2022/03/Libro-comunidades-y-AP-de-la-Patagonia-chilena.pdf.

10. Martinic, *La trapanada al Aysén*, 321.

11. Sepúlveda and Lara, *Comunidades y áreas protegidas de la Patagonia Chilena*, 229.

12. Claudia Sepúlveda Luque, *Línea de base social de las áreas protegidas de la Patagonia Chilena* (Valdivia, Chile: Programa Austral Patagonia de la Universidad Austral de Chile, 2020), 150.

13. Martinic, *La trapanada al Aysén*, 156.

14. William Thiesenhusen, *Broken Promises: Agrarian Reform and the Latin American Campesino* (Boulder: Westview Press, 1995), 90.

15. Thiesenhusen, *Broken Promises*, 89–90; Michael Albertus, *Autocracy and Redistribution: The Politics of Land Reform* (Cambridge: Cambridge University Press, 2015).

16. Antonio Bellisario, "The Chilean Agrarian Transformation: Agrarian Reform and Capitalist 'Partial' Counter-Agrarian Reform, 1964–1980: Part 1: Reformism, Socialism and Free-Market Neoliberalism," *Journal of Agrarian Change* 7, no. 1 (2007): 1–34.

17. Elena Louder and Keith Bosak, "What the Gringos Brought," *Conservation and Society* 17, no. 2 (2019): 161–172, 165.

18. Author interview with Luisa Galindo, February 5, 2024.

19. Author interview with Luisa Galindo, February 5, 2024, and with Elvis Valdes, whose father was hired to hunt pumas for the cooperative, February 5, 2024.

20. Louder and Bosak, "What the Gringos Brought," 165.

21. Author interview with François de Smet, November 22, 2023.

22. Author interview with Charlie de Smet, November 24, 2023.

23. Louder and Bosak, "What the Gringos Brought," 165.

24. Author interview with Charlie de Smet, November 24, 2023.

25. Kris Tompkins, "A History of Valle Chacabuco," Conservacion Patagonica, blog, August 28, 2012, www.conservacionpatagonica.org/blog/2012/08/28/a-history-ofvalle-chacabuco, quoted in Alzar School, "A History of Parque Patagonia," November 17, 2017, https://alzarschool.org/history-of-parque-patagonia.

26. Author interview with Kris Tompkins, December 18, 2023.

27. The philanthropist Peter Buckley assisted with this purchase.

28. Sepúlveda and Lara, *Comunidades y áreas protegidas de la Patagonia Chilena*, 229, 230–231.

29. Bachelet, "Foreword," 27.

30. Author correspondence with Marcelo Mena, December 20, 2023.

31. Antonio Cerrillo, "Cómo se engañó a Franco para salvar Doñana," *La vanguardia*, August 14, 2019.

32. Benigno Varillas, "José A. Valverde, el cientíco que salvó Doñana," *El diario*, August 4, 2023.

33. Carlos López, "La repoblación forestal de Doñana," *Huelva información*, December 29, 2008.

34. World Wildlife Fund, "Doñana, las raíces del panda," *Panda* 145 (October 2019): 11–15.

35. Luc Hoffman, a conservationist who had helped preserve the Rhône Delta and had teamed up with Valverde several years prior, was the WWF's first vice president and a vocal advocate for preserving Doñana.

36. Cerrillo, "Cómo se engañó a Franco para salvar Doñana."

37. Francisco García García, *Doñana en su historia* (Madrid: Organismo Autónomo Parques Nacionales, 2014).

38. Pascual Carrión, *Los latifundios en España* (Barcelona: Ariel, 1975).

39. The reform built on smaller steps in prior years to settle landless farmers on unused agricultural land. While this mainly gave plots to families, in some cases communities collectively occupied lands. Stanley Payne, *The Collapse of the Spanish Republic, 1933–1936: Origins of the Civil War* (New Haven, CT: Yale University Press, 2006), 216–219.

40. Michael Albertus, "The Political Price of Authoritarian Control: Evidence from Francoist Land Settlements in Spain," *Journal of Politics* 85, no. 4 (2023): 1258–1274.

41. Gonzalo Acosta Bono, José Luis Gutiérrez Molina, Angel del Río Sánchez, and Lola Martínez Macías, *El canal de los presos (1940–1962)* (Barcelona: Crítica, 2004).

42. The new towns include Adriano, Chapatales, Maribáñez, Marismillas, Pinzón, Trajano, El Trobal, Vetaherrado, Guadalema de los Quintero, and Troya.

43. Berta Martín-López, Marina García-Llorente, Ignacio Palomo, and Carlos Montes, "The Conservation Against Development Paradigm in Protected Areas: Valuation of Ecosystem Services in the Doñana Social-Ecological System (Southwestern Spain)," *Ecological Economics* 70, no. 8 (2011): 1481–1491, 1482.

44. Cerrillo, "Cómo se engañó a Franco para salvar Doñana."

45. One example of corporation conservation is the restoration of the soils and ecosystems of several degraded Doñana lagoons in 2016–2017 by Spain's Heineken branch, which helped them to retain more water.

46. "Doñana National Park, Spain," UNESCO World Heritage Convention, 2010, https://whc.unesco.org/en/soc/489.

47. Pedro Zorrilla-Miras, Ignacio Palomo, Erick Gómez-Baggethun, Berta Martín-López, Pedro L. Lomas, and Carlos Montes, "Effects of Land-Use Change on Wetland Ecosystem Services: A Case Study in the Doñana Marshes (SW Spain)," *Landscape and Urban Planning* 122 (2014): 160–174, 165.

48. "Doñana bajo plástico: Avanza la invasión de los frutos rojos," World Wildlife Fund, accessed May 27, 2024, www.wwf.es/?51960/Donana-bajo-plastico-avanza-la-invasion-de-los-frutos-rojos.

49. Juanjo Carmona and Pablo Flores, *Doñana y el estuario del Río Guadalquivir: Análisis de WWF españa sobre sus problemas ambientales* (Madrid: WWF Spain, 2020), 5, https://wwfes.awsassets.panda.org/downloads/analisisimpactosdonana.pdf.

50. Rafael Sánchez Navarro, *Environmental Flows in the Marsh of the National Park of Doñana and Its Area of Influence*, Synthesis Report (Madrid: WWF Spain, 2009), http://awsassets.wwf.es/downloads/synthesis_report_final_ecological_flows_1.pdf.

CHAPTER 10: THE RETURN OF THE DISPOSSESSED

1. Lulama Xingwana, "L Xingwana: Tenbosch Land Handover Celebration," speech delivered for the land handover celebration for the greater Tenbosch communities' claim, Mpumalanga, June 19, 2007, South African Government website, www.gov.za/news/l-xingwana-tenbosch-land-handover-celebration-19-jun-2007.

2. Paul James and Philip Woodhouse, "Crisis and Differentiation Among Small-Scale Sugar Cane Growers in Nkomazi, South Africa," *Journal of Southern African Studies* 43, no. 3 (2017): 535–549, 538. Technically, the claims were made by community associations made up of people with verifiable claims to inhabiting areas where the relevant tribal authorities were historically settled.

3. Author interview with Petros Silinda, October 26, 2023. Silinda was chair of the Siphumelele Tenbosch Trust representing the Ngomane Siboshwa community.

4. Author interview with Edward Ndlovu, October 6, 2023.

5. According to RCL Foods, which acquired TSB, as of 2022 about 71 percent of the land growing sugarcane in the Nkomazi region was under Black ownership.

6. Olivia Kumwenda, "New South African Farmers Team Up with Predecessors," Reuters, April 19, 2013, www.reuters.com/article/safrica-farmers-cooperation/new-south-african-farmers-team-up-with-predecessors-idUKL5N0D61BZ20130419.

7. Author interview with Dawie van Rooy, November 16, 2023. Van Rooy accompanied Minister Xingwana on an aerial tour of TSB's operations on the morning of the handover ceremony to impress upon her the area's potential and the importance of the community partnerships to realizing it.

8. Author interview with Dawie van Rooy, November 16, 2023.

9. Great Britain still maintained a degree of influence over South Africa's foreign affairs until 1931.

10. The reserves were expanded slightly following the 1936 Native Trust and Land Act.

11. Cherryl Walker, *Landmarked: Land Claims and Land Restitution in South Africa* (Johannesburg: Jacana Media, 2008), 36.

12. Charles Mather, "Forced Removal and the Struggle for Land and Labour in South Africa: The Ngomane of Tenbosch, 1926–1954," *Journal of Historical Geography* 21, no. 2 (1995): 169–183. This is where the small-scale growers that partner with RCL now reside.

13. Author interview with Sizwe Mkhulu Ngomane, October 18, 2023.

14. James and Woodhouse, "Crisis and Differentiation," 538.

15. Edward Lahiff, "Land Redistribution in South Africa," in *Agricultural Land Redistribution: Toward Greater Consensus*, ed. Hans Binswanger-Mkhize, Camille Bourguignon, and Rogerius van den Brink, 169–200 (Washington, DC: World Bank Publications, 2009), 170.

16. See James Gibson, *Overcoming Historical Injustices* (Cambridge: Cambridge University Press, 2009), 31.

17. Nelson Mandela, "Speech by President Nelson Mandela at the launch of the Kwazulu-Natal Land Reform Pilot Programme," March 26, 1995, transcript at Nelson Mandela Foundation Archive at the Centre of Memory, https://archive.nelsonmandela.org/index.php/za-com-mr-s-237.

18. There was also a third track, land tenure reform, that focused on strengthening land rights within former homelands and providing greater protections for occupants of privately owned farms and state land. This track did not entail significant land transfers and has had less impact than the other tracks.

19. Clarissa Pienaar, "Old- and New-Order Land Claims: What to Expect," *AgriOrbit*, September 9, 2022, https://agriorbit.com/old-and-new-order-land-claims-what-to-expect.

20. For the figure of 10 million acres, see Johann Kirsten and Wandile Sihlobo, "Land Reform in South Africa: 5 Myths About Farming Debunked," *The Conversation*, November 26, 2022. On the difficulties of restitution, murkiness in government statistics on restitution, and reliance on state land, see Lahiff, "Land Redistribution in South Africa," 172–178.

21. Kirsten and Sihlobo, "Land Reform in South Africa."

22. This program started out with a main focus on land reallocation to the poorest. It was reconfigured in 2001 to focus more on promoting commercially oriented agriculture. Beyond voluntary purchases, the government has also engaged in expropriation with market compensation since 2007, but this has been very limited and controversial.

23. Grants required a matching contribution from applicants. Grants and matching contributions were then pooled into funds administered on behalf of applicants to purchase private land for them.

24. James and Woodhouse, "Crisis and Differentiation," 539.

25. Kirsten and Sihlobo, "Land Reform in South Africa."

26. Malcolm Keswell and Michael R. Carter, "Poverty and Land Redistribution," *Journal of Development Economics* 110 (2014): 250–261, 253.

27. For the figure of 6 million acres, see Kirsten and Sihlobo, "Land Reform in South Africa." On the farm failures, see Noko Masipa, "South Africa: ANC's Land Reform Shame—75% of Land Reform Farms Have Failed," All Africa, November 27, 2022, https://allafrica.com/stories/202211270025.html.

28. Michael Albertus and Victor Menaldo, *Authoritarianism and the Elite Origins of Democracy* (Cambridge: Cambridge University Press, 2018), 2.

29. Bernadette Atuahene, "Paying for the Past: Redressing the Legacy of Land Dispossession in South Africa," *Law and Society Review* 45, no. 4 (2011): 955–989; Anna Bohlin, "A Price on the Past: Cash as Compensation in South African Land Restitution," *Canadian Journal of African Studies / Revue canadienne des études africaines* 38, no. 3 (2004): 672–687.

30. Bernadette Atuahene, *We Want What's Ours: Learning from South Africa's Land Restitution Program* (Oxford: Oxford University Press, 2014), 163.

31. Bohlin, "A Price on the Past." For a counterpoint on how delayed and meager financial compensation can carry little significant meaning or even represent the failure of restitution, see Uma Dhupelia-Mesthrie, "Tales of Urban Restitution, Black River, Rondebosch," *Kronos: Journal of Cape History* 32, no. 1 (2006): 216–243.

32. Author discussions with RCL and joint ventures, as well as internal RCL employment data.

33. James and Woodhouse, "Crisis and Differentiation," 541.

34. There are also critics of this deal who argue that TSB and other white-dominated commercial sugar enterprises received handsome payments for land stolen from indigenous Blacks, retained control of sugar operations through their joint ventures, and paid insufficient dividends. And other joint ventures with several communities of this restitution claim (Mhlaba and Lugedlane) not linked to TSB have failed. There are also continuing struggles over governance of the community trusts.

35. Author interview with Edward Ndlovu, October 6, 2023.

36. Nomsa Maphanga, quoted in "Black Sugar Farmers Get a Sweet Deal with TSB," Independent Online, August 13, 2007, www.iol.co.za/business-report/economy/black-sugar-farmers-get-a-sweet-deal-with-tsb-718385.

37. Author interview with Dave Thomson, December 2, 2023.

38. "Giba CPA's Redevelopment Plan at an Advance Stage," South African Government, April 23, 2013, www.gov.za/giba-cpas-redevelopment-plan-advance-stage.

39. Quoted in Walker, *Landmarked*, 103.

40. Tshepiso Mamatela, "Gqeberha Land Initiative Nears Completion After Three Decades," Herald Live, June 9, 2022, www.heraldlive.co.za/business/2022-06-09-gqeberha-land-initiative-nears-completion-after-three-decades.

41. For more on the failures, see, for instance, Lahiff, "Land Redistribution in South Africa," and Eve Fairbanks, *The Inheritors: An Intimate Portrait of South Africa's Racial Reckoning* (New York: Simon and Schuster, 2022).

42. Author interview with Patrick Vilikazi, October 26, 2023.

43. Walker, *Landmarked*, 37–38.

44. Andisiwe Makinana, "No One Will Be Left Out of Land Claims Process, Says Zuma," *Mail and Guardian*, February 27, 2014, https://mg.co.za/article/2014-02-27-no-one-will-be-left-out-of-land-claims-process-says-zuma.

45. Several rural movements sued the government to halt new land claims before the old claims had been entirely resolved.

46. Anthony Albanese, "Eulogy for a Giant," May 18, 2023, PM Transcripts, Australia, https://pmtranscripts.pmc.gov.au/release/transcript-44970.

47. Technically, the land was Crown (public) land, reserved for the use and benefit of Aboriginal people, though the Yolngu had lived there since time immemorial. On their land use, see Nancy Williams, *The Yolngu and Their Land* (Stanford, CA: Stanford University Press, 1986).

48. Yirrkala bark petitions, 1963, transcript, available at Documenting a Democracy, Australia, www.foundingdocs.gov.au/resources/transcripts/cth15_doc_1963.pdf.

49. Giovanni Torre, "Gumatj Clan Welcomes Court Win in Land Rights Case Brought by the Late Yunupingu," *National Indigenous Times*, May 22, 2023, https://nit.com.au/22-05-2023/6054/gumatj-clan-welcomes-court-win-in-land-rights-compensation-case-brought-by-the-late-yunupingu.

50. Author interview with Djawa Yunupingu, June 24, 2024.

51. Josh Nicholas, Calla Wahlquist, Andy Ball, and Nick Evershed, "Who Owns Australia?," *Guardian*, May 17, 2021.

52. "DNA Confirms Aboriginal Culture One of Earth's Oldest," *Australian Geographic*, September 23, 2011, www.australiangeographic.com.au/news/2011/09/dna-confirms-aboriginal-culture-one-of-earths-oldest. Torres Strait Islanders arrived to the region far later, only several thousand years ago.

53. Author interview with Djawa Yunupingu, June 24, 2024. Songlines are story songs passed down across generations that mark routes across the land and put its features and history into cultural context.

54. *Cooper v. Stuart*, cited in Lewis Hinchman and Sandra Hinchman, "Australia's Judicial Revolution: Aboriginal Land Rights and the Transformation of Liberalism," *Polity* 31, no. 1 (1998): 23–51, 29.

55. Hinchman and Hinchman, "Australia's Judicial Revolution," 31.

56. Frank Brennan, *No Small Change: The Road to Recognition for Indigenous Australia* (Brisbane: University of Queensland Press, 2015), 51.

57. Author interview with Djawa Yunupingu, June 24, 2024.

58. There were weaker statutory land rights for Aboriginals in several other states, such as South Australia and New South Wales.

59. Nicolas Peterson, "Common Law, Statutory Law, and the Political Economy of the Recognition of Indigenous Australian Rights in Land," in *Aboriginal Title and Indigenous Peoples*, ed. Louis Knafla and Haijo Westra (Vancouver: University of British Columbia Press, 2010), 171–184, 177.

60. Jaclyn Diaz, "A Historic Rainforest and Other Lands Have Been Returned to Indigenous Australians," National Public Radio, October 5, 2021, www.npr.org/2021/10/05/1043256101/indigenous-australians-get-land-back-queensland.

61. Carli Willis, Dwayne Wyles, and Holly Richardson, "Historic Moment as Daintree National Park Returned to Eastern Kuku Yalanji People," Australian Broadcasting Corporation, September 29, 2021, www.abc.net.au/news/2021-09-30/daintree-handed-back-to-traditional-owners/100498982.

62. Lily Nothling, "Historic Land Handover as 360,000 Hectares Returned to Traditional Owners on Cape York," Australian Broadcasting Corporation, September 6, 2022, www.abc.net.au/news/2022-09-07/cape-york-land-handover-traditional-owners/101414006.

63. "Land Returned to Eastern Maar People in Victoria's First Native Title Decision in a Decade," *Guardian*, March 28, 2023, www.theguardian.com/australia-news/2023/mar/28/land-returned-to-eastern-maar-people-in-victorias-first-native-title-decision-in-a-decade.

64. Emily Bissland, "Eastern Maar Traditional Owners' Land Rights Formally Recognized at Warrnambool," Australian Broadcasting Corporation, March 28, 2023, www.abc.net.au/news/2023-03-28/eastern-maar-native-title-formal-determination-warrnambool/102153426.

65. "Land Returned to Eastern Maar People."

66. Author interview with Djawa Yunupingu, June 24, 2024.

67. Australian Institute of Health and Welfare (AIHW), *Aboriginal and Torres Strait Islander Health Performance Framework: Summary Report* (Canberra: AIHW, July 2023), www.indigenoushpf.gov.au/report-overview/overview/summary-report?ext=. See also, Francis Markham and Nicholas Biddle, *Income, Poverty and Inequality* (Canberra: Centre for Aboriginal Economic Policy Research [CAEPR], Australian National University, 2018).

CONCLUSION

1. Dean Spears, Sangina Vyas, Gage Weston, and Michael Geruso, "Long-Term Population Projections: Scenarios of Low or Rebounding Fertility," *PLoS One* 19, no. 4 (2024): e0298190. There are relatively few demographic projections beyond 2100, but nearly all near-term projections anticipate a population peak before 2100 and population declines in Europe and other locations that are at or past peak. See, for instance, United Nations, *World Population Prospects 2022*, https://population.un.org/wpp.

INDEX

Aboriginal Land Rights (Northern Territory) Act of 1976, 259–260
Aboriginal Land Rights Commission, 259
Africa. *See also* North Africa; *specific countries*
  agriculture in, 17
  climate change in, 267
  decolonization of, 50
  indigenous peoples of, 18
African Americans (Blacks), 4–5, 28, 76, 79
African National Congress (ANC), 235, 243, 244
agriculture. *See also specific topics*
  of Agua Caliente, 58, 70–71
  in Australia, 260
  in Bolivia, 7
  in Brazil, 117–126
  in Chile, 213–219
  in China, 108–117
  climate change and, 267
  in collective reforms, 33, 38–44
  in Colombia, 182, 186, 192–193
  development of, 11–12
  Doñana National Park and, 232–233
  in El Salvador, 99–104
  gender inequality and, 14
  in India, 94–99
  of indigenous peoples, 16–17
  in Italy, 147–150, 152
  in landlord-tenant landholdings, 21
  in Mexico, 135–139
  in Peru, 7, 158, 161–164, 174–175
  population growth and, 15, 31
  rewilding and, 234
  in Rome, 13
  in South Africa, 235–253
  in Ukraine, 267
  in US, 209
  in Venezuela, 144
  in Vietnam, 180
  wilderness and, 106–128
Agua Caliente (Indian Reservation), 4, 55–58, 62, 64–70, *68*
  agriculture on, 58, 70–71
  assimilation of, 70, 72
  casino of, 83
  checkerboarding of, 65–67, 74–75
  Conservatorship and Guardianship Program for, 77–78
  Dawes Act and, 71–75
  Kauisik clan of, 73, 74
  language of, 83–84
  museum of, 82
  Palm Springs and, 76–78, 83
  settler reforms and, 84
  tourism on, 71–72
  zoning for, 77
Albanese, Anthony, 253
Algeria, 50
Allende, Salvador, 216, 217
Amaru, Túpac, 48
Amazon Forest Monitoring Program, 126
Amazon rainforest
  climate change and, 117, 118, 209
  deforestation of, 108, 117–126, *122*, 209
American Revolution, 266
ANC. *See* African National Congress
apartheid. *See* South Africa
Arenas v. United States, 74
Argentina, 24, 36, 211–212
Arnhem Land Aboriginal Reserve, 253–254

INDEX

Asian Tigers, 47
Australia
  agriculture in, 17
  Great Reshuffle in, 5
  racial hierarchy in, 253–264
  settler reforms in, 37
  smallholdings in, 24
  women in, 93
Australian Aboriginals, 18, 26, 253–264
  Dreamtime of, 256
  mining and, 253–260
  Native Title Act and, 260
  segregation of, 257–258

Bachelet, Michelle, 206–207, 222–223
banks. *See also* World Bank
  collective reforms and, 41
  in France, 15
  in Great Britain, 16
  Inter-American Development Bank, 169, 170
  in Peru, 176
Bartolina Sisas, 195–202
Belaúnde, Fernando, 164–165
Berlingieri family, 145–146
Bernhard, Prince, 223–224
Bernis, Francisco, 224, 230
Binnie-Clark, Georgina, 90–91, 92
biodiversity, 5, 16
  in Amazon rainforest, 117
  in Brazil, 108
  in China, 108
  climate change and, 209
  deforestation and, 108
  indigenous peoples and, 233
Bismarck, Otto von, 19–20
Black Lives Matter, 6
Blacks. *See* African Americans
Black South Africans, 235–253
  citizenship of, 242
  education for, 237
  Natives Land Act and, 235, 239–240, 244, 251
Bogert, Frank, 77
Bolivia, 7
  collective reforms in, 43
  cooperative reforms in, 50, 51
  feudalism in, 196–197
  settler reforms in, 36, 197
  women in, 185, 194–204
Bolsheviks, 39
bounty lands, 62
Brazil, 26
  biodiversity in, 108
  climate change in, 267
  cooperative reforms in, 125
  deforestation in, 108, 117–126, *122*
  land-to-tiller reforms in, 121
  road-building in, 118, 121–122, *122*, 125
Bridges, Lucas, 212–214, 216
Bureau of Indian Affairs, 4, 69, 70, 72, 73

cadaster, 170
Cahuilla Indians, 3–4, 57–69
  Dawes Act and, 71–75
  language of, 83–84
  museum of, 82
California, 3–4, 63. *See also* Agua Caliente (Indian Reservation); Cahuilla Indians; Palm Springs
  missions in, 61–62
Calles, Plutarco, 130, 134
Canada
  environmental degradation in, 127
  First Nations of, 85, 93–94
  gender inequality in, 85–94
  indigenous peoples of, 26
  Mexico and, 139
  property rights in, 86–94
  settler reforms in, 36, 37
  smallholdings in, 24
  women in, 86–94
Caribbean. *See also specific countries*
  plantation system in, 22
  settler reforms in, 36
Cassa per il Mezzogiorno (Fund for the South), 149
Castillo, Pedro, 177
Castro, Yira, 183
Catholic Church, 29–30, 61, 185
Chacabuco Valley. *See* Chile
Charles II, King, 60
Chávez, Hugo, 139–141, 142, 144
checkerboarding, 65–67, 74–75
Cherokee, 63, 80
Chickasaw, 63, 80
Chile
  Argentina and, 211–212
  cooperative reforms in, 50, 51, 216–218

Doñana National Park in, 210, 224–233
landlord-tenant landholding in, 215–216
rewilding in, 206–223, *214*, 274
China, 132
agriculture in, 108–117
Brazil and, 123
civil war in, 32
collective reforms in, 40, 42, 105–117, 127
communism in, 43, 106, 108, 110–111, 127
cooperative reforms in, 111
deforestation in, 14, 107, 108–117, 126–127
desertification in, 112, 115, 117
indigenous peoples of, 26
landlord-tenant landholding in, 21–22, 110–111
land reallocation in, 32
land-to-tiller reforms in, 45, 111
population decline in, 268
population growth in, 14
property rights in, 106–107
reforestation in, 127–128
settler reforms in, 37
women in, 204
Choctaw, 63
Christian Democracy (Democrazia Cristiana), in Italy, 146–150, 153
Chúngara, Domitila, 203
citizenship, 2, 16
of Black South Africans, 242
in Bolivia, 203
in France, 30
in Venezuela, 143
civil war
in China, 32
in Colombia, 186, 189–190, 197
in El Salvador, 101, 103
in Spain, 210, 224
in US, 22, 28
climate change, 16, 52, 234
Amazon rainforest and, 117, 118, 209
biodiversity and, 209
Doñana National Park and, 226, 231, 233
Patagonia and, 211
population growth and, 267
coercion, 41, 50
COFOPRI. *See* Commission for the Formalization of Informal Property
Cold War, 46, 48, 50
collective reforms, 33, 38–44
in China, 40, 42, 105–117, 127
communism and, 43–44
cooperative reforms and, 50
in Cuba, 40
environmental degradation in, 42–43
in Mexico, 43, 130–131, 134–138, 179–180
in South Africa, 244, 245
in Soviet Union, 39, 42
underdevelopment with, 41–42
in Venezuela, 143
in Vietnam, 179–180
women in, 42
Colombia, 26
civil war in, 186, 189–190, 197
collective reforms in, 43
land-to-tiller reforms in, 187, 189
plantation system in, 267
settler reforms in, 187
women in, 181–194
colonialism
by France, 37, 50
by Great Britain, 35–36, 60–61, 239, 255–257
indigenous peoples and, 18, 26, 30–31
landlord-tenant landholding and, 20
of Latin America, 22–24
in Mexico, 133
by Spain, 36, 48–49, 161, 178, 196, 197
Commission for the Formalization of Informal Property (COFOPRI), 171
communism, 26
in China, 40, 42, 105–117, 127
collective reforms and, 43–44
in India, 95–96, 148
in Italy, 145, 146–147
land-to-tiller reforms and, 44, 47
in Soviet Union, 39–40
in Vietnam, 180
Congo, 267
conservation. *See* rewilding
Conservation Reserve Program, 234
Conservatorship and Guardianship Program, 77–78

Cook, James, 255
cooperative reforms, 33, 48–53
  in Brazil, 125
  in Chile, 216–218
  in China, 111
  in El Salvador, 101–102
  environmental degradation from, 51
  gender inequality in, 51, 52
  in Nicaragua, 102
  in Peru, 102, 158–180
  racial hierarchy in, 51
  in Venezuela, 143
Corcovado National Park, 220
Corporación Jurídica Yira Castro (Yira Castro Legal Corporation), 182–183
Costa Rica, 36
COVID-19 pandemic, 174
Cree, 17
Crown Estate, 27–28
Cuba, 40, 191
Cultural Revolution, in China, 112, 114–115
Cupeño, 64

Daintree National Park, 261
Dakota, 80
Dakota Access Pipeline, 82
Dawes Act of 1887 (General Allotment Act), 71–75
Dazhai, 114
DDT, 137, 229
decolonization, 26, 50
Decree on Land, 39
deforestation
  of Amazon rainforest, 108, 117–126, *122*, 209
  biodiversity and, 108
  in Chile, 213–214, 215
  in China, 14, 107–117, 126–127
  on Easter Island, 14
  in Mexico, 137
  population growth and, 31
Delaware, 60
Democrazia Cristiana (Christian Democracy), in Italy, 146–150, 153
desertification, 112, 115, 117
development
  in Chile, 223
  Doñana National Park and, 232
  Great Reshuffle and, 129–154, 157–180
  in Italy, 145–153
  in Mexico, 133–139, 153
  in Peru, 157–180
  population growth and, 153
  property rights and, 154
  racial hierarchy and, 129
  in Venezuela, 139–145, 153
Díaz, Porfirio, 133–134
Las Dignas (The Dignified), 103
Dominion Lands Act of 1872, 86–87, 90, 92, 93
Doñana National Park, 210, 224–233
Dreamtime, 256
Dust Bowl, 115
Dutch East India Company, 239

East Asia, 5. *See also specific countries*
  Great Reshuffle in, 26
  landlord-tenant landholding in, 20
  land-to-tiller reforms in, 45, 47, 149
  population growth in, 268
Easter Island, 14
Ecologists in Action (Ecologístas en Acción), 232
Ecuador, 204
education
  for Black South Africans, 237
  of Native Americans, 81
  of women, 93
Egypt, 36
ejidatarios, 131
ejidos, 130–139, *136*
El Niño, 174
El Salvador
  agriculture in, 99–104
  civil war in, 101, 103
  cooperative reforms in, 50, 101–102
  gender inequality in, 88, 99–104
  land-to-tiller reforms in, 45–46, 102–103
  sharecropping in, 102
emancipation, 30
eminent domain, 2
Enríque Ignacio, 130, 131, 134
environmental degradation, 5, 8, 16. *See also* deforestation; rewilding
  in Canada, 127
  in collective reforms, 42–43
  from cooperative reforms, 51

from industrialization, 107
in land-to-tiller reforms, 47–48
in Mexico, 27
population growth and, 14
from settler reforms, 38
in US, 127, 209
in Venezuela, 143
wilderness and, 106–128
Equalization Act of 1959, 74
Europe. *See also specific countries*
colonialism by, 30–31
feudalism in, 18–19
indigenous peoples of, 18
settler reforms in, 33–39
European Union, 151, 231
extinctions, 14, 209, 221, 234

Farabundo Martí National Liberation Front (FMLN), 103
FARC. *See* Revolutionary Armed Forces of Colombia
fascism, 6–47, 148, 224
fertility rates, 14, 268
fertilizers, 27, 43, 47–48, 51
in China, 112, 115, 116–117, 127
in Mexico, 137
in US, 209
feudalism (lord-peasant landholding), 16
agriculture in, 18–19
in Bolivia, 196–197
collective reforms and, 40–41
cooperative reforms and, 51
in Europe, 18–19
in France, 30
in Great Britain, 27–28
haciendas and, 158
land-to-tiller reforms and, 45–46
in Poland, 25
in Prussia, 19–20
in Russia, 25
First Nations
of Australia, 254–255, 260–263
of Canada, 85, 93–94
FMLN. *See* Farabundo Martí National Liberation Front
"Forty Acres and a Mule," 28
Fragalà, 145–146
France, 15. *See also* French Revolution
Catholic Church in, 29–30
colonialism by, 37, 50
settler reforms in, 33, 36–37
Francis (Pope), 61
Franco, Francisco, 104, 223–224, 232–233
Frei, Eduardo, 216
French Revolution, 26, 29–32, 266
Fujimori, Alberto, 166–167, 169–170, 171, 176

García, Alan, 165–166, 169
gender inequality, 8, 16, 269. *See also* patriarchy; women
agriculture and, 14
in Bolivia, 184–185, 194–205
in Canada, 85–94
in Colombia, 184, 185–194
in cooperative reforms, 51, 52
in El Salvador, 88, 99–104
in Great Reshuffle, 85–105
in India, 88, 94–99
in land-to-tiller reforms, 47
in Mexico, 27
General Allotment Act (Dawes Act of 1887), 71–75
Germany, 15, 19, 268
globalization, 267
Gold Rush, 63–64, 67
gold standard, 16
González-Gordón, Mauricio, 224, 230
Goulart, João, 121
Grain First, in China, 114
Grain Growers' Guide, 92
Grand Teton National Park, 207
Great Britain, 15
banks in, 16
Canada and, 86, 89
colonialism by, 35–36, 60–61, 239, 255–257
feudalism in, 27–28
gold standard in, 16
India and, 94
Ireland and, 20–21, 46
settler reforms of, 33, 35–36
Great Depression, 66, 92, 120
Great Famine, in China, 42, 114
Great Fear, 29
Great Green Wall, 127–128
Great Leap Forward, in China, 106, 107, 112, 113

Great Reshuffle, 3, 5–8, 29–52. *See also specific topics*
collective reforms of, 33, 38–44
cooperative reforms, 33, 48–53
development and, 129–154, 157–180
gender inequality in, 85–105
land-to-tiller reforms in, 33, 44–48
return of dispossessed land and, 235–265
rewilding and, 206–233, *214*, 274
settler reforms in, 33–39
wilderness and, 106–128
women and, 181–205
Great Sparrow Campaign, 113–114
Great Steel Making Campaign, 106, 113
Greece, 1, 12–13, 14
Greenpeace, 232
groundwater, 65, 108, 116–117

hacienda system, 16, 24, 40–41, 49
in Colombia, 185
in Mexico, 133, 180
in Peru, 22–23, 157–158, 162, 163
Han dynasty, 14, 109
health/health care
of Aboriginal Australians, 263
of Native Americans, 81
in Venezuela, 145
Hindu Succession Act of 1956, 98
Holland Land Company, 25
Homestead Act of 1962, 25, 35, 65, 66–67, 86
Homesteads for Women, 87, 92
Household Responsibility System, in China, 115–116
House of Windsor, 28
Huarán, Hacienda, 22–23
Hudson's Bay Company, 85
hunter-gatherers, 11, 17–18, 211, 256
hyperinflation, 144, 168, 199

IMF. *See* International Monetary Fund
indentured servants, 21
India, 132
gender inequality in, 88, 94–99
Great Britain and, 36
landlord-tenant landholding in, 20, 94–95, 96
land-to-tiller reforms in, 88, 95
settler reforms in, 94
sharecropping in, 88, 95–97
South Africa and, 240
women in, 204
Indian Act of 1876, 94
Indian Gaming Regulatory Act of 1987, 83
Indian Relocation Act of 1956, 80
Indian Removal Act of 1830, 63
Indian Reorganization Act of 1934, 74–75
Indian Territory, 35, 63
indigenous peoples, 32. *See also* Australian Aboriginals; Black South Africans; Native Americans
agriculture of, 16–17
in Amazon rainforest, 117, 119
biodiversity and, 233
in Bolivia, 194–197, 201
in Chile, 211–212
collective reforms and, 43
in Colombia, 185
colonialism and, 18, 26, 30–31
as hunter-gatherers, 17–18, 211
in Mexico, 133
in Peru, 160, 172–173, 176, 178
population growth and, 26
settler reforms and, 33–39
industrialization
in Brazil, 120
collective reforms and, 42
Doñana National Park and, 232–233
environmental degradation from, 107
in Italy, 147, 151
Industrial Revolution, 30
Innu, 17
INRA. *See* National Institute for Agrarian Reform
Institute of Colonization and Agrarian Reform, 122
Institutional Revolutionary Party (PRI), 130–131, 134–137, 139
Inter-American Development Bank, 169, 170
International Monetary Fund (IMF), 139
Bolivia and, 199
Mexico and, 180
Peru and, 160, 165–166, 169, 179
Ireland, 5, 14
landlord-tenant landholding in, 20–21
land-to-tiller reforms in, 46, 47, 148
Land War in, 20–21
women in, 204

Irish Land Acts, 46
Iron Curtain, 32
Italy, 15, 43
  development in, 145–153
  land-to-tiller reforms in, 104, 148–153

Jackson, Andrew, 63
Jamaica, 36
Japan, 5–6, 132, 268
  land-to-tiller reforms in, 44–45, 47, 176
  Peru and, 169, 171
Jefferson, Thomas, 25
Jim Crow, 22, 28
Johnson, Andrew, 28
Junkers, 19–20

KaNgwane, 241
Katari, Túpac, 198
Kauisik clan, 73, 74
Keystone XL Pipeline, 82
Korea, 43. *See also* South Korea
Kruger National Park, 235, 241, 248
Kuomintang, 110

Labor Party, 258–259
Lakota, 80
Land Back, 6
Landless Rural Workers' Movement (MST), 124–125, 126
landlord-tenant landholding, 40–41, 44–48
  in Chile, 215–216
  in China, 21–22, 110–111
  in India, 94–95, 96
  in Ireland, 20–21
  in Japan, 44–45
land reallocation. *See* Great Reshuffle
land-to-tiller reforms, 33, 44–48
  in Brazil, 121
  in China, 111
  in Colombia, 187, 189
  cooperative reforms and, 50
  in East Asia, 149
  in El Salvador, 102–103
  environmental degradation in, 47–48
  in India, 88, 95
  in Ireland, 148
  in Italy, 104, 148–153
  in Japan, 176
  in South Africa, 244, 245
  in South Korea, 176
  in Taiwan, 176
  in Venezuela, 141, 143
land trusts, 81, 259, 269
Land War, in Ireland, 20–21
Latin America. *See also specific countries*
  cooperative reforms in, 50
  decolonization in, 26
  hacienda system of, 16, 22–24
  indigenous peoples of, 26
  settler reforms in, 93
Law 30, Colombia, 187–188
Law of Land and Agrarian Development, Venezuela, 140–143
Lazarte, Silvia, 194–195, 196, 198–199, 201
Learn from Dazhai, in China, 114
Lenin, Vladimir, 39
Lincoln, Abraham, 28
lord-peasant landholding. *See* feudalism
Louis XVI, King, 29, 30
Luiseño, 64

Mabo, Eddie, 260
MacArthur, Douglas, 44
Macdonald, John, 86
Maduro, Nicolás, 141, 144
Mandan, Hidatsa, Sahnish (Indian nation), 69
Mandela, Nelson, 243, 244, 246
manifest destiny, 63
Mao Zedong, 106, 107, 114, 115
March to the West, in Brazil, 120
Marshall Plan, 149
Mashpee Wampanoag, 60
Massachusetts, 60
Maxwell, Adrian, 70–71
Mayflower, 60
measles, 61, 69
Mena, Marcelo, 208
Mesopotamia, 1, 12, 14
Mexican-American War, 3, 63
Mexico
  Cahuilla and, 59
  collective reforms in, 43, 130–131, 134–138, 179–180
  colonialism in, 133
  development in, 133–139, 153
  economic miracle of, 138
  ejidos in, 130–139, *136*
  land reallocation in, 26–27, 32

Mexico (*cont.*)
rancheros of, 59
revolutions in, 129–130, 133–134
settler reforms in, 36, 37
Zapotec of, 13
Middle East, 26
Miguel, Eileen, 76
Milanovich, Richard, 55, 75
Milirrpum, 258
Miller, Loren, Jr., 78
mining
Australian Aboriginals and, 253–260
in Congo, 267
Doñana National Park and, 231
in Peru, 174, 175, 178
modernization, 24, 52, 153
Morales, Evo, 195–196, 198–199, 201, 202
Morocco, 50
Movement Toward Socialism, 201–202
Mpoti, Chief, 241
MST. *See* Landless Rural Workers' Movement
Muscogee Creek, 63
Mussolini, Benito, 148

Nabalco, 258
NAFTA. *See* North American Free Trade Agreement
Napoleon, 19
National Forest Protection Program, in China, 128
National Institute for Agrarian Reform (INRA), Bolivia, 200–201
National Party, South Africa, 240, 242, 243, 244
nation-building, 85
nation-states, 15–16, 31, 266
Native Americans. *See also* First Nations; *specific tribes*
in California, 3–4
census of, 79
child mortality of, 80
education of, 81
health of, 81
Indian Gaming Regulatory Act and, 83
Indian Relocation Act and, 80
Indian Removal Act and, 63
Indian Reorganization Act and, 74–75
Indian Territory for, 35, 63
life expectancy of, 79
New Deal for, 74
poverty of, 80, 81
settler reforms and, 35
taxes and, 79
in US, 4–5, 59–62, 79
women, 81–82
Natives Land Act of 1913, 235, 239–240, 244, 251
Native Title Act, 260
Navajo Nation, 69
neoliberalism, 168, 170–172
Nepal, 204
New Deal for Native Americans, 74
New England, 17
settler reforms in, 34
smallholdings in, 24–25
NGOs. *See* nongovernmental organizations
Nicaragua, 50, 102, 105
Nixon, Richard, 116
nongovernmental organizations (NGOs), 160, 172, 200
Norris, William, 212
North Africa
cooperative reforms in, 50, 51
decolonization in, 26
France and, 37
North America. *See also* Canada; Mexico; United States
Great Reshuffle in, 5
indigenous peoples of, 18
North American Free Trade Agreement (NAFTA), 139

Obregón, Álvaro, 130, 134
OECD. *See* Organisation for Economic Co-operation and Development
Oklahoma, 35
Oliver, Frank, 91
Operation Amazonia, 118, 121, 122, 123–124
Operation Barga, 95–98
Oregon Country, 63
Organisation for Economic Co-operation and Development (OECD), 160, 174
The Other Path (de Soto), 167–168

Pacific Railway Acts of 1862
and 1871, 66
Palestinian territories, 37
Palm Springs, 4, 55–58
African Americans in, 76
Agua Caliente and, 76–78, 83
hospital in, 75
Latinos in, 76
museum in, 82
population growth in, 74
tourism in, 73
Patagonia National Park, 206–207, *214*, 223
patriarchy, 154
in Bolivia, 194–204
in Canada, 93
in Colombia, 184
in El Salvador, 88, 100
in India, 99
Peasant Leagues, in Brazil, 120
peasants, 7. *See also* feudalism
in Bolivia, 195, 197–198
in China, 106, 107
in Colombia, 182, 186, 188, 197–198
in French Revolution, 29
in Italy, 145–148, 151
in Mexico, 131, 135–138
in Peru, 158, 162–163, 171
in Soviet Union, 39–40, 42–43
Penn, William, 60
Pennsylvania, 60
Peru, 6–7
cooperative reforms in, 48–51, 102,
158–180
COVID-19 pandemic in, 174
development in, 157–180
hacienda system in, 22–23, 157–158,
162, 163
property rights in, 159–180
settler reforms in, 36
women in, 105
pesticides, 27, 43
in Chile, 231
in China, 112, 116–117, 127
in cooperative reforms, 51
in land-to-tiller reforms, 47–48
in Mexico, 137
PETT. *See* Special Land Titling and
Cadaster Project
Pilgrims, 60
Pinochet, Augusto, 217
plantation system, 4
in Colombia, 267
in hacienda system, 22–24
in United States, 28
plow, 14
Poland, 25
population growth, 1, 3, 12, 85
agriculture and, 15
in Brazil, 118
climate change and, 267
development and, 153
environmental degradation and, 14
after French Revolution, 31
implosion of, 268
indigenous peoples and, 26
in Palm Springs, 74
peaking of, 267
rewilding and, 209
in Venezuela, 141–142
populism, 32
in Brazil, 121
in Peru, 177
in South Africa, 246
Portugal, 22–24, 50, 119
PRI. *See* Institutional Revolutionary Party
primogeniture, 30
property rights. *See also specific topics*
in Brazil, 125–126
in Canada, 86–94
in China, 106–107
in collective reforms, 42
development and, 154
in Great Reshuffle, 52
indigenous peoples and, 18
in Italy, 150
in Mexico, 132, 135, 136, 138, 180
in Peru, 159–180
tradability of, 168
in Venezuela, 132, 141–144
in Vietnam, 180
of women, 89–90, 92
Prussia, 19–20
Public Land Survey System, 65
Pumalín Douglas Tompkins National Park,
208, 220

Quebec, 17, 34
Queensland Parks and Wildlife Service, 262

racial hierarchy, 8, 16, 55–84, 269. *See also* indigenous peoples
in Australia, 253–264
in collective reforms, 43
in cooperative reforms, 51
development and, 129
in land-to-tiller reforms, 46
in settler reforms, 36, 37
in South Africa, 235–253
in United States, 28
railroads, 3, 65–67, 69, 74–75, 76
rancheros, 59
RCL Foods, 236, 241, 245, 247–248
Reconstruction, 5
redlining, 5
reforestation
in China, 127
in Peru, 107
in Spain, 224–225
Revolutionary Armed Forces of Colombia (FARC), 186, 191
rewilding
agriculture and, 234
in Chile, 206–223, *214*, 221, 274
population growth and, 209
in Spain, 210, 223–233
Rhode Island, 60
Roche, William, 91
Rockefeller, John D., Jr., 207
Rome, 1, 12–13, 14
Roosevelt, Franklin Delano, 74
Roosevelt, Teddy, 72–73
Rosales, Manuel, 144
Rupert's Land, 85
Russia, 132. *See also* Soviet Union
feudalism in, 18–19, 25
land reallocation in, 32
Russian Revolution, 129

Salvadoran Institute of Agrarian Transformation, 99–100
Santos, Juan Manuel, 190
Scanlon, Meaghan, 261–262
sea level rise, 267
segregation
of Australian Aboriginals, 257–258
in South Africa, 239
Sendero Luminoso (Shining Path), 164, 171
SEO Birdlife. *See* Spanish Ornithological Society
serfdom. *See* feudalism
Serra, Junípero, 61
Serrano, 64
settler reforms, 33–39. *See also* Homestead Act of 1962
agriculture and, 38
Agua Caliente and, 84
in Bolivia, 197
in Colombia, 187
environmental degradation from, 38
in India, 94
in Latin America, 93
racial hierarchy in, 36, 37
in South Africa, 244
in Spain, 104
in Venezuela, 141, 142
sharecropping, 22
by African Americans, 28
in El Salvador, 102
in India, 88, 95–97
in South Africa, 240
Sherman Institute, 70
Shining Path (Sendero Luminoso), 164, 171
Sisa, Bartolina, 198
slash-and-burn agriculture, 109, 117–126
slavery. *See also* plantation system
in Brazil, 119
in Mesopotamia, 12
in Rome, 13
in United States, 63
Sloping Land Conversion Program, in China, 128
smallholdings
in Brazil, 119
Great Reshuffle and, 27
in India, 94
in New England, 24–25
smallpox, 61, 69
social hierarchy/status, 2, 13–14, 16
in collective reforms, 43
in land-to-tiller reforms, 46
Sociedad Explotadora del Baker, 211–212
Sociedad Hobbs y Compañia, 212–214
Sociedad Valle Chacabuco, 214
de Soto, Hernando, 167–170
South Africa. *See also* Black South Africans
collective reforms in, 244, 245
colonialism in, 239
Great Reshuffle in, 5

indigenous peoples of, 26
land-to-tiller reforms in, 244, 245
racial hierarchy in, 235–253
settler reforms in, 34, 244
sharecropping in, 240
sugarcane in, 236–237, 247, 249–250
women in, 249
Southeast Asia, 17, 18. *See also specific countries*
landlord-tenant landholding in, 20
population growth in, 268
Southern Pacific Railroad, 3, 67
South Korea, 5–6, 132
land-to-tiller reforms in, 45, 46, 47, 176
Soviet Union
China and, 114
collective reforms in, 39, 42
women in, 204
Spain, 15
Bolivia and, 196, 197
Catholic Church in, 61
civil war in, 210, 224
colonialism by, 36, 48–49, 161, 178, 196, 197
colonialism in Latin America by, 22–24
Doñana National Park in, 210, 224–233
fascism in, 224
Mexico and, 133
Peru and, 48–49, 161, 178
rewilding in, 210, 223–233
settler reforms in, 33, 36, 104
Spanish Ornithological Society (SEO Birdlife), 232
Special Land Titling and Cadaster Project (PETT), 170, 171
Stalin, Joseph, 39–40, 42
Stein, Baron vom, 19
Sudan, 267
sugarcane, 236–237, 247, 249–250

Taiwan, 5–6, 110, 132
land-to-tiller reforms in, 45, 46, 47, 176
taxes, 16
in France, 30
in Mexico, 133
Native Americans and, 79
in Peru, 177
Tehuelche, 211–212
tenants/tenancy. *See also* landlord-tenant landholding
in Brazil, 120
in collective reforms, 40
in El Salvador, 102
in India, 95–97
in Italy, 149
in Japan, 45
in land-to-tiller reforms, 44–46, 48
in Palm Springs, 77
in South Africa, 240
terra nullius, 4, 257, 260
Texas, 62, 63
Tiberius Gracchus, 13
tiller reforms. *See* land-to-tiller reforms
title deeds, 246
Tocqueville, Alexis de, 25
Tompkins, Doug, 207, 209–210, 219–222
Tompkins, Kristine, 206–210, 219–222
Tompkins Conservation, 208, 220
Torres-Martinez Indian Reservation, 72
Torres Strait Islander people, 254–255, 260, 263
tourism
on Agua Caliente Indian Reservation, 71–72
in Chile, 223
in Palm Springs, 73
townships, 65
Trail of Tears, 63
Trans-Amazonian Highway, 118, 122, *122*, 125
Treaty of Mesilim, 12
Treaty of Temecula, 64
TSB, 236–237, 242, 245, 247, 248, 249–250
Tunisia, 50

Ukraine, 267
Unified Syndical Confederation of Peasant Workers of Bolivia, 197–198
United Nations
Colombia and, 191
Convention on the Elimination of All Forms of Discrimination Against Women of, 187
on urbanization, 6

United States (US). *See also* African Americans; Native Americans
agriculture in, 209
American Revolution of, 266
Blacks in, 4–5
bounty lands in, 62
Brazil and, 123
China and, 116
civil war in, 22, 28
climate change in, 267
Conservation Reserve Program in, 234
Dust Bowl in, 115
environmental degradation in, 127, 209
Great Reshuffle in, 62
indigenous peoples of, 26
Italy and, 148, 149
land-to-tiller reforms by, 44, 46–47
Mexico and, 139
plantation system in, 22, 28
population growth in, 268
railroads in, 65–66, 67, 69, 76
settler reforms in, 35, 37
slavery in, 63
smallholdings in, 24
Vietnam War and, 114, 180
women in, 93
urbanization, 6, 52
in Chile, 215
in Italy, 147, 151
women and, 24
Uribe, Álvaro, 189–190
Uruk, 12

Valverde, José Antonio, 224, 230, 231
Vargas, Getúlio, 120
Vargas Llosa, Mario, 131, 166–167
Velasco Alvarado, Juan, 48, 163
Venezuela
citizenship in, 143
collective reforms in, 143
cooperative reforms in, 143
development in, 139–145, 153
environmental degradation in, 143
land-to-tiller reforms in, 141, 143
property rights in, 132, 141–144
settler reforms in, 141, 142
La Vía Campesina, 200–201
Victims Law, in Colombia, 190–191
Vietnam
collective reforms in, 179–180
land-to-tiller reforms in, 45
women in, 204
Vietnam War, 114, 180

wage labor
by African Americans, 28
in Italy, 147–148
in land-to-tiller reforms, 45, 48
in Prussia, 19
in Rome, 13
in South Africa, 240
in Spain, 228
Wampanoag, 17
wars. *See also* civil war; *specific wars*
on Easter Island, 14
in Mesopotamia, 12
of Zapotec, 13
Washington, George, 62
West Bank, 26
West Papua, Indonesia, 37
Wheat and Woman (Binnie-Clark), 90–91
Whitlam, Gough, 258–259
wilderness. *See also* deforestation; rewilding
environmental degradation and, 106–128
Williams, Gabrielle, 262
women
in Australia, 93
in Bolivia, 185, 194–204
in Canada, 86–94
in collective reforms, 42
in Colombia, 181–194
education of, 93
Great Reshuffling and, 181–205
Native American, 81–82
in Nicaragua, 105
in Peru, 105
property rights of, 89–90, 92
in South Africa, 249
in US, 93
Woodward, Edward, 259
World Bank
Bolivia and, 199
Colombia and, 189
land-to-tiller reforms and, 46, 47
Mexico and, 139, 180
Peru and, 160, 169, 170, 179
South Africa and, 245

World War I, 25
  Homesteads for Women and, 92
World War II, 26
  cooperative reforms after, 50
  Italy after, 148, 152–153
  Japan after, 44
  land-to-tiller reforms after, 47
World Wildlife Fund (WWF), 210, 223–224, 230, 231, 232

Xingwana, Lulama, 235
Xinjiang, 37

Yira Castro Legal Corporation (Corporación Jurídica Yira Castro), 182–183
Yugoslavia, 50
Yunupingu, Djawa, 254–255, 258, 263
Yunupingu, Galarrwuy, 253–254, 263

zamindars, 96
Zamora, Ezequiel, 140
Zapata, Emiliano, 134
Zapotec, 13
Zimbabwe, 40, 132
zoning, 2
  for Agua Caliente Indian Reservation, 77
Zuma, Jacob, 252